MW01592600

# HARBRACE
# COLLEGE
# WORKBOOK
# FORM 12C

## INSTRUCTOR'S EDITION

## Writing for the World of Work

## Melissa E. Barth

Appalachian State University

**Harcourt Brace College Publishers**

Fort Worth  Philadelphia  San Diego  New York  Orlando  Austin  San Antonio
Toronto  Montreal  London  Sydney  Tokyo

*Publisher* • Ted Buchholz
*Senior Developmental Editor* • Sarah H. Smith
*Production Manager* • Debra A. Jenkin
*Text & Cover Design* • Don Fujimoto
*Editorial & Production Services* • Tripp Narup, Monotype
Editorial Services Group

Copyright © 1995, 1990, 1986, 1982, 1979, 1977, 1973, 1972, 1968, 1967, 1962, 1957, 1956 by Harcourt Brace & Company
Copyright 1953, 1952 by Harcourt Brace & Company
Copyright renewed 1990, 1980 by Cornelia S. Hodges
Copyright renewed 1985, 1984, 1981 by Cornelia S. Hodges and J. N. Hodges

All rights reserved. No part of this publication may be reproduced or transmitted in any form or by any means, electronic or mechanical, including photocopy, recording, or any information storage and retrieval system, without permission in writing from the publisher.

Although for mechanical reasons all pages of this publication are perforated, only those pages imprinted with a Harcourt Brace & Company copyright notice are intended for removal.

Requests for permission to make copies of any part of the work should be mailed to: Permissions Department, Harcourt Brace & Company, 6277 Sea Harbor Drive, Orlando, Florida 32887-6777.

Printed in the United States of America

Library of Congress Catalog Card Number, Student Edition:    94-77128
                                     Instructor's Edition:  94-77129
ISBN, Student Edition:    0-15-501465-X
    Instructor's Edition:  0-15-501807-8


4567890123   039   987654321

# TO THE INSTRUCTOR

Welcome to Form 12C of the *Harbrace College Workbook.* Like Forms 12A and 12B, Form 12C is designed to be used either independently or in conjunction with the Twelfth Edition of the *Harbrace College Handbook.* Form 12C focuses on the world of work: all of its examples and exercises deal directly with the working world and illustrate many of the writing skills that students will need as they pursue their careers. For this edition, all of the explanations and exercises have been carefully re-examined. Most of the exercises have been replaced, expanded, significantly revised or entirely rewritten; all of the explanations have similarly been re-evaluated, revised, or substantially rewritten.

**Arrangement**   The materials in Form 12C are arranged in sections that parallel those of the *Harbrace College Handbook,* Twelfth Edition. The numbers and letters denoting subdivisions within the chapters in Form 12C correspond to those of the Handbook, with the following exceptions: Chapter 5 on case, Chapter 7 on verb forms, Chapter 12/13 on the comma, and Chapter 35 on business writing. Because of the special emphasis on certain skills in this version of the Workbook, an organization somewhat different from the Handbook seemed necessary in these chapters. You will also note that the chapter numbering system of Form 12C jumps from Chapter 33 to Chapter 35, omitting the Handbook's Chapter 34 on the research paper, a subject beyond the scope of most courses in which the Form C version of the Workbook is used.

Chapter 1 of Form 12C covers the main points of grammar and punctuation; it is, in other words, a practical minicourse in the grammar and punctuation of sentences. Some students may be able to move directly from Chapter 1 to the later chapters that treat word choice and sentence effectiveness (Chapters 20 through 30) or even to the chapters that go beyond the sentence to longer units of composition (Chapters 31 through 33). Other students will need additional review of basic areas—such as agreement, tense, and the uses of the comma and apostrophe—that is supplied in the intervening chapters (2 through 19). Of course, the needs of the class or the individual student will determine how much time is devoted to Chapters 2 through 19 and how many of the exercises in each chapter are assigned.

**Exercises**   The subject matter of the exercises is the world of work. The exercises cover such topics as the importance of work, the job market, writing on the job, the modern technologies of the work place, and work-related issues such as leisure time, workplace hazards, working women, and persons with disabilities in the working world. Form 12C provides many more exercises related to basic areas of grammar and punctuation than are found in the other forms of the Workbook; students should not run out of exercise material before they have mastered a specific skill. For example, fifteen exercises deal with the use of the comma (six in Chapter 1, six in Chapter

12/13, and three in Chapter 17); and twelve exercises stress the use of sentence-combining techniques to achieve an effective style.

**Writing**    Form 12C includes not only chapters on writing paragraphs and essays but also a chapter (35) on the special kinds of composition students will need to master in order to succeed in the world of work—for example, letters of application, résumés, letters asking for adjustments, and memoranda. Finally, new to this edition of Form C, is a focus on revision skills in conjunction with later writing assignments (especially in Chapter 35) and exercises incorporating collaborative writing, revision, and rewriting (also Chapter 35).

**The Dictionary**    Proper use of the dictionary is stressed throughout Form 12C: in the study of nouns, adjectives, adverbs, and verbs, and in the chapters on capitalization, abbreviations, italics, and numbers. However, unless each member of the class is familiar with the dictionary, the best place to begin teaching and learning dictionary skills is Chapter 19.

**Spelling**    Although most students receive little formal instruction in spelling after elementary school, correct spelling is important to success not only in college but also in the working world. Form 12C does not presume to be a complete spelling manual, but it does emphasize throughout the use of the dictionary to avoid various kinds of misspellings, and it covers all major spelling rules. In addition, it presents two lists of words that are frequently misspelled or misused in professional writing. Perhaps even more important, the "Individual Spelling List" at the end of the Workbook offers a chart on which students can record the words they misspell in their writing assignments and the reasons for the misspellings.

**Note:**    Each of the forms of the Harbrace College Workbook is available in an Instructor's Edition as well as a Student Edition. The Instructor's Edition is an exact replica of the Student Edition with answers and point allocations for all of exercises overprinted in a second color.

**Acknowledgements**    In the previous edition of Form C, I thanked my teachers, past and present, for what they have taught me, sometimes under duress. It seems equally important to thank all of the students who have been my teachers, too; as their most attentive student, I owe them a debt of gratitude for keeping me learning.

The preparation of this edition of the Workbook has also benefited from the insights of my editor, Sarah Helyar Smith, Senior Developmental Editor; Don Fujimoto, Senior Art Director; Debra Jenkin, Production Manager; as well as from Tripp Narup of Monotype Editorial Services. I am grateful also to the guidance of those who reviewed this edition: Robert D. Hoeft, Blue Mountain Community College; Sarah Wooten Pollock, Lenior Community College; and David M. Strain, University of the Ozarks.

# TO THE STUDENT

You learn how to write chiefly by revising your own work. Corrections made for you are of comparatively little value. Therefore the instructor points out the problem but allows you to make the actual revision for yourself. The instructor usually indicates a necessary correction by a number (or a symbol) marked in the margin of your paper opposite the error. If a word is misspelled, the number **18** (or the symbol **sp**) will be used; if there is a sentence fragment, the number **2** (or the symbol **frag**); if there is a faulty reference of a pronoun, the number **28** (or the symbol **ref**). Consult the text (see the guides on the inside covers), master the principles underlying each correction, and make the necessary revisions in red. Draw one red line through words to be deleted, but allow such words to remain legible in order that the instructor may compare the revised form with the original.

In certain cases your instructor may require that you pinpoint your errors by supplying the appropriate letter after the number written in the margin. For example, after the number **12** in the margin you should take special care to supply the appropriate letter (**a, b, c, d,** or **e**) from the explanatory sections on the comma to show why the comma is needed. Simply inserting a comma teaches little; understanding why it is required in a particular situation is a definite step toward mastery of the comma.

## Specimen Paragraph from a Student Theme

Marked by the instructor with numbers:

| | |
|---|---|
| 3 | Taking photographs for newspapers is hard work, it is not the |
| 12 | romantic carefree adventure glorified in motion pictures and novels. For |
| 18 | every great moment recorded by the stareing eye of the camera, there |
| | are twenty routine assignments that must be handled in the same |
| 28 | efficient manner. They must often overcome great hardships. The work |
| 24 | continues for long hours. It must meet dealines. At times they are called |
| | on to risk their lives to obtain a picture. To the newspaper photographer, |
| 2 | getting a good picture being the most important task. |

Marked by the instructor with symbols:

| | |
|---|---|
| cs | Taking photographs for newspapers is hard work, it is not the |
| , / | romantic carefree adventure glorified in motion pictures and novels. For |
| sp | every great moment recorded by the stareing eye of the camera, there |
| | are twenty routine assignments that must be handled in the same |
| ref | efficient manner. They must often overcome great hardships. The work |
| sub | continues for long hours. It must meet dealines. At times they are called |
| | on to risk their lives to obtain a picture. To the newspaper photographer, |
| frag | getting a good picture being the most important task. |

Corrected by the student:

| | |
|---|---|
| 3 | Taking photographs for newspapers is hard work; it is not the |
| 12 | romantic carefree adventure glorified in motion pictures and novels. For |
| 18 | every great moment recorded by the ~~stareing~~ *staring* eye of the camera, there |
| | are twenty routine assignments that must be handled in the same |
| 28 | efficient manner. ~~They must often overcome great hardships. The work~~ *Newspaper photographers must often overcome* |
| 24 | *great hardships and work long hours to meet deadlines.* ~~continues for long hours. It must meet dealines~~. At times they are called |
| | on to risk their lives to obtain a picture. To the newspaper photographer, |
| 2 | getting a good picture ~~being~~ *is* the most important task. |

# CONTENTS

# MECHANICS

# PUNCTUATION

# SPELLING AND DICTION

## 31 Critical Reading and Logical Thinking                 351

# EFFECTIVE WRITING

## 32 The Paragraph                                         359

## SENTENCE SENSE

## 1

### Learn how sentences work.

Most people have a more sophisticated sense of what makes up a sentence than they realize. To demonstrate your own sentence sense, read the following paragraph through several times.

> a person has more than thirty-five thousand different kinds of careers to choose from most people try to choose their careers carefully because they know they will be working for most of their lives they want their careers to be meaningful to themselves and to others each person wants to choose a career that makes the best use of his or her interests and talents clearly the choice of a career is one of the most important and most difficult decisions one makes in life

For this paragraph to have meaning, you must use your sentence sense to group words into separate units of thought. You may have to read the paragraph several times to understand the meaning because the writer did not use the periods and capital letters that show where one sentence ends and another begins. Therefore you, the reader, must supply the markers that the writer neglected to provide. Consider the following revised version of the previous paragraph:

> **A** person has more than thirty-five thousand different kinds of careers to choose from**.** **M**ost people try to choose their careers carefully**.** **B**ecause they know they will be working for most of their lives**,** they want their careers to be meaningful to themselves and to others**.** **E**ach person wants to choose a career that makes the best use of his or her interests and talents**.** **C**learly**,** the choice of a career is one of the most important and most difficult decisions one makes in life**.**

In writing *about* careers, only confusion will result from the writer's failure to follow a standard and accepted form that the reader clearly understands. But what about writing *for* a career? Imagine the harm that would be done if someone wrote this kind of label for a painkilling product:

> Take two tablets every four hours for relief of pain from muscular aches headache and toothache for no more than ten days do not exceed recommended dosage unless advised by a physician keep out of the reach of small children if pain persists consult a physician.

In this case the reader's possible misunderstanding of where sentences begin and end could have serious results for both the producer and the buyer of the product. Whatever the career, the first duty of the writer is to follow a form that will be clear to those who read the writer's message.

Copyright © 1995 by Harcourt Brace & Company. All rights reserved.

**Basic Sentence Parts**   Your plan for learning to write for the world of work begins with developing a strong sentence sense. Almost all sentences are made up of a subject and a predicate. The subject tells who or what the sentence is about, and the predicate says something about the subject.

| SUBJECT | + | PREDICATE |
|---|---|---|
| People | + | once had few choices in careers. |

The subject is often a noun or pronoun—a word such as *people* or *they*. The predicate can be subdivided into two parts: the verb and the complement. The verb expresses an action, an occurrence, or a state of being. The complement receives or completes the action of the verb or says something about the subject. In the following examples, the subject is underlined once; the verb, twice; and the complement, three times. (You will be asked to follow this same pattern as you work the exercises in this chapter of the *Workbook*.)

| SUBJECT | + | VERB | + | COMPLEMENT |
|---|---|---|---|---|
| People | + | once had | + | few choices in careers. |

[*Had* is the verb; it expresses an occurrence. The complement completes the action of the verb.]

| SUBJECT | + | VERB | + | COMPLEMENT |
|---|---|---|---|---|
| Choosing a career | + | is | + | an important decision. |

[The complement says something about the subject.]

*Order of Sentence Parts*   The normal order for the three main sentence parts is subject, verb, complement (S–V–C).

NORMAL ORDER

S–V–C    Today's world offers many careers.

Some sentences have only a subject and a verb.

S–V    Prospective employers advertise in many places.

Although most sentences follow the S–V–C or S–V patterns, writers will sometimes vary the usual order for variety or emphasis.

NORMAL ORDER

S–V–C    The possibilities are many.

Copyright © 1995 by Harcourt Brace & Company. All rights reserved.

EMPHATIC ORDER

C–V–S          Many are the possibilities.   [The subject comes last.]

The writer also varies the normal order when asking most questions.

V–S–V–C        Have you investigated various career opportunities?

               [A part of the verb precedes the subject].

C–V–S–V        How many career opportunities have you investigated?

               [The complement and part of the verb precede the subject.]

And the normal word order varies when a sentence begins with *there* or *it*.

V–S            There are books about careers in the library.

               [The verb precedes the subject.]

V–S            It is likely that you will find helpful information in the library.

The order of the main sentence parts is very important in a language such as English because the function of a word often depends on its position in the sentence. In the following examples, *employer* is a subject in the first sentence and a part of the predicate in the second; on the other hand, *employees* is a part of the predicate in the first sentence and a subject in the second. Only the *position* of these two words tells you what part they play in the sentence.

The employer praised the employees.

The employees praised their employer.

Both the subject and the verb will be explored in depth in the following pages of Chapter **1**.

Copyright © 1995 by Harcourt Brace & Company. All rights reserved.

Deduct 5 for each incorrect answer.

**Basic Sentence Parts**                                            Exercise 1–1

NAME _____ SCORE _____

DIRECTIONS   In the following sentences, the subject is underlined once, the verb is underlined twice, and the complement (when there is one) is underlined three times. If the main parts of the sentence are in the usual word order (S–V–C), write *usual* in the blank; if they vary from the usual order, write *varied* in the blank. When you finish the exercise, answer the questions and complete the revisions called for on the next page.

EXAMPLE
What would you have done to make a living during the 1700s?    *varied*

1.  Your career in colonial America would probably have been farming.    usual

2.  In the early days of colonial America, most families worked a farm
    for a living.    usual

3.  Every person in these farm families had his or her work on the
    family farm.    usual

4.  There were many chores to be done each day.    varied

5.  Of necessity, families were very large.    usual

6.  Some of the people in a farm-centered community made their
    living running the general store.    usual

7.  Have you seen record books from a colonial store?    varied

8.  An account book from the Cades Cove Community in Tennessee
    lists the purchases families in the area made.    usual

9.  What supplies would most families purchase?    varied

10. Things like tobacco, coal oil, coffee, and shoes were typical
    purchases.    usual

Copyright © 1995 by Harcourt Brace & Company. All rights reserved.

11. Most families paid for their purchases with products from their

    farms.                                                          _usual_

12. During the 1800s, the Agricultural Revolution began to affect farm

    life in North America.                                          _usual_

13. Because of improved farming methods, fewer people were needed

    to work a farm.                                                 _usual_

14. Being built everywhere were factories.                          _varied_

15. Many people who had been farmers now found many types of jobs

    in the factories.                                               _usual_


QUESTIONS

1. Which sentence varies from the usual S–V–C word order for the
   sake of emphasis?                                                _14_

   Rewrite the following sentences in the usual S–V–C word order:


4. Many chores were to be done each day.


7. You have seen record books from a colonial store.


9. Most families would purchase supplies.


14. Factories were being built everywhere.


*6*

Copyright © 1995 by Harcourt Brace & Company. All rights reserved.

## 1a  Learn to recognize verbs.

Every sentence has a verb, even one-word sentences that trainers use to communicate with their dogs: *Stay. Fetch. Sit.* Even though the verb is usually the second main part of a sentence, when you look for sentence parts, find the verb first since no sentence can be a sentence without one.

*Function*     Like the words spoken by a dog trainer, most verbs express action. But other kinds of verbs express occurrences or states of being.

ACTION                Most people now *work* eight hours a day.

OCCURRENCE            Many people *choose* their careers during their teenage years.

STATE OF BEING        Sometimes people *become* unhappy with their careers.

**Note:**   The verb may appear as part of a contraction: I'*m* (I *am*), we'*re* (we *are*), he'*d* (he *had* or he *would*).

Sometimes a word looks like a verb because its meaning is associated with action, but it functions as some other sentence part—quite often as the subject or a modifier. Take the word *work*, for example, which is an action word but which can serve as a subject, a verb, or a modifier.

SUBJECT              *Work* is important to most people.

VERB                People *work* for reasons other than pay.

MODIFIER             The five-day *work* week may become obsolete.

To distinguish between *work* as a verb and *work* as some other sentence part, try putting an article (*a*, *an*, or *the*) in front of the word; if the sentence still makes sense, then the word is probably functioning as some other sentence part, but if the sentence does not make sense with the article included, the word is functioning as a verb.

SUBJECT              [*The*]   Work is important to most people.

VERB                People   [*the*]   work for reasons other than pay.

MODIFIER             [*The*] five-day work week may become obsolete.

The verb determines the kind of complement that the sentence will have: either a word or words that receive the action of the verb or a word or words that say something about the subject.

*Transitive Verbs*     Many verbs serve as transitive verbs; they pass their action along to the object or objects. (See also **1b(2)**.)

TRANSITIVE           Fortunately, people can change their careers.

                     [Can change what? *Careers* receives the action of the verb.]

Copyright © 1995 by Harcourt Brace & Company. All rights reserved.

TRANSITIVE     An internship showed me the need to change my career plans.

[*Showed* whom what? *Me* and *need* receive the action of the verb.]

*Intransitive Verbs*     If, on the other hand, the verb does not pass its action along to the complement, it is referred to as an *intransitive verb*. One type of intransitive verb is complete in itself; it has no complement.

INTRANSITIVE     The internship ended.

[The verb, *ended*, is complete in itself; it needs no complement.]

Another type of intransitive verb, the *linking verb*, introduces material in the predicate that gives more information about the subject. The most common linking verbs are *be* (*is, are, am, was, were, has been, have been, will be*, and so on), *seem, appear*, and verbs that refer to the senses, such as *taste, look*, and *feel*.

LINKING VERBS     I was grateful for the internship program.   [*Was* links the subject

with a complement, *grateful*, that says something about the subject.]

*Position*     The verb (underlined twice) is usually the second main part of a sentence; however, in questions, emphatic sentences, or sentences beginning with *there* or *it*, the verb may come first or may come before the subject (underlined once).

USUAL ORDER     Interns *can gain* valuable work experience.

QUESTION     *Can* interns *gain* valuable work experience?

EMPHATIC     Valuable *is* the experience that interns can gain.

THERE     *There is* valuable experience that interns can gain.

*Form*     Verbs can change their form to show number (one or more) and tense (the time of the action, occurrence, or state of being). Singular verbs in the present tense usually end in *s* or *es*, and past tense verbs usually end in *d* or *ed*. (The dictionary shows all unusual changes in verb form.)

A person usually *shows* a natural inclination to work with people or with things. [singular number; present tense]
People *show* their preferences in many ways.   [plural number; present tense]
She *has decided* on a career in counseling.   [past tense shown by *d* ending of main verb; singular number shown by helping verb, *has*]
They *have selected* accounting as their major.   [past tense shown by *ed* ending of main verb; plural number shown by helping verb, *have*]

     Copyright © 1995 by Harcourt Brace & Company. All rights reserved.

*Auxiliary (Helping) Verbs*     Often the main verb—which shows action, occurrence, or state of being—is accompanied by one or more helping verbs—usually forms of *be* (*is, are, was, were, has been, will be,* and so on) or *has, have, do, can,* or *could* (the Appendix contains a more complete list of helping verbs). The helping verb or verbs (also called *auxiliary verbs*) may come immediately before the main verb or may be separated from the main verb.

> Fortunately, people today *can change* their careers.   [The helping verb, *can,* immediately precedes the main verb, *change.*]
> They *do* not *have* to remain in the same career forever.   [The helping verb, *do,* is separated from the main verb, *have,* by *not.*]
> *Have* you *found* your career yet?   [The helping verb, *have,* is separated from the main verb, *found,* by the subject, *you.*]

Notice that a verb such as *have, has, be, can,* and *do* works either as the main verb of the sentence or as a helping verb. In the second example above, *have* is the main verb; in the third example, it is the helping verb.

**Note:**   The helping verb, like the main verb, may be a part of a contraction: *can't* find (*can*not find), *she's* coming (she *is* coming), *we've* gone (we *have* gone).

*Verb + Particle*     The main verb may also be accompanied by a particle—a word (or words) like *to, in, with, up,* and *of* that adds to or changes the meaning of the main verb.

> We *put* our names on the list of applicants for the job.   [main verb]
> We *cannot put up with* the company's delay much longer.   [The main verb, *put,* is accompanied by a helping verb, *can,* and the particles *up* and *with.*]

*Compound Verbs*     Often a sentence has two verbs connected by *and, but, or,* or *nor.*

> We *applied for* summer work but *did* not *hear* from the company for a month.
> We *waited* and *waited* for some word.

Copyright © 1995 by Harcourt Brace & Company. All rights reserved.

Deduct 3 1/2 for each incorrect item on the list.

**Identifying Verbs**                                          Exercise 1–2

NAME _____ SCORE _____

DIRECTIONS   The following famous quotations about work illustrate the various functions of verbs—to express action, occurrence, or state of being. The subject of each verb is already underlined once; you should underline each verb twice. (Most sentences have more than one verb.) Then make a list of the twenty-nine verbs that you have located in these quotations.

EXAMPLE
Work is the refuge of people who have nothing better to do.   —OSCAR WILDE

1. I'm [I am] a great believer in luck, and I find the harder I work the more I have of it.   —THOMAS JEFFERSON

2. When a man tells you that he got rich through hard work, [you] ask him whose. —DON MARCUS

3. If everything about work is so wonderful, why, then, is it so much work for me to get there when it's [it is] raining?   —R. ANNE DAHL

4. A human being must have occupation if he or she is not to become a nuisance to the world.   —DOROTHY L. SAYERS

5. Apparently we all work for ourselves, but in reality we are always working for others.   —DR. WILLIAM STEKHEL

6. When I think of work, I think of my cat: she works by sleeping on my desk. —F. FREDERICK SKITTIE

7. [You] never give away your work. People don't [do not] value what they don't [do not] have to pay for.   —NANCY HALE

8. I thought [work] was a very bad thing that the human race had invented for itself. —AGATHA CHRISTIE

9. A society in which everyone works is not necessarily a free society and may indeed be a slave society.   —ELEANOR ROOSEVELT

10. I never forget that work is a curse—which is why I've [I have] never made it a habit.   —BLAISE CENDRARS

Copyright © 1995 by Harcourt Brace & Company. All rights reserved.

LIST OF VERBS

1. am
2. find
3. work
4. have
5. tells
6. got
7. ask
8. is
9. is
10. is raining
11. must have
12. is
13. work
14. are working
15. think

16. think
17. works
18. give
19. do value
20. do have
21. thought
22. was
23. had invented
24. works
25. is
26. may be
27. forget
28. is
29. have made

Copyright © 1995 by Harcourt Brace & Company. All rights reserved.

Deduct 10 for each incorrectly filled blank.

**Identifying Helping Verbs and Particles**                    Exercise 1–3

NAME _____ SCORE _____

DIRECTIONS    In the following sentences the main verbs are underlined twice. Find the helping verbs and particles that go with these main verbs and also underline them twice. Then write the entire verb or verbs in the blank.

EXAMPLE
People should study the job market and match up their skills with the available positions.

should study, match up

1. You can often learn about jobs from friends and relatives. *can learn*

2. Or you can look up job listings at your school's Job Information and Placement

   Center. *can look up*

3. Sending out unsolicited application letters will also help you identify jobs.

   *will help*

4. This sort of letter should clearly identify the type of job you want to apply for since

   the company will have sent out no job announcement. *should identify,*

   *will have sent out*

5. These letters do locate employment opportunities, but you will want to research

   the companies you contact in this way. *do locate, will want*

6. Because a company did not advertise a job, your job will be to convince them that

   they need your skills. *did advertise, will be*

Copyright © 1995 by Harcourt Brace & Company. All rights reserved.

7. You can either call or write a potential employer about a job interview. _____

   *can call, (can) write* _____

8. Because your application will offer the employer a first, and usually a lasting,

   impression of you, you must certainly make an effort to make yours perfect. ____

   *will offer, must make* _____

9. Your letter must clearly describe the skills you have that make you the right candi-

   date for the job. *must describe* _____

10. The last paragraph of your letter should ask for an interview and should give your

   phone number. *should ask, should give* _____

Copyright © 1995 by Harcourt Brace & Company. All rights reserved.

Deduct 10 for each incorrectly filled blank.

**Main Verbs, Helping Verbs, and Particles**                    Exercise 1–4

NAME _____    SCORE _____

DIRECTIONS   In the following sentences the subjects have been underlined once. Underline the complete verbs twice—that is, the main verbs and, if there are any, the helping verbs and particles. Some sentences have compound verbs. Write the complete verb or verbs for each sentence in the blank.

EXAMPLE
The applicant may send in a résumé with the letter of application.

__may send in_____

1. Rather than mailing in your résumé ahead of time, you may wish to take it along

   with you to the interview.  _may wish_____

2. On your résumé your education, special skills, and job experience should all be

   clearly outlined for the employer.  _should be outlined_____

3. Because most readers are busy people, you must try to limit your résumé to one or

   two pages.  _are, must try_____

4. Your name, address, and telephone numbers will normally appear at the top of

   your résumé.  _will appear_____

5. The educational record and employment background of an applicant, as well as

   other information—honors and activities—constitute the body of the résumé.

   _constitute_____

Copyright © 1995 by Harcourt Brace & Company. All rights reserved.

6. You will most certainly want to list the names of three to five references.

   _will want_

7. If you list a person as a reference, you must, of course, be sure they can speak of

   your qualifications for the job. _list, must be_

8. Can you now put together a convincing résumé? _can put_

9. Before you have your résumé printed to mail out, you should print it out and look

   it over carefully. _have printed, should print out,_

   _(should) look over_

10. To make the best impression on an employer, your résumé should probably be

    typeset and professionally printed. _should be typeset, (should be) printed_

Copyright © 1995 by Harcourt Brace & Company. All rights reserved.

Deduct 5 for each blank incorrectly filled.

## Forms of Verbs

Exercise 1–5

NAME _____ SCORE _____

DIRECTIONS   In each of the following sentences one verb has been omitted. Fill in the blank with the present tense (present time) of the verb that appears in parentheses after the sentence. The subjects of the sentences are printed in italics.

EXAMPLE

Many college *courses* _____**present**_____ theory rather than applied practice. (presented)

*Putting* theory into practice _____**comes**_____ with the job.   (came)

1. *People* _____**think**_____ of their work in different ways.   (thought)

2. Many *arguments* _____**arise**_____ over the importance of work.   (arose)

3. Some *people* _____**see**_____ their families as more important than their jobs.   (saw)

4. *Others* _____**feel**_____ their careers are the most important part of their lives.   (felt)

5. "All *work* and no *play* _____**make**_____ Jack a dull boy" is a familiar saying. (made)

6. "*Idle hands are the devil's workshop*" _____**is**_____ another well-known expression.   (was)

7. Other *people* _____**say**_____ that work is just something that people do to make the money they need to do the important things in life.   (said)

8. One *person* _____**asserts**_____ that work is life itself.   (asserted)

9. The *importance* of work _____**depends**_____ on a person's values.   (depended)

10. For every one hundred lazy workers there _____**is**_____ at least one *workaholic*.   (was)

Copyright © 1995 by Harcourt Brace & Company. All rights reserved.

11. Most *people* in the work force _____ fall _____ somewhere in between these two extremes.   (fell)

12. Still, most *people* _____ spend _____ many hours a day at work.   (spent)

13. A *workaholic*, however, _____ finds _____ it difficult to stop working. (found)

14. The *workaholic* _____ stays _____ on at the office long after the end of the eight-hour day.   (stayed)

15. The workaholic's *characteristics* _____ include _____ an inability to accept failure, guilt about their level of productivity, and almost constant worry about performance.   (included)

16. For the workaholic, all *relationships* and leisure *activities* _____ become _____ unimportant when measured against success at work.   (became)

17. Such a *person* rarely _____ enjoys _____ a vacation.   (enjoyed)

18. Most *workaholics* _____ die _____ before they reach retirement age. (died)

19. *Heart attacks* among workaholics _____ are _____ extremely common. (was)

20. There _____ are _____ more *workaholics* than most of us realize.   (was)

Copyright © 1995 by Harcourt Brace & Company. All rights reserved.

**Verbals**   Like verbs, verbals express action, occurrence, or a state of being. And the endings they have—*ing*, *ed*, and *en*—are the same endings that verbs can have. Here, for example, are four verbal forms for the verb *take*:

*taking, taken, having taken, to take*

(Notice that *taking* and *taken*, when accompanied by helping verbs, are true verbs: *are taking* and *have taken*, for example.)

Finally, like verbs, verbals are often followed by words that complete their meaning.

*Taking* my **time**, I found just the job I wanted. [Taking what? *Time* completes the meaning of the verbal.]

*Having* taken a vocational aptitude **test**, I was better able to *plan* a **career.** [Having taken what? *Test* completes the meaning of the first verbal. To plan what? *Career* completes the meaning of the second verbal.]

But in spite of its similarities to a true verb, a verbal cannot serve as the main verb of a sentence. Consider, for example, this sentence with its verb *have taken*.

We have taken our time.

Notice that when a verbal replaces the verb, the word group is no longer a sentence. (See also **2a**.)

we *taking* our time
we *having taken* our time
we *to take* our time

Thus whenever there is a verbal (or verbals) in a sentence, there must also be a main, or true, verb.

*Taking* our time, we filled out the application carefully.

*Having taken* our time, we answered each question completely.

*To take* our time we carried our applications home *to fill out*.

Copyright © 1995 by Harcourt Brace & Company. All rights reserved.

Deduct 10 for each incorrect verb (the second blank).

**Recognizing Verbs and Verbals**                    Exercise 1–6

NAME _____ SCORE _____

DIRECTIONS   Here are ten famous quotations about work. The verbals have been printed in italics. Find the true verbs and underline them twice. In the first blank, write the verbal or verbals; in the second, write the verb or verbs.

EXAMPLE

*Working* with people is difficult, but not impossible.   —PETER DRUCKER

_____ Working _____          _____ is _____

1. We work *to become,* not *to acquire.*   —ELBERT HUBBARD

_____ to become, to acquire _____          _____ work _____

2. Work expands so as *to fill* the time available for its completion.

—NORTHCOTE PARKINSON

_____ to fill _____          _____ expands _____

3. If there is one thing better than the thrill of *looking* forward, it is the exhilaration

that follows the *finishing* of a long and exacting piece of work.   —ALEC WAUGH

_____ looking, finishing _____          _____ is, is, follows _____

4. Many men are hard workers: they're [they are] always looking around *to find* some-

thing for others *to do.*   —EVAN ESAR

_____ to find, to do _____          _____ are, are looking around _____

Copyright © 1995 by Harcourt Brace & Company. All rights reserved.

5. Next to *doing* a good job yourself the greatest joy is in *having* someone else do a

   first-class job under your direction.   —WILLIAM FEATHER

   | doing, having | is, do |
   |---|---|

6. I go on *working* for the same reason that a hen goes on laying eggs.   —H. L. MENCKEN

   | working, laying | go on, goes on |
   |---|---|

7. Anyone can do any amount of work *provided* it isn't [is not] the work he is supposed

   *to be doing* at the moment.   —ROBERT BENCHLEY

   | provided, to be doing | can do, is, is supposed |
   |---|---|

8. No man is obliged *to do* as much as he can do; a man is *to have* part of his life

   to himself.   —SAMUEL JOHNSON

   | to do, to have | is obliged, can do, is |
   |---|---|

9. *Thinking* and *fretting* about work to be done often uses up more energy than

   *completing* the actual task.   —JEFF BARTH

   | thinking, fretting, completing | to be done, use up |
   |---|---|

10. A great many people have...asked how I manage *to get* so much work *done* and

    still keep *looking so dissipated.*   —ROBERT BENCHLEY

    | to get done, looking so dissipated | have asked, manage, keep |
    |---|---|

   Copyright © 1995 by Harcourt Brace & Company. All rights reserved.

## 1b  Learn to recognize subjects, objects, and complements.

### 1b(1)  Learn to recognize subjects of verbs.

A sentence that has a verb but no stated subject is a command. In a command, the subject is understood to be *you*, though it is not actually written down.

[You] Fill out the application form and return it to the personnel director.

In all other kinds of sentences, the subject is stated, even in the shortest of sentences.

*I quit*!

*Function*     The subject is who or what the sentence is about. Once you have located the verb in a sentence, all you need to do then is to ask who or what is *doing, occurring,* or *being*. Your answer will be the complete subject. To find the simple subject, ask specifically who or what the verb is talking about.

Many important rewards are derived from work.   [What are derived? *Many important*

*rewards*. What specifically are derived? Not "many important" but *rewards*.]

One of my friends wants a high income more than anything else.   [Who wants? *One of my*

*friends*. Who specifically wants? Not "of my friends" but *one*.]

It is important to be able to find the simple subject in a sentence so that you can make the number of the verb and the subject the same. If you mistake "friends" as the subject of the last example above, you will probably make the verb plural—"want"— and thus make an error in agreement because the simple subject is *one* and the verb must be singular (*wants*) to agree with it in number. (See also Chapter **6**.)

*Compound Subjects*     Like the verb, the subject of a sentence may be compound. The parts of the compound subject are connected by a word like *and, but, or,* or *nor* (printed in boldface below).

*Income, recognition,* **and** *adventure* are three goals sought by workers.
Not *income* **but** *adventure* is my main concern now.

## Noun Subjects
A majority of simple subjects are nouns, words that name persons, places, things, and ideas. Since people first appeared on the earth, they have been interested in nouns. We are told that the first job Adam had was to name the things he saw in the Garden of Eden: *sky, bird, flower, tree, apple, snake*. (Adam's name, of course, was a noun, too, as was the name of Eve.)

Modern people are still giving names to things. As soon as something new comes along, we rush to give it a name: *Skylab, astronaut, détente, rock and roll, Amtrak*.

Copyright © 1995 by Harcourt Brace & Company. All rights reserved.

*Types of Nouns*   Proper nouns begin with capital letters and name particular people, places, things, and ideas: *Columbus, New World, Mayflower, Thanksgiving, Declaration of Independence.* Common nouns are not capitalized; they are everyday names for general classes of people, places, things, and ideas: *explorer, continent, ship, holiday, capitalism.* Both common and proper nouns are often made up of more than one word: *tennis court, mother-in-law, oil well, Holy City, Bill of Rights.*

Many nouns name things that can be touched; these are called concrete nouns: *contract, report, insurance, corporation.* Other nouns refer to matters that cannot be touched; these are called abstract nouns: *praise, safety, satisfaction, plan, hostility.*

As you can see, we need nouns to say almost anything, even to speak a nonsense sentence like "*Peter Piper* picked a *peck* of pickled *peppers.*"

*Noun Signals*   Certain words signal that a noun is coming. Articles (*a, an, the*) and possessive pronouns (*my, your, his, her, its, our,* and *their*) are followed by nouns.

**The** *supervisor* gave us **a** *copy* of **our** latest *reports.*

*Form*   Nouns change their endings to show two things: plural number and posses-sion. When we name more than one of anything, we usually add an *s* or *es* to show that the noun is plural. (Remember that verbs act in just the opposite way: an *s* or *es* ending means that the verb is singular.)

> I wrote one report; Ethan wrote two reports.
> I read one memo; Ethan read two memos.
> I hired one woman; Ethan hired two women.
> I have one brother-in-law; Ethan has two brothers-in-law.   [Note that the chief word, *brother*, shows the sign of the plural.]

The dictionary shows you the plural for all nouns that form their plurals in some way other than the addition of *s* (for example, *man*→*men, calf*→*calves, sheep*→*sheep*).

Singular nouns add an apostrophe and an *s* (*'s*) to show possession, or ownership: *Ethan's job* or *Ethan's house* (we do not write *Ethan house* or *Ethan job*). The possessive noun is placed in front of the person, place, thing, or idea possessed.

If the possessive noun is plural, we usually add only the apostrophe:

| | | |
|---|---|---|
| jobs' requirements | teachers' salaries | guests' arrival |
| potatoes' roots | cities' problems | wolves' howling |

But if the plural of the noun does not end in *s* (*women, children,* and *alumni,* for example), we add *'s* to form the plural possessive:

| | | |
|---|---|---|
| women's rights | children's absences | alumni's contributions |

When a compound noun is made possessive, the last word shows the sign of the possessive case:

| | |
|---|---|
| sons-in-law's jobs | the Queen of England's biography |

**Note:**   When we give a noun the possessive form, whether singular or plural, we change it to a modifier—a descriptive or qualifying word. (You will study modifiers in **1d**.)

Copyright © 1995 by Harcourt Brace & Company. All rights reserved.

Deduct 2 for each blank incorrectly filled.

## Recognizing Nouns

Exercise 1–7

NAME _____ SCORE _____

DIRECTIONS   Use *a*, *an*, and *the* to decide which of the following words are nouns; if a word sounds right with *a*, *an*, or *the* in front of it, write its plural form in the blank. If it does not, the word is not a noun; in that case, leave the blank empty. (If you are uncertain how to make the plural of the noun, consult your dictionary. When no plural form is given, the noun forms its plural in the usual way—by adding an *s* or *es*. See also **18d (5)**.)

EXAMPLES

into         _____

laugh        _____laughs_____

1. potato      _____potatoes_____          13. ski         _____skis_____

2. believe     _____           14. on          _____

3. story       _____stories_____           15. right       _____rights_____

4. such        _____           16. with        _____

5. artist-in-      artists-in-             17. carton      _____cartons_____

   residence       residence               18. some        _____

6. wolf        _____wolves_____            19. child       _____children_____

7. big         _____           20. happy       _____

8. penny       _____pennies_____           21. account     _____accounts_____

9. belief      _____beliefs_____           22. percentage  _____percentages_____

10. sock       _____socks_____             23. slowly      _____

11. boss       _____bosses_____            24. blessing    _____blessings_____

12. bagful     _____bagfuls_____           25. object      _____objects_____

Copyright © 1995 by Harcourt Brace & Company. All rights reserved.

DIRECTIONS   Use a possessive pronoun—*our*, for example—to decide which of the following words are nouns. If a word sounds right with *our* in front of it, write its plural in the blank. If it does not sound right with *our* in front of it, leave the blank empty because the word is not a noun. Use your dictionary to help you form the plurals of nouns that do not follow the usual pattern of adding *s* or *es*.

| | | | |
|---|---|---|---|
| 1. toy | toys | 14. reception | receptions |
| 2. remedy | remedies | 15. crisis | crises |
| 3. receive | | 16. fulfill | |
| 4. cargo | cargos or cargoes | 17. industry | industries |
| 5. fox | foxes | 18. ox | oxen |
| 6. only | | 19. brother- | brothers- |
| 7. separate | | in-law | in-law |
| 8. moth | moths | 20. business | businesses |
| 9. mosquito | mosquitoes or mosquitos | 21. compute | |
| 10. bus | buses or busses | 22. tendency | tendencies |
| 11. company | companies | 23. monkey | monkeys |
| 12. church | churches | 24. bench | benches |
| 13. patio | patios | 25. excellent | |

Copyright © 1995 by Harcourt Brace & Company. All rights reserved.

Deduct 5 for each blank incorrectly filled.

**Recognizing Simple Subjects**                          Exercise 1–8

NAME _____ SCORE _____

DIRECTIONS   The complete subject in each of the following sentences is italicized. Find the simple subject that tells specifically who or what the verb (underlined twice) is speaking about. Underline the simple subject with one line and write it in the blank. (Remember that a simple subject may be compound.)

EXAMPLES

*A poorly prepared job candidate* entered the office.                _candidate_

*This person's résumé, with its many typographical errors,* was

   difficult to read.                                                _résumé_

1. *The sloppy clothes that the applicant wore* created an

   unfavorable first impression.                                     _clothes_

2. *Both the person and the résumé* looked untidy.            _person, résumé_

3. *Poor preparation for the interview* also did not help to

   improve the candidate's image.                                    _preparation_

4. *The job applicant's vague, halting replies to the inter-*

   *viewer's questions* were other problems.                         _replies_

5. *The main requirements for the job that the applicant*

   *sought* were neatness and self-confidence.                       _requirements_

6. *This particular person's interview with the personnel*

   *director* lasted just ten minutes.                               _interview_

7. Needless to say, *this inappropriately dressed and poorly*

   *prepared applicant* did not get the job.                         _applicant_

8. *The things on which people base their decision about*

   *whom to offer a job* often relate to first impressions.          _things_

Copyright © 1995 by Harcourt Brace & Company. All rights reserved.

9. *Many well-qualified people may apply for a job.*  —— people ——

10. *The person who is determined to land a good job must* carefully prepare for each interview.  —— person ——

11. *The self-confidence and fluency gained by careful preparation will help any job applicant.*  —— self-confidence, fluency ——

12. *A neatly filled-out application, a carefully typed résumé, and a businesslike appearance are three* especially valuable assets for any job applicant.  —— application, résumé, appearance ——

13. *Various methods of preparing for an interview can* benefit any job seeker.  —— methods ——

14. *One way to get ready for an interview is to make a list* of questions the interviewer might ask.  —— way ——

15. *The effort devoted to rehearsing possible answers to such questions will generally pay off.*  —— effort ——

16. *Another thing that the applicant might do is to write out* an autobiography.  —— thing ——

17. *The details included in the autobiography usually* provide answers to questions one may be asked.  —— details ——

18. *The interests and abilities of the applicant come out in* the autobiography.  —— interests, abilities ——

19. *These two important areas are usually covered during* an interview.  —— areas ——

20. *Some especially well-prepared applicants have actually* staged mock interviews.  —— applicants ——

Copyright © 1995 by Harcourt Brace & Company. All rights reserved.

Deduct 10 for each incorrect subject and verb.

**Mastering Noun Subjects and Verbs**                    Exercise 1–9

NAME _____    SCORE _____

DIRECTIONS    Rewrite the subject and verb parts of the following sentences, changing the simple subjects and verbs from singular to plural or plural to singular. Underline the subjects with one line and the verbs with two lines.

EXAMPLE
A person trains for a job in various ways.

People (or Persons) train for

1. Students acquire skills (for example, typing and bookkeeping) through high-school and college courses.

    Student acquires

2. Classes sometimes require outside work in the field of the student's intended occupation.

    Class requires

3. For example, would-be teachers do student teaching during the last year of college.

    teacher does

4. Prospective computer repair technicians also participate in apprenticeships.

    technician participates

5. The on-the-job experiences in the field show the trainee what his or her future job is really all about.

    experience shows

6. Sometimes after the internship the apprentices change occupational goals.

    apprentice changes

7. More often, the intern decides to continue with his or her chosen career.

    interns decide

8. Sometimes the student gets additional training in a specialized occupation through a summer job.

    students get

9. Summer positions often pay little or nothing at all, but give valuable experience.

    position pays

10. Thus the trainees are rewarded twice: in money and in extra, hands-on experience.

    trainee is rewarded

Copyright © 1995 by Harcourt Brace & Company. All rights reserved.

**Pronoun Subjects**   Besides the noun, the pronoun is the other common type of simple subject. The use of pronouns avoids the unpleasant and often tedious repetition of nouns; substituting pronouns for some of the nouns will also add variety to your sentences. The skillful use of pronouns will help you avoid repetitious sentences such as

> The *manager* reads *reports*.
> The *manager* evaluates the information the *reports* provide.
> The *manager* bases the *manager's* decisions on the *reports'* recommendations.

Clearly, that discussion of decision making would have been much improved if the writer had used pronouns—words that substitute for nouns.

> The *manager* reads *reports*.
> *She* evaluates the information that *they* provide.
> *She* bases her decisions on *their* recommendations.

*Function*   Pronouns take the place of nouns. The meaning of a pronoun is clear only when the reader is sure what noun is being referred to (usually called the pronoun's *antecedent* or its *referent*). For this reason, careful writers always make sure that each pronoun they use has an easily identifiable antecedent.

NOUNS   All graduating *seniors* must take a one-hour *course* in "How to Get a Job."

PRONOUNS   *They* must take *it* so that *they* will be prepared for job interviews. [*They* refers to *seniors*; *it* refers to *course*.]

*Types of Pronouns*   Unlike the almost limitless number of nouns, there are only a certain number of pronouns. The most frequently used ones are called personal pronouns: *I, me, you, he, him, she, her, it, we, us, they,* and *them*. As their name indicates, these pronouns refer to people or to living things.

Other pronouns refer only to things: *something, nothing, everything,* and *which*, for example. A few pronouns can refer to either persons or to things: *one, each, most, some, many, all, both,* and *that*.

A few important pronouns that you will study in depth later—*who, whom, which, that, what, whose, whoever,* and *whomever*—help to expand sentences. These pronouns sometimes serve as the subjects of their own word clusters, and they, too, take their meaning from the nouns to which they refer.

> The students *who* take this course are well prepared for their job interviews.
> [*Who* is the subject of the verb *take*; it refers to the noun *students*.]
> This course, *which* is offered several times a semester, is invaluable to students.
> [*Which* is the subject of the verb *is offered*; it refers to the noun *course*.]

These same pronouns may be used to ask questions—and are called interrogative pronouns when they are so used (in which case they need not always refer to particular nouns).

> *Who* is your supervisor?
> *What* is your job?

Copyright © 1995 by Harcourt Brace & Company. All rights reserved.

*Form*    Unlike nouns, pronouns do not form their plural by adding *s* or *es*. Instead, *I* becomes *we*; *he*, *she*, and *it* become *they*. One personal pronoun—*you*—does not change form at all to show plural number. Other pronouns can only be singular: for example, *each* and *one*; still others can only be plural: for example, *both* and *many*.

A few pronouns, like nouns, form their possessive by adding an *'s*: someone*'s* hat, everyone*'s* concern, anyone*'s* hope. All personal pronouns, however, have a distinct form for the possessive case: *my*, *mine*; *your*, *yours*; *his*; *her*, *hers*; *its*; *our*, *ours*; and *their*, *theirs*. And personal pronouns, unlike nouns, change their form to show whether they are being used as subjects or as objects of verbs (receivers of the action of the verb).

SUBJECT    *He* asked James for a raise.

OBJECT    James gave *him* his raise last month.

Copyright © 1995 by Harcourt Brace & Company. All rights reserved.

Deduct 5 for each incorrect pronoun.*

## Pronouns as Replacements for Nouns

Exercise 1–10

NAME _____   SCORE _____

DIRECTIONS   Work with the following paragraph to substitute pronouns for at least twelve of the nouns or noun phrases to reduce the weak repetition. All of the nouns in the paragraph have been underlined to help you locate them. Remember not to create confusing antecedent problems; make sure that each pronoun that you use has a clear antecedent.

                                      *she*

The one thing that April Miller knew when April was a little girl was that she wanted

           *She*                                              *ones*

to be a veterinarian. April Miller explored many occupations, but the occupations that

*her*             *ones*          *her*

suited April Miller best were the occupations that allowed Miller to work with animals.

                      *They*                      *her*

April Miller had always loved animals. Animals seemed to relate well to Miller. When

            *she*                                   *She*

April was in high school April worked for a veterinarian named Annie Gray. Annie told

              *her*

April Miller that it had taken Annie many years to get through veterinarian school.

Annie Gray was the first female to apply for admission to the veterinary school at the

            *It*                               *they*

State University. The State University had women students, but the women students

mainly studied teaching and nursing. The State University did not have a policy against

                                      *it*

admitting women students to the veterinary college; the State University had just never

         *them*

had women students apply for admission before. The veterinary professors at the

                                *she*

State University gave Gray a hard time once Gray finally got to study to be a vet, but

      *one*                                     *they*

being a vet was a goal Annie Gray had set for herself, and the veterinary professors

weren't going to stand in Annie Gray's way. As April Miller listened to Annie Gray's

    *she*

story, April realized that much had changed in the forty years since Annie Gray opened

her veterinary practice as the first "lady vet" in Montana.

*Students' answers will vary depending on the nouns they choose to replace. This key identifies one possible series of nouns a student might replace.

Copyright © 1995 by Harcourt Brace & Company. All rights reserved.

Deduct 10 for each incorrectly filled blank.

**Recognizing Pronoun Subjects**                     Exercise 1–11

NAME _____   SCORE _____

DIRECTIONS   The verbs in the following sentences have been underlined twice. Underline all subjects with one line, and write the pronoun subjects in the blanks. Many sentences have more than one subject.

EXAMPLE
The occupations that people with disabilities fill are many.              _____that_____

1. What people with disabilities can do is limitless.                      _____What_____

2. Virtually everything is open to them that anyone else can do.           _everything_

3. You and I will more than likely work alongside many persons

   with disabilities.                                                      ____You, I____

4. That will be a reality because of the Americans with

   Disabilities Act.                                                       ____That____

5. It requires employers to refrain from discriminating against

   persons with disabilities.                                             _____It_____

6. A person with a disability who has the same education, train-

   ing, and experience as other people has a legal right to be

   considered equally.                                                    _person, who_

7. Everyone should be able to pursue whatever career they

   desire.                                                                 ___Everyone___

8. My friend, who specializes in treating children with cancer

   and who uses a wheelchair, works in a teaching hospital in

   Seattle, Washington.                                                    _friend, who_

9. Many times, as she interacts with the children, she says they

   will climb onto her lap.                                               ___she, she___

10. In her work with severely ill children, she thinks her wheel-

    chair makes them see her as being more like them.                     _____she_____

Copyright © 1995 by Harcourt Brace & Company. All rights reserved.                     *35*

Deduct 5 for each incorrect subject (the first blank).

**Mastering Subjects: A Review**                    Exercise 1–12

NAME _____    SCORE _____

DIRECTIONS    All verbs in the following sentences are underlined twice. You are to underline once the noun or pronoun subjects that tell who or what is doing, occurring, or being. Then write the subject in the first blank and the verb in the second blank. (Remember that a sentence may have a compound subject and/or verb.)

EXAMPLE
A funny movie, *9 to 5,* paints a grim picture for working women.

_____ movie _____        _____ paints _____

1.  In this film, three women who have jobs in an office endure the tyranny of their boss.

_____ women _____        _____ endure _____

2.  This powerful man treated the many women working for him with disrespect.

_____ man _____        _____ treated _____

3.  The boss, played by Dabney Coleman, made rude remarks about one woman's figure.

_____ boss _____        _____ made _____

4.  Dolly Parton played the woman who was harassed for romantic attention.

_____ Dolly Parton _____        _____ played _____

5.  Courts have now labeled that kind of treatment as "sexual harassment."

_____ Courts _____        _____ have labeled _____

6.  The second female character, created by Jane Fonda, is also unappreciated by

the boss.        _____ character _____        _____ is _____

7.  Unlike Parton's character, this woman is afraid to speak up for herself.

_____ woman _____        _____ is _____

8.  The boss taunts her and shouts at her about little mistakes.

_____ boss _____        _____ taunts, shouts _____

Copyright © 1995 by Harcourt Brace & Company. All rights reserved.

9. But what really bothers her are his demeaning remarks about her gender.

<u>what really bothers her, remarks</u>    <u>are</u>

10. The arrogant boss puts her work down because she is not aggressive.

<u>boss</u>    <u>puts down</u>

11. Men and women have also won court cases for this kind of sexual harassment.

<u>men, women</u>    <u>have won</u>

12. In these cases, persons experience discrimination in what is called a hostile working environment.

<u>persons</u>    <u>experience</u>

13. The third woman in *9 to 5* orchestrates the working women's revenge.

<u>woman</u>    <u>orchestrates</u>

14. To her, their boss's unfair treatment of them does not deserve to go unpunished.

<u>treatment</u>    <u>does deserve</u>

15. Lily Tomlin, the actress who plays this woman, has the role of a single working mother.    <u>Lily Tomlin</u>    <u>has</u>

16. The hold her boss exerts over her is strong since she has a child to support.

<u>hold</u>    <u>is</u>

17. Many times people are harshly criticized for remaining in a hostile working environment.    <u>people</u>    <u>are criticized</u>

18. Why would anyone tolerate such types of abuse?

<u>anyone</u>    <u>would tolerate</u>

19. As the characters in *9 to 5* illustrate, sometimes they need the job to support themselves.    <u>they</u>    <u>need</u>

20. No matter what form it takes, sexual harassment, or gender discrimination, is against the law.    <u>harassment</u>    <u>is</u>
    <u>discrimination</u>

Copyright © 1995 by Harcourt Brace & Company. All rights reserved.

**1b(2)  Learn to recognize objects of verbs.**

Ask the subject and verb "who?" "whom?" or "what?" to find the complement of a sentence. If a sentence provides an answer when you follow the subject and verb with *whom* or *what*, the sentence has a complement or complements.

NO COMPLEMENT      Our workday ends at 4:30.   [Workday ends whom or what? There is

no answer in the sentence. The words that follow the verb answer a

different question—"when?"]

COMPLEMENT      Our schedule gives us a head start on the afternoon traffic.

[Our schedule gives whom? *Us.* Gives us what? *A head start.*]

Sometimes a sentence may have a complement that remains unstated.

The trainee understood.   [A complement may be added to this sentence because the

verb, *understood*, is a *transitive verb*, one that can take an object: The trainee under-

stood the manual.]

*Function*      A complement (or complements) that follows a *transitive verb* is a word (or words) to which the verb's action is transferred or passed along. There are three types of complements that may follow transitive verbs: *direct objects, indirect objects,* and *object complements*.
   Direct objects are the most frequent complement to follow a transitive verb.

DIRECT OBJECT      My supervisor, Mr. Tom McMahon, manages twenty employees in our

laboratory.   [The direct object, *employees*, shows whom the verb,

*manages*, is acting upon.]

Direct objects can also be accompanied by an indirect object, which precedes it, or by an object complement, which follows it.

INDIRECT AND      He gives us careful instructions for each experiment.   [The first
DIRECT OBJECTS
object, *us*, is the indirect object. The second object, *instructions*, is

the direct object. An indirect object shows *to* or *for* whom (or what)

the action is done.]

Copyright © 1995 by Harcourt Brace & Company. All rights reserved.

| DIRECT OBJECT AND OBJECT COMPLEMENT | Attention to instructions made the lab a safe place to work.<br><br>[The object complement, *a safe place to work*, describes the direct object, *lab*.] |
|---|---|

**Note:** Some verbs such as *give, buy, send, call, consider,* or *find* may have a direct or an indirect object.

### 1b(3)  Learn to recognize subject and object complements.

If a complement (or complements) follows a linking verb (forms of *be* and verbs such as *see, taste, feel, appear,* and *look*), the complement refers back to the subject of the sentence. These *subject complements* refer to, identify, or qualify the subject. Subject complements that rename the subject are either nouns or pronouns (also called *predicate nominatives* or *predicate nouns*); those subject complements that describe the subject are adjectives (also called *predicate adjectives*).

| SUBJECT COMPLEMENT | The lab manager is Lynne.  [*Lynne* is a predicate nominative giving more information about the subject, *manager*.] |
|---|---|

| SUBJECT COMPLEMENT | The lab equipment looks modern.  [*Modern* is a predicate adjective describing the subject, *equipment*.] |
|---|---|

An *object complement* refers to, identifies, or qualifies the direct object. It helps to complete the meaning of verbs such as *make, name, elect, call, paint.*

| OBJECT COMPLEMENT | The lateness made the bill *useless.* |
|---|---|

| OBJECT COMPLEMENT | They called the product *Dolly Dingle.* |
|---|---|

**Note:** Often you must be able to pick out the exact complement or complements in a sentence in order to avoid making mistakes in the form of the pronoun or the modifier. (See also Chapters **4** and **5**.)

*Basic Formula*  Now you have the basic formula for a sentence:

SUBJECT–VERB–(and usually) COMPLEMENT(S)

Copyright © 1995 by Harcourt Brace & Company. All rights reserved.

Deduct 3 1/3 for each incorrect underlining and each blank incorrectly filled.

**Recognizing Complements**                                    Exercise 1–13

NAME _____    SCORE _____

DIRECTIONS    In the following sentences underline the simple subject once, the verb twice, and the simple complement three times. Write *subject* in the blank if the complement (or complements) refers to the subject; write *object* if the complement (or complements) receives the action of the verb. If there is no complement, write a zero (*0*) in the blank.

> EXAMPLES
> The employee had high blood pressure.                    _____*object*_____
>
> James Ng is the company's wellness coordinator.          _____*subject*_____

1. The wellness coordinator offers the employees advice.    _____*object*_____

2. Large companies spend a lot of money on health

   promotion.                                               _____*object*_____

3. Wellness training often seems peculiar to more conser-

   vative, traditional employers.                           _____*subject*_____

4. Yet they, too, complain when employees miss work.        _____*0*_____

5. James Ng offers his company's employees health

   counseling.                                              _____*object*_____

6. In his work, he stresses prevention first.               _____*object*_____

7. For example, employees learn cholesterol control and

   stress management.                                       _____*object*_____

8. The wellness coordinator offers managers and workers

   helpful information.                                     _____*object*_____

9. Some employees attend many wellness workshops.           _____*object*_____

10. Usually, the ones who go like the classes.              _____*object*_____

Copyright © 1995 by Harcourt Brace & Company. All rights reserved.

11. Healthy employees will actually save a company money.     *object*

12. Why are pills and crash diets not the answer?     *subject*

13. They only treat symptoms or existing conditions.     *object*

14. The wellness coordinator's role, on the other hand, will

    generally be teaching people how to prevent problems.     *subject*

15. Those who talk to Mr. Ng will soon learn how to make

    wellness a part of their life.     *object*

 Copyright © 1995 by Harcourt Brace & Company. All rights reserved.

Deduct 2 for each sentence part incorrectly underlined.

## Recognizing Subjects, Verbs, and Complements: A Review

Exercise 1–14

NAME _____ SCORE _____

DIRECTIONS    In the following sentences underline the simple subject once, the verb twice, and the simple complement or complements three times. Remember that one or more of the sentence parts may be compound.

EXAMPLES

The Wellness Center offers the employees information about diet and exercise.

What information do you want?

1. At the Wellness Center, I found helpful information about losing weight.

2. The services at the Wellness Center at work can help you, too.

3. The Wellness Center is a place where you can have your cholesterol checked.

4. The professionals working at the Wellness Center also evaluate blood pressure, stress levels, and many other things.

5. The primary goal of the Wellness Center is the education of our employees and the prevention of disease.

6. What use have you made of the Wellness Center?

7. It furnished me with helpful lists of foods I could avoid to reduce my daily fat consumption.

8. One important service of the Wellness Center offers both employees and their supervisors a Stop-Smoking program.

9. Have you ever visited your company's Wellness Center?

10. At the Wellness Center, you will certainly find information about your concerns.

Copyright © 1995 by Harcourt Brace & Company. All rights reserved.

11. The Wellness Center encourages people to take charge of their good health.

12. Often supervisors recommend these programs to their employees.

13. Many times, when someone goes to the Wellness Center for one concern, they will also learn other healthy tips.

14. A company's Wellness Center generally charges employees who use its services no fee.

15. I highly recommend the Wellness Center to my co-workers.

Copyright © 1995 by Harcourt Brace & Company. All rights reserved.

**1c Learn to recognize all the parts of speech.**

Now that you have learned about the basic structure of a sentence, you are ready to begin working with all of the elements that combine to give a sentence its meaning. The following chart lists the various functions words can perform in a sentence and the types of words that perform each function.

| *Function* | *Kinds of Words* |
| --- | --- |
| Naming | Nouns and Pronouns |
| Predicating (stating or asserting) | Verbs |
| Modifying | Adjectives and Adverbs |
| Connecting | Prepositions and Conjunctions |

The next chart summarizes the parts of speech that you will study in detail in the rest of this chapter (except for interjections).

| *Parts of Speech* | *Uses in Sentences* | *Examples* |
| --- | --- | --- |
| 1. Verbs | Indicators of action, occurrence, or state of being | Tom *wrote* the report. Mary *evaluated* the stocks. They *are* executives. |
| 2. Nouns | Subjects and objects | *Kay* gave *Ron* the *list* of *clients.* |
| 3. Pronouns | Substitutes for nouns | *He* will return *it* to *her* later. |
| 4. Adjectives | Modifiers of nouns and pronouns | The *detailed* prospectus is the *convincing* one. |
| 5. Adverbs | Modifiers of verbs, adjectives, other adverbs, or whole clauses | presented *clearly* a *very* interesting study *entirely* too long *Indeed,* we are ready. |

Copyright © 1995 by Harcourt Brace & Company. All rights reserved.

| Parts of Speech | Uses in Sentences | Examples |
|---|---|---|
| 6. Prepositions | Words used before nouns and pronouns to relate them to other words in the sentence | *in* a hurry<br>*with* no thought *to* them |
| 7. Conjunctions | Connectors of words, phrases, or clauses; may be either coordinating or subordinating | reinvest *or* sell<br>before the meeting *and* after it<br>*since* the sale of the stock |
| 8. Interjections | Expressions of emotion (unrelated grammatically to the rest of the sentence) | *Good grief!*<br>*Ouch!*<br>*Well,* we tried. |

**1d  Learn to recognize phrases and subordinate clauses.**

You are already familiar with a group of words that may function as the verb of a sentence—the verb phrase (*will be writing*) and the verb with a particle (*put up with*). Other word groups may function as the subject or object (**1d(1)** below) or as modifiers (**1d(2)**).

**1d(1)  Learn to recognize phrases and subordinate clauses used as subjects and objects.**

| | |
|---|---|
| SUBJECT | *Keeping a careful record of expenses* was a part of our job. |
| OBJECT | We decided *to keep a log of our daily expenditures.* |
| SUBJECT AND OBJECT | *Whoever examined our log* could find *how we had spent our money each day.* |

The main types of word groups that function as subjects and as objects are verbal phrases and noun clauses.

*Verbal Phrases*    A phrase is a series of grammatically related words (words grouped together) that lacks a subject, a predicate, or both. The verbal phrase is the kind that most frequently functions as a subject or object. The main part of the verbal phrase is the verbal itself—a word that shows action, occurrence, or state of being as a verb does but that cannot function as the verb of a sentence. You may remember from your study of verbs and verbals in **1b(1)** that verbals usually end in *ing, ed, en,* or are preceded by *to*. The verbal, along with the other words in the phrase, can function as a subject, an object, or as a subject complement, just as an individual noun or pronoun can.

    Copyright © 1995 by Harcourt Brace & Company. All rights reserved.

| | |
|---|---|
| NOUN | *Machines* have eliminated many jobs.  [subject] |
| VERBAL PHRASE | *Using machines in the place of workers* has eliminated many jobs. [subject] |
| NOUN | Machinery has increased the *efficiency* of many jobs.  [direct object] |
| VERBAL PHRASE | Machinery helps *to increase the efficiency of many jobs.*  [direct object] |
| NOUN | Their business was *agricultural equipment sales.* [subject complement] |
| VERBAL PHRASE | Their business was *selling agricultural equipment.* [subject complement] |

*Noun Clauses*     A clause is a series of related words (words grouped together) that has both a subject and a verb. One kind of clause, referred to as a *main clause* or an *independent clause,* can stand alone as a sentence. The other, called a *subordinate clause* or *dependent clause,* may function as a noun—either a subject or object—or as a modifier in a sentence. (**1d(2)** discusses the use of phrases and subordinate clauses as modifiers. In fact, they are more commonly used as modifiers than as subjects or objects.) As nouns, subordinate clauses usually are introduced by one of these words: *who, whom, whose, which, that, whoever, whomever, what, whether, how, why,* or *where.* These introductory words are clause markers; they are printed in boldface in the following examples.

| | |
|---|---|
| NOUN | An *applicant* must fill out an application.  [subject] |
| NOUN CLAUSE | **Whoever** *wants a job* must fill out an application.  [subject] |
| NOUN | Applicants' responses to questions often show their *skills* as writers. [direct object] |
| NOUN CLAUSE | Applicants' responses to the questions often show **whether** *they can write well or not.*  [direct object] |

OR

Applicants' responses to the questions often show **how** *well they can write.*  [direct object]

| | |
|---|---|
| NOUN | The group's *findings* pleased their boss.  [subject] |
| NOUN CLAUSE | **What** the group found out *pleased their boss.*  [subject] |
| NOUN | He observed the factory *workers.*  [object] |
| NOUN CLAUSE | He observed **what** the factory workers did.  [object] |

Copyright © 1995 by Harcourt Brace & Company. All rights reserved.

Like verbal phrases, noun clauses can also function as subject complements.

| | |
|---|---|
| NOUN | The group's interest was *industrial productivity*. |
| VERBAL PHRASE | The group's interest was *evaluating industrial productivity*. |
| VERBAL PHRASE | The group's interest was *to evaluate industrial productivity*. |
| NOUN CLAUSE | Their belief was *that more agencies should evaluate industrial productivity*. |

Copyright © 1995 by Harcourt Brace & Company. All rights reserved.

Deduct 5 for each incorrect underlining and each incorrectly filled blank.

**Recognizing Phrases and Clauses
Used as Subjects and as Complements**　　　　　　　Exercise 1–15

NAME _____ SCORE _____

DIRECTIONS　In the first of each of the following pairs of sentences, the complete subject is underlined once or the complete object is underlined three times. In the second sentence of each pair, underline once the clause or phrase that functions as the subject or underline three times the clause or phrase that functions as the object. Then in the blank identify the phrase or clause with a *P* or *C*.

EXAMPLE

Future growth is important when one plans a career.

Knowing future growth possibilities is important when one plans a career.　　*P*

1. For the next decade, some corporations project fewer employees.

   For the next decade, some corporations project that they will

   employ fewer people.　　　　　　　　　　　　　　　　　　*C*

2. An exact forecast for a specific occupation is difficult.

   Forecasting employment opportunities exactly for a specific occu-

   pation is difficult.　　　　　　　　　　　　　　　　　　　*P*

3. Changes in national policy determine the growth rate of certain

   areas of employment.

   Changes in national policy determine whether certain areas of

   employment will grow.　　　　　　　　　　　　　　　　　*C*

4. For example, the government might decide that an area of scientific

   research should receive more funding.

   For example, the government might decide to give more funding to

   an area of scientific research.　　　　　　　　　　　　　　*P*

Copyright © 1995 by Harcourt Brace & Company. All rights reserved.

5. The expanded government-sponsored program would increase the demand for scientists and laboratory personnel.

The government's sponsoring of an expanded research program would increase the demand for scientists and laboratory personnel.  _____P_____

6. Predictions about employment are based on certain assumptions.

Predicting employment is based on certain assumptions.  _____P_____

7. When experts make employment projections, they generally assume a peacetime economy.

When experts make employment projections, they generally assume that the country will not be involved in a major war.  _____C_____

8. The changes that a war might bring about no one can accurately predict.

What changes would occur as a result of war no one can accurately predict.  _____C_____

9. Stability in other areas of the economy is also a basic assumption.

That other areas of the economy will remain stable is also a basic assumption.  _____C_____

10. People's basic attitudes about work, education, income, and leisure must remain unchanged.

That people's attitudes about work, education, income, and leisure will not change is another basic assumption.  _____C_____

Copyright © 1995 by Harcourt Brace & Company. All rights reserved.

**1d(2) Learn to recognize words, phrases, and subordinate clauses used as modifiers.**

A modifier is a word or word group that describes, limits, or qualifies another word or word group, thus expanding the meaning of the sentence. A sentence made up only of the two main parts (the basic pattern of subject + predicate) is always short and direct, but it may lack the information necessary to be entirely clear, as the following sentence illustrates:

The applicant had qualifications.

Almost any reader would want to know "what applicant" and "qualifications for what." The basic formula is not very satisfying in this example. The addition of modifiers makes the sentence more exact in meaning. Adjectives modify nouns or pronouns; adverbs modify verbs, adjectives, other adverbs, and sometimes whole sentences. A single word, a phrase, or a subordinate clause can function as an adjective or as an adverb.

|  | **1** | **2** | **3** |
|---|---|---|---|

ADJECTIVES      The *best* applicant *for the job that the interviewers saw today* was

Jane Troy.

[All three adjectival modifiers (a word, a prepositional phrase, and a subordinate clause) qualify the subject, *applicant*.]

ADVERBS      *At the interview's end*, the personnel director *briefly* talked *about the*

*site visit while the candidate listened.*

[The first adverbial modifier (a prepositional phrase) qualifies the whole sentence. The second (a word), the third (another prepositional phrase), and the fourth (a subordinate clause) all modify the verb, *talked*.]

Often you can combine two choppy sentences into a single, more effective sentence by making the essential information in one an added modifier in the other.

TWO SENTENCES      The report was poorly written. It was rejected by the manager.

COMBINED      The *poorly written* report was rejected by the manager.

TWO SENTENCES      The report contained several noticeable errors in grammar and spelling. It probably had not been proofread carefully by the writer.

COMBINED      *Since it contained several errors in grammar and spelling*, the report probably had not been proofread by the writer.

THREE SENTENCES      The manager examined the first page of the report. He did not bother to read any farther. The report did not represent careful work on the part of the writer.

COMBINED      *After the manager had examined the first page of the report*, he did not bother to read any farther *because it did not represent careful work on the part of the writer.*

Copyright © 1995 by Harcourt Brace & Company. All rights reserved.

**Single-Word Modifiers**   Nearly all sentences have one or more articles—*a, an,* and *the*—which modify nouns or elements functioning as nouns. In addition to *a, an,* and *the,* most sentences contain other words that modify various elements.

> A *large* increase in employment is expected in the field of landscape architecture.   [*Large* modifies *increase.*]
>
> The increase is *largely* due to the *continued* interest in *city* and *regional environmental* planning.   [*Largely* modifies *due; continued* modifies *interest; city, regional,* and *environmental* modify *planning.*]

*Punctuation*      Single-word modifiers are punctuated only if they are placed in an unusual position in the sentence or if they modify the whole sentence.

> *Attractive,* the grounds for the building contribute to a happy work environment.   [usual position; *the attractive grounds*]
>
> *Surprisingly,* no employee objects to the long walk through the trees to enter the building. [*Surprisingly* modifies the whole sentence.]

Two modifiers in succession are usually punctuated when there is no *and* between them if *and* is understood. Where no *and* would fit, no comma is used.

> The *large, well-landscaped* grounds surrounding the building make the work environment pleasant.   [You could say "large and well-landscaped grounds."]
>
> *Beautiful flower* gardens are also nearby.   [You would not say "beautiful and flower gardens." *Beautiful* modifies *flower gardens,* not just *gardens.*]
>
> *Both large* and *small* plants line the street curving up to the building.   [You would not say "both and large plants."]

(See also **12c.**)

     Copyright © 1995 by Harcourt Brace & Company. All rights reserved.

Deduct 5 for each incorrectly filled blank and 5 for each incorrect reason.*

## Using Single-Word Modifiers

Exercise 1–16

NAME _____ SCORE _____

DIRECTIONS   In each blank write the required modifier or modifiers that fit smoothly into the sentence. Punctuate with commas where necessary. After each sentence explain the reason for punctuating each modifier you have added.

EXAMPLE
A modifier describing *newsletter*

The _____ current _____ newsletter was sloppily designed and hard to read.

Reason:  Modifier is in its usual place.

1. A modifier describing the attitude of the boss

   _____ Concerned, _____ the Marketing Director, Ms. Cowles, told her sales

   staff to design a more appealing one.

   Reason:  Modifier is out of its usual position—"The

   concerned Marketing Director."

2. A modifier of *information*

   The _____ included _____ information sent to clients should be interesting

   and useful.

   Reason:  Modifier is in its usual place.

3. A modifier of *needed* and a modifier of *advice*

   The clients _____ certainly _____ needed to get _____ helpful _____

   advice about their investments.

   Reason:  Modifiers are in their usual places.

*Students' word choices will vary.

4. A modifier of *suggestions*

 Ms. Cowles' suggestions for revisions _____ , clear _____ and

 _____ precise, _____ showed the sales staff how to improve the newsletter.

 Reason: Modifiers are out of their usual position—"Clear
 and precise suggestions." There is no comma
 between the modifiers because of the use of <u>and</u>.

5. Two modifiers describing *newsletter*

 Both she and her staff wanted a _____ neat, _____

 _____ informative _____ newsletter.

 Reason: There are two modifiers in succession with <u>and</u>
 omitted.

6. A word modifying *other*

 Besides stock performance data, they decided there were _____ many _____
 other subjects they could cover.

 Reason: Modifier is in its usual place.

7. A modifier of the entire sentence and a modifier of *information*

 _____ Certainly, _____ they wanted the clients to have

 _____ useful _____ information about the company's services.

 Reason: "Certainly" modifies the whole sentence; modifier
 is in its usual place.

   Copyright © 1995 by Harcourt Brace & Company. All rights reserved.

**Using Single-Word Modifiers**                    Exercise 1–16 (continued)

8.  A modifier describing *ideas*

    The sample newsletters Ms. Cowles had collected gave them ___other___ ideas.

    Reason:  Modifier is in its usual place.

9.  A modifier of the entire sentence

    ___Obviously,___ the clients would react favorably to the new format.

    Reason:  "Obviously" modifies the whole sentence.

10.  Two modifiers describing *newsletter*

    The ___new,___ ___sophisticated___ newsletter received

    many compliments from Ms. Cowles.

    Reason:  There are two modifiers in succession with <u>and</u> omitted.

Copyright © 1995 by Harcourt Brace & Company. All rights reserved.

**Phrases as Modifiers**   You learned in **1d(1)** that a phrase is a series of grammatically related words that lacks a subject, a predicate, or both. Three types of phrases are commonly added as modifiers: appositives, prepositional phrases, and verbal phrases.

**Appositives**   An appositive is a word or phrase that identifies, explains, or supplements the meaning of a noun or pronoun that it is placed next to. Usually the appositive follows the noun or pronoun it identifies or explains. Appositives are set off by commas—or sometimes by dashes or a colon (see Chapter **17**)—except on the few occasions when they are essential to the meaning of the noun or pronoun to which they refer (see **12d**).

> *Megatrends, a best-seller about business,* has influenced people's thinking about the corporate world.   [The appositive, *a best-seller about business,* explains what *Megatrends* is.]
> Mr. Coulthard, *the business professor,* assigns *Megatrends* as required reading. [The appositive, *the business professor,* explains who Mr. Coulthard is.]

The appositive allows the writer to combine ideas that would otherwise be stated in two sentences.

| | |
|---|---|
| TWO SENTENCES | *Megatrends* is a best-seller about business. It has influenced people's thinking about the corporate world. |
| APPOSITIVE ADDITION | *Megatrends, the best-seller about business,* has influenced people's thinking about the corporate world. |

**Prepositional Phrases**   The prepositional phrase is the most frequent type of phrase modifier added to the sentence. It begins with a preposition—a word like *in, on, between,* or *to*—-and ends with a noun, a pronoun, or an *ing* verbal: *in* the report, *on* the desk, *between* the machines, *to* everyone, *without* our knowing.

A prepositional phrase used to modify one word within a sentence is usually not punctuated. But a prepositional phrase that modifies the entire sentence is usually set off by a comma or commas (the comma may be omitted after a prepositional phrase that begins a sentence if no misreading would result).

| | |
|---|---|
| MODIFIER OF NOUN | They read the book *about business law.* |
| MODIFIER OF VERB | They discussed the book *over the next week.* |
| MODIFIER OF SENTENCE | They examined, *in fact,* every case study carefully. |
| MODIFIER OF SENTENCE | The case studies, *in addition to the theory,* are necessary to teach how business law works in practice. |
| MODIFIER OF SENTENCE | *In a case study,* a specific law is illustrated by a real-world example. |

Copyright © 1995 by Harcourt Brace & Company. All rights reserved.

**Verbal Phrases**   A verbal phrase includes a verbal and the other words related to it—usually a modifier or modifiers and an object.

> *Applauding the speaker enthusiastically*, the audience rose to their feet.   [The verbal, *applauding*, is followed by an object, *speaker*, and a modifier, *enthusiastically*.]
>
> *To show its appreciation*, the audience remained standing until the speaker had left the platform.   [The verbal, *to show*, is followed by an object, *appreciation*, and a modifier, *its*]

Adding a verbal phrase allows the writer to combine ideas that would otherwise be stated in two separate sentences.

| | |
|---|---|
| TWO SENTENCES | The audience applauded the speaker enthusiastically. They rose to their feet. |
| VERBAL PHRASE ADDITION | *Applauding the speaker enthusiastically*, the audience rose to their feet. |

*Punctuation*     Verbal phrases used as modifiers are usually punctuated by commas, whether they appear at the beginning, in the middle, or at the end of sentences.

| | |
|---|---|
| BEGINNING | *Having limited herself to five main points*, the speaker finished her presentation in fifteen minutes. |
| MIDDLE | The speaker, *having limited herself to five main points*, finished her presentation in fifteen minutes. |
| END | The speaker finished her presentation in fifteen minutes, *having limited herself to five main points.* |

*Placement*     Verbal phrases used as modifiers must be placed so that they clearly modify one word in the sentence, usually the subject. If the writer puts a verbal phrase in the wrong place or includes no word for the phrase to modify, the verbal phrase is called a dangling modifier (see also Chapter **25**). A dangling modifier is sometimes laughable and is always confusing.

| | |
|---|---|
| DANGLING MODIFIER | *Having always enjoyed books*, the library was where Dean chose to work.   [*Dean*, not *the library*, enjoyed books.] |
| CLEAR MODIFIER | *Having always enjoyed books*, Dean chose to work in the library. |
| DANGLING MODIFIER | *While flying over Washington, D.C.*, the government buildings were an amazing sight.   [There is no word for the verbal phrase to modify.] |
| CLEAR MODIFIER | *While flying over Washington, D.C.*, I found the government buildings an amazing sight.   [The verbal phrase now has a word to modify—*I*.] |

**Note:**   The verbal phrase can also function as an appositive.

| | |
|---|---|
| EXAMPLE | His goal, *to start his own business*, is still a long way off. |

   Copyright © 1995 by Harcourt Brace & Company. All rights reserved.

Deduct 10 for each incorrect revision.

**Using Appositives**                              Exercise 1–17

NAME _____ SCORE _____

DIRECTIONS   Combine each of the following pairs of sentences by making the essential information in one an appositive in the other. Place the appositive next to the noun it identifies or explains, and punctuate the appositive with commas. (**Note:** Sometimes the appositive may precede the noun it identifies.)

EXAMPLE
Paralegal writers can carry out much of the routine work in a law office. Paralegal writers

are professionals who have become more numerous in recent years.

Paralegal writers, professionals who have become more numerous in recent years, can carry out much of the routine work in a law office.

1. A paralegal writer is often a college graduate who has obtained additional training in the field. The paralegal is involved in conducting specialized research and other

fact-finding activities for attorneys.

A paralegal writer, often a college graduate who has obtained additional training in the field, is involved in conducting specialized research and other fact-finding activities for attorneys.

2. The paralegal is a skilled writer. The paralegal often must communicate with

clients, judges, and opposing attorneys.

A skilled writer, the paralegal often must communicate with clients, judges, and opposing attorneys.

Copyright © 1995 by Harcourt Brace & Company. All rights reserved.

3. The paralegal helps the attorney to prepare cases. The paralegal is often the person who composes rough drafts of complicated legal documents.

The paralegal, often the person who composes rough drafts of complicated legal documents, helps the attorney to prepare cases.

4. The attorney depends on the paralegal to do much of the initial information-gathering work for a case. The attorney is the person who must evaluate the evidence in the case.

The attorney, the person who must evaluate the evidence in the case, depends on the paralegal to do much of the initial information-gathering work for a case.

5. The lawyer is responsible for planning and developing the work on a case. The lawyer makes all of the final decisions.

The lawyer, responsible for planning and developing the work on a case, makes all of the final decisions.

Copyright © 1995 by Harcourt Brace & Company. All rights reserved.

## Using Appositives

DIRECTIONS    The appositive often says as much as a longer construction does. Reduce the number of words in each of the following sentences by making the *who* or the *which* clause into an appositive. Cross out the words to be eliminated and add commas wherever necessary. Below the original sentence, write the appositive that results from your revision, including any needed commas.

EXAMPLE

The number of liberal arts majors, ~~who are~~ students in fields such as history, English, and philosophy, entering technical occupations has increased in the past decade.

*, students in fields such as history, English, and philosophy,*

1.  Students majoring in these disciplines, ~~which were~~ traditionally viewed as ones for teachers rather than businesspersons, are currently in high demand as future employees in "high tech" fields.

    *, traditionally viewed as ones for teachers rather than businesspersons,*

2.  Highly specialized technical corporations, ~~which were~~ the ones that formerly interviewed only graduates in such fields as computer science, mathematics, and engineering, now seek out liberal arts majors, principally for their strong communication skills.

    *, the ones that formerly interviewed only graduates in such fields as computer science, mathematics, and engineering,*

3.  One such company—EDS, ~~which is~~ involved in developing customized software systems, provides its newly hired liberal arts majors with up to two years' technical on-the-job training.

    *, involved in developing customized software systems,*

Copyright © 1995 by Harcourt Brace & Company. All rights reserved.

4. On a recent campus tour, one of the EDS recruiters, ~~who is~~ a former English major, paid a special visit to the English Department to publicize their program.

   *, a former English major,*

5. The prospective employee ideally brings with him or her two attributes, ~~which are~~ an ability to write clearly and effectively and a good foundation in a technical subject.

   *, an ability to write clearly and effectively and a good foundation in a technical subject.*

Copyright © 1995 by Harcourt Brace & Company. All rights reserved.

Deduct 10 for each incorrectly filled blank.

**Using Prepositional Phrases**                                  Exercise 1–18

NAME _____     SCORE _____

DIRECTIONS   In the blanks on the left, indicate whether the italicized prepositional phrase in each of the following sentences modifies a sentence part (*P*) or modifies the entire sentence (*S*). Punctuate with commas those prepositional phrases that modify entire sentences. In the blanks on the right, write the italicized prepositional phrases and include the punctuation marks that you have added for the phrases that modify entire sentences.

EXAMPLES
*To many people's surprise,* the area of health care delivery is not as limited as they

had believed.

_____S_____     To many people's surprise,

More and more people enter branches *of this field* every year.

_____P_____     of this field

1. *In fact,* a student with an associate's degree can enter the health care delivery field.

_____S_____     In fact,

2. Most college dental hygiene or respiratory therapy programs provide on-the-job

   training *for their students*.

_____P_____     for their students

3. People preparing for careers in these fields receive valuable training *as they work*

   with patients.

_____P_____     as they work

4. *Besides reading about how things should be done,* students watch experienced

   teaching staff deliver the treatments they study.

_____S_____     Besides reading about how things should be done,

Copyright © 1995 by Harcourt Brace & Company. All rights reserved.

5. People in these occupations express a high level of satisfaction *with their jobs*.

    P      with their jobs

6. Other types of medical practitioners will also be needed in increasing numbers *during the coming decade*.

    P      during the coming decade

7. *As the baby boom generation ages and requires additional health care,* more and more jobs will open up in the health care professions.

    S      As the baby boom generation ages and requires additional health care,

8. Many Americans work harder *at staying* in good health.

    P      at staying

9. Some people think of our contemporary times *as the Fitness-Conscious Era*.

    P      as the Fitness-Conscious Era

10. Moreover, concern about fitness is growing among people *of all ages and occupations*.

    P      of all ages and occupations

Copyright © 1995 by Harcourt Brace & Company. All rights reserved.

Deduct 10 for each incorrect combination.

**Using Verbal Phrases**                                      Exercise 1–19

NAME _____     SCORE _____

DIRECTIONS   Each of the following sentences has a verbal phrase written after it. Rewrite the
sentence using the verbal phrase as a clear modifier. Be sure to include the punctuation needed.
(Often, verbal phrases may be inserted in more than one place in their sentences.)

EXAMPLE
Industries may be divided into two categories. looked at from a broad perspective
Looked at from a broad perspective, industries may be
    divided into two categories.

1. One type of industry involves the production of goods. expected to show little

   growth in the next ten years
   Expected to show little growth in the next ten years, one
       type of industry involves the production of goods. or One
       type of industry, expected to show little growth in the
       next ten years,...

2. The growth rate of industries providing goods is not expected to increase as

   dramatically as that of those providing services. currently employing less than one-

   half of all workers
   Currently employing less than one-half of all workers, the
       growth rate of industries providing goods is not expected
       to increase as dramatically as that of those providing
       services.

3. Some industries produce both goods and services. not so easily categorized
   Some industries, not so easily categorized, produce both
       goods and services. or Not so easily categorized, some...

4. Service-producing industries include such divisions as government, transportation,

   public utilities, finance, insurance, and real estate. requiring more and more

   college graduates
   Service-producing industries, requiring more and more
       college graduates, include such divisions as government,
       transportation, public utilities, finance, insurance, and real
       estate. or Requiring more and more college graduates,
       service-producing industries...

Copyright © 1995 by Harcourt Brace & Company. All rights reserved.

5. Citizens of the United States demand more service industries than ever before. to keep up their standard of living

To keep up their standard of living, citizens of the United States demand more service industries than ever before. or Citizens of the United States, to keep up their standard of living, demand...

6. Government at the state and local levels has shown the largest growth of all service-producing industries. having increased by about 90 percent in the last twenty years

Government at the state and local levels, having increased by almost 90 percent in the last twenty years, has shown the largest growth of all service-producing industries. [The verbal phrase may also be placed at the beginning or end of this sentence.]

7. State and local government is expected to need more and more college-trained employees. to meet the public's demand for education, health, and protective services

State and local government is expected to need more and more college-trained employees to meet the public's demand for education, health and protective services. or State and local government, to meet...

8. Employment at the federal level of government will not be so readily available during the coming decade. increasing by only a small percentage in the last twenty years

Increasing by only a small percentage in the last twenty years, employment at the federal level of government will not be so readily available during the coming decade.

9. You can determine the service areas that hold the most promise for future employment. studying graphs that show projected rates of growth

Studying graphs that show projected rates of growth, you can determine the service areas that hold the most promise for future employment.

10. Health services are expected to expand more rapidly than any others. to satisfy the public's demand for more and better health care

To satisfy the public's demand for more and better health care, health services are expected to expand more rapidly than any others. [Other arrangements of this sentence are acceptable.]

Copyright © 1995 by Harcourt Brace & Company. All rights reserved.

**Subordinate Clauses as Modifiers** In **1d(1)** you studied one kind of subordinate clause—the noun clause, which can function as a subject or object. (As you may remember, a subordinate clause contains both a subject and a verb, but, unlike a main clause, cannot stand by itself as a sentence because of the subordinator that introduces it.) Other kinds of subordinate clauses—the adjective clause and the adverb clause— act as modifiers.

*Adjective Clauses* Adjective clauses are introduced by a subordinator such as *who, whom, that, which,* or *whose*—often referred to as *relative pronouns*. A relative pronoun relates the rest of the words in its clause to a word in the main clause, and, as a pronoun, also serves some noun function in its own clause, often as the subject. (Remember that a clause, unlike a phrase, has both a subject and a verb.)

> Another field *that interests students* is health science. [The relative pronoun *that* relates the subordinate clause to the subject of the main clause, *field*, and also serves as the subject of the verb, *interests*, in its own clause.]

An adjective clause follows the noun or pronoun that it modifies. It cannot be moved elsewhere without confusing either the meaning or the structure of the sentence.

| | |
|---|---|
| CORRECT PLACEMENT | The best-paying occupations, *which students are most likely to want*, are listed in various directories. |
| INCORRECT PLACEMENT | The best-paying occupations are listed in various directories *which students are most likely to want*. |
| CONFUSING STRUCTURE | *Which students are most likely to want*, the best-paying occupations are listed in various directories. |

Sometimes the relative pronoun is omitted when the clause is short and no misreading could result.

| | |
|---|---|
| WITH RELATIVE PRONOUN | Zoo management is a career *that* few students have considered. |
| WITHOUT RELATIVE PRONOUN | Zoo management is a career few students have considered. |

An adjective clause may be either restrictive or nonrestrictive. A restrictive (defining) clause is not punctuated because it limits the meaning of the words it follows and is, consequently, essential to the meaning of the sentence. A nonrestrictive (nondefining) subordinate clause, on the other hand, is punctuated, usually with commas, because it is not essential to the meaning of the sentence. When used as a relative pronoun, the word *that* usually introduces a restrictive (defining) subordinate clause.

| | |
|---|---|
| RESTRICTIVE CLAUSE | The person *who decides to be a farmer* faces many hardships. [The clause defines or identifies the kind of person who faces many hardships.] |
| NONRESTRICTIVE CLAUSE | My nearest neighbor, *who is a farmer*, faces many hardships. [The word, *neighbor*, is identified or defined by the modifier *nearest*.] |

Copyright © 1995 by Harcourt Brace & Company. All rights reserved.

RESTRICTIVE CLAUSE    My neighbor is not discouraged by the hardships *that he endures.*    [The word *that* introduces a restrictive clause.]

*Adverb Clauses*    An adverb clause is introduced by a subordinator such as *since, when, if, because, although,* or *so that* (see the Appendix for a list of the most commonly used subordinators). Like the adjective clause, the adverb clause adds another subject and verb (and sometimes other elements) to the sentence. But unlike the relative pronoun that introduces the adjective clause, the subordinator of an adverb clause does not function as a main part of its own clause. The adverb clause usually modifies the verb of the main clause, but it may also modify an adjective or adverb in the main clause.

> *If economists could only capture the economy in a bottle*, they could explain it more accurately.    [The subordinator, *If* introduces the adverb clause, which modifies the verb *could explain.*]

> Economists are seldom as confident *as they appear.*    [The subordinator, *as*, introduces the adverb clause, which modifies the adjective *confident.*]

> Nevertheless, economists can predict changes in the economy better *than anyone else can predict them.*    [The subordinator, *than*, introduces the adverb clause, which modifies the adverb *better.*]

Adverb clauses may be added to a sentence at various places. When an adverb clause is added in front of a main clause, it is followed by a comma; when it is added in the middle of a main clause, it is usually set off by commas (a comma at the beginning and end of the clause); when it is added after a main clause, it is usually unpunctuated.

BEGINNING    *When our country was first settled*, almost every worker was a farmer.

MIDDLE    Almost every worker, *when our country was first settled*, was a farmer.

END    Almost every worker was a farmer *when our country was first settled.*

In general, subordinate clauses introduced by clause markers like *which, that, who, whom,* and *whose* may be added to sentences only after the words they modify; otherwise, the clauses are misplaced modifiers.

Copyright © 1995 by Harcourt Brace & Company. All rights reserved.

Deduct 5 for each incorrect combination and 5 for each incorrectly filled blank.

# Using Subordinate Clauses

Exercise 1–20

NAME _____ SCORE _____

DIRECTIONS   A subordinate clause appears after each of the following main clauses (sentences). Combine the subordinate clause with the main clause, using commas whenever necessary. If the subordinate clause may be added at more than one place, write a check mark (✓) in the blank at the right.

EXAMPLES

College graduates will continue to face stiff competition in most occupations if present trends continue.      ✓ _____

Many students train for their professions in two-year colleges. who do not want a B.S. or a B.A. degree      _____

1.  The number of students entering junior and community colleges is increasing rapidly because these colleges can successfully train students for many occupations in two years or less.      ✓ _____

2.  The outlook for jobs during the late 1990s will vary according to the occupation although there is a general shortage of openings for graduates of both four-year and two-year colleges.*      ✓ _____

3.  A need for graduates in most engineering fields is expected. if past trends continue.      ✓ _____

4.  On the other hand, there is a surplus of graduates who are trained in political science and philosophy.      _____

5.  Obviously, students must pay careful attention to the changing demands of the job market if they expect to find suitable work after graduation.      ✓ _____

6.  Today's students must think of marketing their skills. who want jobs      _____

7.  Careful planning must be a part of a student's education, which considers the skills in demand on the job market.      _____

*Note that a dependent clause introduced by *although* is usually punctuated even if it is added to the end of the sentence.

Copyright © 1995 by Harcourt Brace & Company. All rights reserved.

8. Thus students must choose their subjects carefully. when they
   are scheduling their classes for the semester or quarter.       ✓

9. Certain subjects, like composition, mathematics, and computer
   science, are a must. since the skills they teach will be required in
   most occupations.                                                ✓

10. For the rest of the 1990s there will be jobs for all graduates. who
    have trained themselves for   the openings in the available
    occupations.                                                    _____

Copyright © 1995 by Harcourt Brace & Company. All rights reserved.

## 1e  Learn to recognize main clauses and the various types of sentences.

Sometimes a writer has two or more related ideas to set forth. Depending on the relationship of the ideas and on the desired emphasis, the writer may choose to express the ideas in separate sentences or to combine them in one of several ways.

**Types of Sentences**   There are four types of sentences: *simple, compound, complex,* and *compound-complex*. Which of these types a given sentence is depends on the number of main and subordinate clauses it includes.

*Simple Sentences*   The simple sentence consists of only one main clause and no subordinate clauses. A simple sentence is often short, but not always, since one or more of the basic sentence parts—the subject, verb, or objects—may be compound and since many single-word and phrase modifiers may be attached to the main clause.

SIMPLE   Computers handle many routine office chores.

SIMPLE   **Once used only by scientists,** computers now help *to reduce the amount of*

*repetitious work in the modern office.*   [The main clause, or basic formula,

*Computers help reduce work,* has been expanded by the addition of one adjec-

tive (underlined), one verbal phrase (in boldface), and three prepositional

phrases (in italics).]

SIMPLE   In the modern office, complicated word processing, routine accounting work,

and complex data processing all are done with a computer.   [The subject is

compound; single-word modifiers and prepositional phrases also expand the

main clause.]

*Compound Sentences*   A compound sentence consists of two or more main clauses (but no subordinate clauses) connected by a coordinating conjunction*(*and, but, or, for, nor, so, yet*) or by a conjunctive adverb**(such as *thus* or *therefore* and others listed in the Appendix) or other transitional expressions (such as *as a matter of fact* and others listed in the Appendix). In a compound sentence the connecting word (in boldface below) acts like a fulcrum on a seesaw, balancing grammatically equivalent structures.

COMPOUND   Computer experience will help a person get a clerical position, **but** some

people still refuse to learn this skill.   [The first main clause is balanced by the

*Coordinating conjunctions are always three letters or fewer in length.
**Conjunctive adverbs are always four letters or more in length.

Copyright © 1995 by Harcourt Brace & Company. All rights reserved.   *71*

grammatically equivalent second main clause. The clauses are connected by

the coordinate conjunction *but*.]

COMPOUND    Most businesses still keep records; **however,** employees must now use com-

puters to handle many filing jobs.    [The conjunctive adverb, *however*, balances

the first main clause against the grammatically equivalent second main clause.]

**Caution:**   If you overdo the joining of main clauses with *and*, your style will be childish. Save the *and*'s for ideas that should be stressed equally. Use a subordinate clause and main clause when one idea is dependent upon another. Or use two separate sentences when there is no strong relationship between the two ideas.

CHILDISH    I went to college so that I could get a good job, and I wanted to find work writing for a large corporation. I thought I would like the challenge of preparing reports, and I knew I could communicate ideas clearly. I learned about technical writing in an English course, and I took advanced classes to gain the skills I needed to be a technical writer.

BETTER    I went to college so that I could get a good job. I wanted to find work writing for a large corporation. I thought I would like the challenge of preparing reports, and I knew that I could communicate ideas clearly. After I learned about technical writing in an English course, I took advanced classes to gain the skills I needed to be a technical writer.

You will notice that the better paragraph has only one sentence in which two main clauses are joined by *and*, whereas the childish paragraph has three such sentences.

**Punctuation**   Either a comma or a semicolon shows the reader that one main clause has ended and another is about to be added. The punctuation mark is written after the first main clause, just *before* the joining word. When two main clauses are joined by a coordinating conjunction (a word such as *and* or *but*), a comma is used. When the two main clauses are joined by a conjunctive adverb (a word such as *however*) or other transitional expressions (a phrase such as *for instance*), a semicolon is used. A comma normally follows the conjunctive adverb or other transitional expression. (However, this comma is sometimes omitted when it is not needed to prevent misreading.)

Finally, when no conjunction joins two main clauses, a semicolon is used.

AND    The opportunities for receptionists are expected to increase during the late 1990s, and this occupation, unlike file clerking, should not be affected by automation.

HOWEVER    Thousands of job openings are expected for cashiers during the next few years; however, future growth may slow because of the widespread use of automated checkout systems.

Copyright © 1995 by Harcourt Brace & Company. All rights reserved.

NO JOINING WORD    Some clerical occupations depend on people more than on machinery; job openings in these areas will be increasing rapidly during the 1990s.

*Complex Sentences*    A complex sentence consists of one main clause and one or more subordinate clauses. The subordinate clause in a complex sentence may function as the subject, an object, or a modifier. Like the compound sentence, the complex sentence contains more than one subject and more than one verb; however, at least one of the subject–verb pairs is introduced by a subordinator such as *what, whoever, who, when*, or *if* (in boldface below) which makes its clause dependent on the main clause.

COMPLEX    ***Whoever** has visited Epcot Center in Florida* has had a glimpse into the future.    [The subordinate clause functions as the subject of the sentence.]

COMPLEX    ***When** we stop to think about it*, even the nineties resemble a "science fiction" world.    [The subordinate clause functions as a modifier—as an adverb clause.]

*Compound-Complex Sentences*    A compound-complex sentence consists of two or more main clauses and at least one subordinate clause. Thus it has three or more separate sets of subjects, verbs, and sometimes objects.

COMPOUND-COMPLEX    No one can predict what the machines of the future will do, but it is

safe to say that businesses of the future will undoubtedly rely heavily

on the new machine technology.

Copyright © 1995 by Harcourt Brace & Company. All rights reserved.

Deduct 10 for each incorrectly constructed sentence. (Main clauses may be combined in more than one way.)

## Combining Main Clauses                    Exercise 1–21

NAME _____ SCORE _____

DIRECTIONS    In each of the following cases, write a sentence combining two main clauses joined by the type of conjunction required in italics. Be sure to punctuate the sentence correctly. Then write the conjunction (and any punctuation surrounding it) in the blank.

EXAMPLE
*transitional expression*

People who enjoy sales work can choose
from a variety of occupations; for
example, they can become insurance
agents, real estate brokers, or retail
trade salesworkers.                                    __; for example,__

1. *use no conjunction*




                                                        _____

2. *conjunctive adverb*




                                                        _____

3. *coordinating conjunction*

_____

4. *transitional expression*

_____

5. *coordinating conjunction*

_____

Copyright © 1995 by Harcourt Brace & Company. All rights reserved.

**Combining Main Clauses**

6. *conjunctive adverb*

_____

7. *use no conjunction*

_____

8. *conjunctive adverb*

_____

Copyright © 1995 by Harcourt Brace & Company. All rights reserved.

9. *use no conjunction*

_____

10. *transitional expression*

_____

 Copyright © 1995 by Harcourt Brace & Company. All rights reserved.

Deduct 10 for each incorrectly constructed sentence.

**Building Sentences**                                    Exercise 1–22

NAME _____    SCORE _____

DIRECTIONS   In each of the following cases, write a sentence of the type specified in the space provided. Where indicated, use the connecting word given in italics. Be sure to punctuate the sentence correctly.

> EXAMPLE
>
> COMPOUND   use *but*
>
> Many people have several interests, but they do not know where to look for advice about combining them into one career.

1. SIMPLE

2. COMPLEX   use *but*

3. COMPOUND–COMPLEX   use *however*

4. SIMPLE

Copyright © 1995 by Harcourt Brace & Company. All rights reserved.

5. COMPOUND   use *and*

6. COMPOUND–COMPLEX

7. COMPLEX

8. COMPOUND   use *therefore*

9. SIMPLE

10. COMPLEX

   Copyright © 1995 by Harcourt Brace & Company. All rights reserved.

## 2

### Write complete sentences and revise fragments.

A sentence fragment is a nonsentence beginning with a capital letter and ending with a period. A sentence fragment is usually a phrase (a group of related words that lacks a subject and/or a verb) or a subordinate clause (a group of related words that has both a subject and a verb but that is introduced by a clause marker—a word such as *who*, *which*, *that*, *if*, *since*, or *because*).

| | |
|---|---|
| PHRASE | needing to prepare a report for your employer |
| SUBORDINATE CLAUSE | when you need to prepare a report for your employer |
| SENTENCE | You need to prepare a report for your employer. |

Few people write isolated fragments; rather they write fragments as parts of a paragraph. They separate what should be sentence additions from the main clauses with which they belong. Notice that the writer of the following has mistakenly separated what should be sentence additions from the main clause with which they belong.

> *When you need to prepare a report for your employer.* You may panic at the assignment. *Realizing that your writing skills as well as your knowledge of your field will be examined carefully.*

When the italicized words are treated as additions to the main clause, and are punctuated with commas, the fragments are avoided.

> *When you need to prepare a report for your employer,* you may panic at the assignment, *realizing that your writing skills as well as your knowledge of your field will be examined carefully.*

Of course, the fragments may also be avoided by making the italicized words into main clauses themselves, but the writing that results sounds childish.

> You need to prepare a report for your employer. You may panic at the assignment. You realize that your writing skills as well as your knowledge of your field will be examined carefully.

Usually, then, the best correction for a sentence fragment is to
(1) supply missing elements
         OR
(2) connect it with the main clause from which it has been separated.

The exercises in this section will provide you with experience in making fragments into additions to main clauses and in correctly punctuating these additions.

Copyright © 1995 by Harcourt Brace & Company. All rights reserved.

Deduct 5 for each incorrect revision and 5 for each incorrectly filled blank.

## Avoiding Phrase Fragments

Exercise 2–1

NAME _____ SCORE _____

### 2a Revise phrases punctuated as sentences.

To avoid fragments, connect verbal phrases, prepositional phrases, and appositives to the independent clauses with which they belong.

DIRECTIONS   Join the sentence fragment to the main or independent clause from which it has been separated. Use a comma either before or after the fragment. (You will need to change the capitalization of one of the word groups.) In the blank write either *a* or *b* to show which word group is the fragment.

EXAMPLES

ᵃAn important part of many jobs, ᵇ*t*he business report is usually presented

in written form.                                                                                   ____a____

ᵃMost reports are quite simple, ᵇ*r*equiring no more than one page of

composition.                                                                                        ____b____

1. ᵃBusiness reports help the reader make any number of decisions,
   ᵇ*w*hether a project can be undertaken or a contract offered to a

   bidder, for instance.                                                                     ____b____

2. ᵃAs a part of a permanent record kept on file, ᵇ*a* report may serve as

   a resource for the writer preparing a later report on the same matter.  ____a____

3. ᵃThe writer must clearly understand the use to which the informa-

   tion in any report will be put, ᵇ*p*rior to writing up the findings.        ____b____

4. ᵃBusiness letters usually alert the reader to their main point first,
   ᵇ*u*nlike reports that may not present their main point until the end.   ____b____

5. ᵃMost reports follow a general-to-specific format, ᵇ*t*he main point

   being presented first and the supporting facts following.                   ____b____

Copyright © 1995 by Harcourt Brace & Company. All rights reserved.

6. <sup>a</sup>In a report that ends with its recommendations, <sup>b</sup>*t*The facts or sup-

    porting evidence are listed first to help the reader see the validity of

    your point of view.                                                                                        _____a_____

7. <sup>a</sup>The reader may be ready to accept the report's recommendation,

    <sup>b</sup>*s*Since you prepared the way with a clear presentation of the

    evidence first.                                                                                              _____b_____

8. <sup>a</sup>Staff technical writers often compose a company's reports, <sup>b</sup>*e*Even

    those destined to be read by clients or stockholders.                           _____b_____

9. <sup>a</sup>Unlike complicated formal reports, <sup>b</sup>*a*Almost any employee can

    expect to write short informal reports on a regular basis.                     _____a_____

10. <sup>a</sup>Many short reports help an individual or members of a group arrive

    at a consensus/ <sup>b</sup>*b*By presenting the facts needed to support a rec-

    ommendation or a conclusion.                                                                 _____b_____

Copyright © 1995 by Harcourt Brace & Company. All rights reserved.

In problems 1–10, deduct 3 1/3 for each incorrect revision and 3 1/3 for each incorrectly filled blank; in problems 11–15 deduct 3 1/3 for each incorrect compound element and 3 1/3 for each incorrectly punctuated compound element or list.

## Avoiding Phrase Fragments—Continued

Exercise 2–2

NAME _____   SCORE _____

To avoid fragments, connect a list of items or the second part of a compound verb or compound direct objects to the main clause with which it belongs.

DIRECTIONS   Join a list of items or the second part of the compound verb or compound direct object to the main clause with which it belongs. Use no comma before the second part of the compound verb or compound direct object. Use a comma or a colon before a list that you attach to the main clause: use a comma if the list is introduced by a phrase like *such as*; use a colon if there is no introductory phrase. (You will need to change the capitalization of each word group that you join to the main clause.) In the blank, write *compound verb* if the fragment that you join to the main clause is the second part of the verb or *compound object* if the fragment that you join to the main clause is the second part of the object; write *list* if the fragment is a series of items.

EXAMPLES

Sources of information for reports can include data obtained

firsthand, Ór material obtained through gathering and

assembling the research done by others.                    *compound object*

Information from primary sources is obtained in several

ways, Questionnaires, experiments, and surveys.            *list*

1. Information from primary sources is obtained firsthand,
   And has not been analyzed by someone else.              *compound verb*

2. Gathering information from primary sources takes
   more time, And costs more than consulting secondary
   sources.                                                 *compound verb*

3. Thus, when writing a report, you should consult secondary sources first, And should use them to avoid
   duplicating someone else's work.                         *compound verb*

Copyright © 1995 by Harcourt Brace & Company. All rights reserved.

4. Secondary sources are found in three places; Libraries,
   research departments in some companies, and, occasionally, data-gathering firms.                          list

5. There are many kinds of libraries available, Such as
   school, college, and municipal.                          list

6. The information from sources may be taken in one of
   two ways; Copied word-for-word from books or articles
   or summarized.                                            list

7. You may obtain information about office equipment
   and supplies from several primary sources; By studying
   manufacturers' brochures, by observing other offices,
   and by attending sales and professional conventions.     list

8. As you collect your information, you will need to organize your findings, And evaluate them.                    compound verb

9. If you do your research carefully, you may have more
   information than you need, Or more than your supervi-
   sor will care to read about.                              compound object

10. Before writing a report you must decide on a final plan
    for presentation, As well as eliminate all the informa-
    tion that does not suit your plan.                       compound verb

       Copyright © 1995 by Harcourt Brace & Company. All rights reserved.

**Avoiding Phrase Fragments**                                   Exercise 2–2 (continued)

DIRECTIONS   In the following, write sentences containing the appropriate constructions—be sure to punctuate them correctly.

EXAMPLE

sentence containing a list with an introductory clause

> Material for a report can be obtained from many sources, such as trade journals, annual reports, and interviews with experts.[*]

11. sentence containing a compound verb

12. sentence containing a compound object

13. sentence containing a list with no introductory clause

14. sentence containing a compound verb

15. sentence containing a list with an introductory clause

[*]Answers will vary.

Copyright © 1995 by Harcourt Brace & Company. All rights reserved.

In problems 1–10, deduct 3 1/3 for each incorrect revision and 3 1/3 for each incorrectly filled blank. In problems 11–15, deduct 6 2/3 for each incorrectly written sentence.

## Avoiding Clause Fragments

Exercise 2–3

NAME _____ SCORE _____

### 2b Revise clauses punctuated as sentences.

To avoid fragments, connect subordinate clauses to the main clauses to which they belong.

DIRECTIONS   Join the subordinate clause to the main clause from which it has been separated. Use a comma after the subordinate clause if it comes before the main clause; use no comma if the subordinate clause follows the main clause unless it is introduced by the clause marker *although*. (You will need to change the capitalization of one of the clauses.) In the blank write either *a* or *b* to show which word group is the fragment.

EXAMPLES

[a]A report's probable usefulness to the company should be considered/
   [b]̶B̶efore a report is assigned.                                          ___b___

[a]Because they are expensive and time-consuming to prepare and
   distribute/ [b]U̶nnecessary reports should be eliminated.                  ___a___

1. [a]Since routine reports are written frequently,/[b]M̶any companies use

   prepared forms.                                                           ___a___

2. [a]A prepared form providing the information requested saves both

   time and energy,/[b]I̶f a company receives frequent inquiries about its

   products or services.                                                     ___b___

3. [a]Most medical fields use prepared forms,/[b]S̶ince definite informa-

   tion must be presented and requested.                                     ___b___

4. [a]When reporting for dental or medical examinations,/[b]P̶atients must

   usually supply answers to specific questions.                             ___a___

5. [a]Patients' answers recorded on these standard forms may become the

   basis for a doctor's final written report,/[b]W̶henever the dental or med-

   ical caregiver must supply claim information to insurance carriers.       ___b___

Copyright © 1995 by Harcourt Brace & Company. All rights reserved.

6. ᵃWhereas formal reports often require a long time to prepare/,

   ᵇ**s**Short routine reports usually can be completed in minutes.          _____a_____

7. ᵃNo report is useful unless the information it presents is accurate,

   objective, and well-organized/**a**, ᵇAlthough the design of reporting

   forms can vary.          _____b_____

8. ᵃA writer must first determine the audience for the report/, ᵇ**b**Because

   who will read the report and the purpose it will serve determine

   each report's structure.          _____b_____

9. ᵃThe writer should read reports carefully/, ᵇ**i**If similar ones have been

   compiled in the past.          _____b_____

10. ᵃA past report can keep the writer from wasting much valuable time

    reinventing the wheel/**a**, ᵇAlthough, unfortunately, previous reports

    often get lost in someone's files.          _____b_____

Copyright © 1995 by Harcourt Brace & Company. All rights reserved.

**Avoiding Clause Fragments**        Exercise 2–3 (continued)

DIRECTIONS    In the following, write sentences according to the required pattern.

EXAMPLE

A subordinate clause preceding the main clause.

> While previous reports can be helpful, you must be careful not to copy someone else's work.*

11. A subordinate clause introduced by the word *if* following the main clause

12. A subordinate clause introduced by the word *although* following the main clause

13. A subordinate clause introduced by the word *if* preceding the main clause

14. A subordinate clause following the main clause

15. A subordinate clause that precedes the main clause

*Answers will vary.

Copyright © 1995 by Harcourt Brace & Company. All rights reserved.    

In problems 1–10, deduct 3 1/3 for each incorrect revision and 3 1/3 for each incorrectly filled blank; in problems 11–15, deduct 6 2/3 for each incorrectly written sentence.

## Avoiding Clause Fragments—Continued

Exercise 2–4

NAME _____ SCORE _____

DIRECTIONS   For the following sentences, join the subordinate clause to the main clause from which it has been separated. If the subordinate clause defines or limits in some way the meaning of the term to which it refers, use no comma before it. If the subordinate clause simply adds useful but not necessary information about the term to which it refers, use a comma before the clause marker. No comma should be used before the clause marker *that*. (See **1d(2)** on restrictive and nonrestrictive clauses.) You will need to change the capitalization in each subordinate clause. In the blank write the clause marker, if one is included, that signals the beginning of the subordinate clause fragment. (**Note:** Sometimes *that* is omitted when the subordinate clause is joined to the main clause.)

EXAMPLES

[a]As an employee of any business, you may be asked to write reports/ [b]That
must be prepared according to certain specifications.

_____that_____

[a]If the request comes to you in written form, carefully note the authorization/ [b]Which should make clear the exact nature of the report you
are to prepare.

_____which_____

1. [a]After underlining all major points listed in the authorization,
make a note of any questions/ [b]That you have about what you are
expected to do.

_____that_____

2. [a]To find the answers to your questions, it is appropriate to call or
write the person/ [b]Who requested the report.

_____who_____

3. [a]You may wish to follow up any telephone conversation with a
memo/ [b]That spells out the understandings you reached with the
person who authorized the report.

_____that_____

4. [a]Let us assume that Ms. Phillips has written to you requesting a
report/ [b]Which should evaluate the effectiveness of recent ads for
your company's new product line.

_____which_____

Copyright © 1995 by Harcourt Brace & Company. All rights reserved.

5.  <sup>a</sup>After reading the request carefully, you find that you have several
    questions about the exact information wanted by Ms. Phillips, <sup>b</sup>Who
    is your immediate supervisor and also the manager of the company.     _who_

6.  <sup>a</sup>Your first step would be to make a list of the questions/ <sup>b</sup>That you
    want her to answer.     _that_

7.  <sup>a</sup>Your questions might concern the meaning of "recent" ads and the
    amount of detail that should be given about each one/ <sup>b</sup>That you
    plan to list.     _that_

8.  <sup>a</sup>To write an effective study, you consult any reports covering past
    years/ <sup>b</sup>Your predecessors have prepared.     _____

9.  <sup>a</sup>Then you call Ms. Phillips/ <sup>b</sup>Who is happy to respond to any ques-
    tions left unanswered by your reading of previous reports.     _who_

10. <sup>a</sup>By doing your "homework," you save your supervisor the trouble
    of giving you information/ <sup>b</sup>That you could easily have found on
    your own.     _that_

Copyright © 1995 by Harcourt Brace & Company. All rights reserved.

**Avoiding Clause Fragments**                    Exercise 2–4 (continued)

DIRECTIONS    In the following, write sentences according to the required pattern.

EXAMPLE
A sentence containing a subordinate clause that limits the meaning of the term to which it refers.

The materials that I received through the mail were helpful to me.*

11. A sentence containing a clause starting with the word *that*

12. A sentence containing a subordinate clause that adds useful but not necessary information about the term to which it refers

13. A sentence containing a subordinate clause starting with the word *who* that limits the meaning of the term to which it refers

14. A sentence containing a subordinate clause starting with the word *which* that adds useful but not necessary information about the term to which it refers

15. A sentence containing a subordinate clause that *could* start with the word *that* but which omits it where it is joined to the main clause

*Answers will vary.

Deduct 5 for each incorrect circle and 5 for each incorrect revision.

**Avoiding Sentence Fragments:  A Review**          Exercise 2–5

NAME _____     SCORE _____

DIRECTIONS    Each sentence or fragment in the following paragraphs is numbered. Circle the numbers of the ten fragments. Then connect the fragments to the main clauses with which they belong. (In a few cases a fragment can be joined to either of two main clauses. Also, a few fragments occur in succession.) Change the capitalization and include commas and colons as needed.

[1]Your final written report will probably fall into one of three categories. [2]The memorandum, the letter, or the short informal report. [3]The memorandum and letter forms are alike, [4]Except that the letter is slightly more formal, [5]And will probably be read by people outside the company. [6]Most likely, though, the information you gathered will be presented in the form of the short informal report, [7]Which is usually no longer than ten pages. [8]If, for example, your subject is limited to a consideration of advertising strategies, [9]You should have little trouble organizing your material, [10]Since the various types of ads can serve as the basis for your paragraphing.

[11]Your report probably should include several sections, [12]The title page, followed by the letter or memorandum requesting or authorizing the report, [13]Or by a statement indicating who requested or authorized it. [14]The first section of the body of the report states the purpose of the report clearly and concisely. [15]The next section should give a summary of your findings, [16]Including a description of the method or sources used to arrive at the conclusions, [17]Such as surveys, questionnaires, direct observations, and research. [18]Finally, you should present your recommendations, [19]Which will include the ways in which you think the ads could be improved, together with information about the most successful ad formats, their particular features, and how

Copyright © 1995 by Harcourt Brace & Company. All rights reserved.

they are an improvement over the present advertising campaign. [20]Headings should be used within the body of the report to identify its three main divisions: purpose, findings, and recommendations.

Copyright © 1995 by Harcourt Brace & Company. All rights reserved.

## 3

**Join independent clauses with a coordinating conjunction or a semicolon to prevent misreading and to show relationships clearly.**

When one main clause is added to another, either a comma or a semicolon is used between the main clauses whenever the main clauses are connected by a coordinating conjunction: *and, but, or, nor, so, for,* or *yet.*

When writing compound or compound–complex sentences, using a comma between main clauses not connected by a coordinating conjunction creates a comma splice error. Using no punctuation mark at all creates a fused sentence (also called a comma fault or a run-on sentence).

> COMMA SPLICE    Most people think of a report as a written document, in reality, employees present almost as many oral reports as written ones.

> FUSED SENTENCE    Most people think of a report as a written document in reality employees present almost as many oral reports as written ones.

If the coordinating conjunction is omitted between main clauses, then a semicolon is placed between the main clauses. On the other hand, if a colon is used, the second clause generally explains the first one.

> Most people think of a report as a written document; in reality, employees present almost as many oral reports as written ones.

> Employees may present oral reports to a variety of people: they may be called on for oral presentations by their immediate supervisors, by the upper management of their companies, and even, on occasion, by the general public.　[Here the second main clause does not present a related point but rather explains the idea of the first main clause.]

If the coordinating conjunction is replaced by another type of connecting word—a conjunctive adverb (*thus, then, therefore, however*) or a transitional expression (*on the other hand, in fact, for example, to sum up*)—the standard mark of punctuation between the main clauses is still the semicolon.

> Most people think of a report as a written document; *however,* in reality, employees present as many oral reports as written ones.

**Note:**    Remember that a conjunctive adverb or a transitional expression may be used as an added modifier in a main clause *rather than* as a connector between main clauses. In such a case, the conjunctive adverb or transitional expression is normally set off by commas: "Few employees, however, escape the task of preparing some written reports."

In addition to the use of the semicolon, there are two other ways to correct a comma splice or fused sentence: write two separate sentences or make one of the main clauses into a subordinate clause.

Copyright © 1995 by Harcourt Brace & Company. All rights reserved.

TWO SENTENCES    Most people think of a report as a written document. In reality, employees present almost as many oral reports as written ones.

SUBORDINATION    Although most people think of a report as a written document, in reality, employees present almost as many oral reports as written ones.

The exercises in this chapter will give you practice in correcting comma splices and fused sentences in all three ways: by using a semicolon or colon, by writing two separate sentences, and by subordinating one idea to another.

Copyright © 1995 by Harcourt Brace & Company. All rights reserved.

Deduct 5 for each incorrect caret and 5 for each incorrectly filled blank.

**Avoiding Comma Splices and Fused Sentences**          Exercise 3–1

NAME _____   SCORE _____

**3a  Use a comma between main clauses *only* when connecting them with the coordinating conjunctions *and, but, or, nor, for, so,* or *yet.***

If no coordinating conjunction is used, do one of the following:
(1)  use a semicolon (but only if the statements made by the two main clauses are closely related);
(2)  use a colon (but only if the second main clause explains the first);
(3)  make the two main clauses separate sentences, each beginning with a capital letter and ending with a period;
(4)  rewrite one of the main clauses to make it a subordinate clause addition to the other main clause.

**Note:**  Be especially careful to avoid fused sentences and comma splices when dividing a quotation.

> "Prepare an oral report as carefully as you would a written one," my technical writing instructor advised.  [Do not use a comma here.]  "Be especially conscious of your audience in preparing an oral report."

DIRECTIONS    In the following fused and comma-spliced sentences, insert an inverted caret (**V**) where two main clauses come together. Then correct the error in the way you think best. Write **;** in the blank if you use a semicolon to make the correction, **:** if you use a colon, **.** if you use two sentences, and *sub* if you make one of the clauses subordinate.

EXAMPLE
According to a recent survey, the drafting of written reports occupies

                           **V**

24.5% of a technical expert's time;preparing oral reports takes up 25.4%.*      _____**;**_____

1.  All sorts of information is processed by technical experts;fact-find-

ing presentations and progress reports are two such documents.      _____**:**_____

2.  For example, a computer systems troubleshooter will generally

write up what she found to be causing the problem, this memo

helps the customer understand what had been going wrong with

their system and how it was repaired.      _____**.**_____

3.  In smaller companies, technicians write most of the descriptive lit-

erature about their company's products,and they may also write

consumer information such as labels and user's manuals.      _____**,**_____

*Answers will vary.

Copyright © 1995 by Harcourt Brace & Company. All rights reserved.          *101*

**Because or Since**

4. *V* **R**eports that outline new product specifications are needed by con-

r

sumers and workers in the field, they help both groups keep up with

the latest innovations.                                                       sub,

5. Analytical reports also are important pieces of technical communi-

*V*

cation; they present material about an important issue, product or

process.                                                                      ;

**since**

6. A technical report must be precise and clearly worded *V* readers of

these documents expect accuracy.                                              sub

7. Computerized record keeping has not eliminated the need to write

*V*

analytical reports in small companies; for instance, technicians pre-

pare and distribute test results.                                             ;

*V*

8. Errors are unacceptable; readers can be confused, make mistakes in

carrying out a procedure a report outlines, and even sustain an

injury.                                                                       :

**because**

9. A report with misspelled words makes the writer look bad *V* this type

of error implies carelessness and calls into question the writer's

accuracy in other areas.                                                      sub

10. A sloppy writer, no matter how skilled in the technical aspects of the

*V*

job, won't last long; one company president remarked, "mistakes like

misspellings of common words in the description of our product

make the customer doubt the quality of the product and the

accuracy of those directions."                                                ;

Copyright © 1995 by Harcourt Brace & Company. All rights reserved.

Deduct 10 for each incorrectly filled blank.

## Avoiding Comma Splices and Fused Sentences—Continued   Exercise 3–2

NAME _____   SCORE _____

**3b  Use a semicolon before a conjunctive adverb (such as *however* or *therefore*) or a transitional expression (such as *for example* or *on the other hand*) that is placed between independent clauses.**

DIRECTIONS   In the following fused and comma-spliced sentences, insert an inverted caret (**V**) where the two main clauses come together. Then add a semicolon if no mark of punctuation is there; if a comma is there, cross it out and insert a semicolon. In the blank write the semicolon and the word or phrase that follows it as well as any punctuation that follows the word or phrase.

EXAMPLE

The memo is the shortest, most direct form of business com-

munication;therefore, it is the form most frequently used

within companies.                                          ____; therefore,____

1.  In a memo the main point usually comes first;however,

the sequence of points depends on the writer's purpose.   ____; however,____

2.  The memo next briefly supplies important details about

the conclusion,;then it offers further assistance or infor-

mation.                                                   ____; then____

3.  A memo's purpose is to give information;therefore, it

does not have to present recommendations.                 ____; therefore,____

4.  A memo is generally short;in fact, it should seldom run

more than two pages.                                      ____; in fact,____

5.  Information can, of course, be communicated orally,;

however, a memo provides the writer and reader with a

lasting record.                                           ____; however,____

Copyright © 1995 by Harcourt Brace & Company. All rights reserved.   *103*

6. Memos should include a date and headlines;ordinarily,

   *To*, *From*, *Date*, and *Subject* (rather than *Re*) are placed

   at the head of the memo. .                                    ; ordinarily,

7. Recording information via a memo is important,; for

   instance, the reader can refer to it again to refresh her

   memory.                                                       ; for instance,

8. What is known as a letter report can also work like a

   memo;thus, such a report uses internal headings in the

   same way as a memo.                                           ; thus,

9. A letter-report often omits standard business letter

   parts,;consequently, it may leave out the inside address,

   the salutation and the complimentary close.                  ; consequently,

10. Readers appreciate either memos or letter-reports;

    moreover, they often base important decisions on the

    material these documents present.                           ; moreover,

Copyright © 1995 by Harcourt Brace & Company. All rights reserved.

Deduct 5 for each incorrect caret and 5 for each incorrect revision.

## Avoiding Comma Splices and Fused Sentences: A Review    Exercise 3–3

NAME _____    SCORE _____

DIRECTIONS    In the following paragraphs insert an inverted caret (**V**) where two main clauses are incorrectly joined. Then correct the fused and comma-spliced sentences by writing in semicolons or colons, by adding a period and a capital letter to make two separate sentences, or by rewriting one of the sentences as a subordinate clause.

[1]A report writer must observe certain conventions of style. [2]First, and most important, a simple, straightforward presentation is essential ᵥ*or since*:poetic words and roundabout phrasing have no place in reports. [3]The main purpose of a report is to communicate information clearly ᵛ;therefore, anything that interferes with clarity should be avoided. [4]Sentences in memos and reports are usually much shorter and less complex in structure than are those in other types of writing ᵛ;again clarity, not variety, is the primary aim of a report writer.

[5]Report writers should avoid the personal or subjective approach. [6]They should avoid personal pronouns, especially the first person *I* or *we* ᵛᵀ.these pronouns often make the report appear to give only the writer's opinion rather than information presented by an objective reporter. [7]For example, it is weak to say, "We found errors" ᵛ;however, you could say that "The investigators found errors." [8]Furthermore, vague evaluations such as *expensive* and *superior* should be avoided because these words can mean different things to different readers. [9]A writer must give concrete details, ᵥ*since or because* ~~and~~ the reader will make

Copyright © 1995 by Harcourt Brace & Company. All rights reserved.

judgments based on the facts the report presents. [10]"This product is the most wonderful thing our company has ever manufactured," one enthusiastic technician wrote, "it is a *must* for every household." [11]Needless to say, the supervisor reading the technician's report was not impressed with these subjective opinions furthermore, the technician's gushy, biased description of the product's operation annoyed the supervisor.

[12]Finally, like any other writer, a report writer must give credit for all facts and ideas gained through the research of others otherwise, the writer is guilty of plagiarism, as serious an offense in business and industry as it is in college. [13]Footnotes or source iden-tifications, which are enclosed in parentheses within the body of the report, must be included to acknowledge sources used to develop the final report of course, note pages and, usually, a bibliography section are provided at the end of the report.

Copyright © 1995 by Harcourt Brace & Company. All rights reserved.

## 4

**Distinguish between adjectives and adverbs. Use the conventional forms.**

In **1d** you learned how a modifier can make a word in the basic formula more exact in meaning.

> Writing a *good business* letter is not the *extraordinarily difficult* task *most* people feel that it is.

Without the modifiers—not to mention the articles—this sentence would not even have the same meaning, as is clearly shown when the sentence is written without any modifiers.

> Writing a letter is the task people feel that it is.

The modifiers (*good, business,* and *most*) of the subjects (*letter* and *people*), the modifier (*not*) of the verb (*is*), the modifier (*difficult*) of the complement (*task*), and the modifier (*extraordinarily*) of another modifier (*difficult*) are all necessary to make the meaning of the sentence clear.

**Adjectives**    Modifiers of nouns and pronouns are called adjectives.

> Of all the types of *business* letters, the *most difficult* one for *most* people to write is the
>
> letter of introduction.

**Note:** The pronouns *everyone* and *everybody* are often modified by adverbs rather than adjectives because they are compound words made up of a pronoun (*one* and *body*) and an adjective (*every*): "*Almost* everyone can learn to write an effective business letter to a friend as well as to a stranger."

An adjective may also be used either as a *subject complement* or as an *object complement.*

*Subject Complements*    Adjectives used as subject complements follow linking verbs—mainly forms of *be* (*am, is, are, was, were, has been, have been, will be,* and so on) and verbs like *appear, seem, look, feel,* and *taste*—and describe or show something about the subject of the sentence. (Because they appear as part of the predicate, they are also called predicate adjectives.)

> SUBJECT COMPLEMENT The supervisor is fair and reasonable. [*fair* and *reasonable*
>
> describe the subject, *supervisor.*]

**Note:** Some subject complements are nouns: The computer is the *solution.*

Copyright © 1995 by Harcourt Brace & Company. All rights reserved.

*Object Complements*     Adjectives used as object complements are also found in the predicate, but they describe or refer to the direct object of the verb.

OBJECT COMPLEMENT   Our boss finds competition healthy.   [The object complement,

*healthy*, modifies the direct object, *competition*.]

**Note:**   Some object complements are nouns: Our boss considers us a *team*.

**Adverbs**   Adverbs modify verbs or modify other modifiers, verbals, a phrase, a clause, or even the rest of the sentence in which they appear.

A business letter written to a friend or an acquaintance is *quite often highly* informal. [*Often* modifies the verb *is*; *quite* modifies the adverb *often*; and *highly* modifies the adjective *informal*.]

Writers often have special difficulty with sentences that include linking verbs and their modifiers and other verbs that function as linking verbs.

In sentences with linking verbs (*be, seem*, and so forth) or with verbs sometimes used as linking verbs (for instance, *feel* or *look*), it is especially important to determine whether a modifier refers to the verb or to the subject. If it refers to the verb, an adverb must be used; if it refers to a subject, an adjective must be used.

When the modifier refers to a verb like *be, seem, feel*, or *look* rather than to the subject, an adverb, not an adjective, is used.

The client read *hurriedly* through the contractors' bids.   [*Hurriedly*, an adverb, modifies the verb, *read*.]

The client looked *hurried* as he searched through the contractors' bids.   [*Hurried*, an adjective, modifies the subject, *client*.]

**Form**   Both adjectives and adverbs change their form when two or more things are being compared. An *er* on the end of a modifier or a *less* or *more* in front of it indicates that two things or groups of things are being compared (the comparative degree); an *est* on the end of a modifier or a *least* or *most* in front of it indicates that three or more things or groups of things are being compared (the superlative degree). Some desk dictionaries show the *er* and *est* ending for those adjectives and adverbs that form their comparative and superlative degrees in this way (for example—old, old*er*, old*est*). Most dictionaries show the changes for highly irregular modifiers (for example—good, *better, best*). As a rule of thumb, most one-syllable adjectives and most two-syllable adjectives ending in a vowel sound (*tidy, narrow*) form the comparative with *er* and the superlative with *est*. Most adjectives of two or more syllables and most adverbs form the comparative by adding the word *more* and the superlative by adding the word *most*.

COMPARATIVE DEGREE   Writing a business letter to a customer is *more difficult* than writing a personal letter to a friend.

SUPERLATIVE DEGREE   The *most difficult* letter to write is the one requesting a job interview.

   Copyright © 1995 by Harcourt Brace & Company. All rights reserved.

**Caution:** Many dictionaries do not list the *er* or *est* endings. Double-check if you are uncertain.

**Note:** For many adjectives the choice of *er* and *est* or *more* and *most* is optional.

The work grows *more* and *more* easy as time passes.

OR

The work grows *easier* and *easier* as time passes.

**Note:** Current usage, however illogical it may seem, accepts comparisons of many adjectives or adverbs with absolute meanings, such as *"a more perfect* report," "the *deadest* campus," and *"less* completely exhausted." But many writers make an exception of *unique*—using *"more nearly* unique" rather than "more unique." They consider *unique* an absolute adjective—one without degrees of comparison.

Copyright © 1995 by Harcourt Brace & Company. All rights reserved.

Deduct 10 for each incorrectly filled blank.

## Distinguishing Between Adjective and Adverb Modifiers     Exercise 4–1

NAME _____     SCORE _____

**4a  Use adverbs to modify verbs, adjectives, and other adverbs.**

**4b  Use adjectives as subject or object complements.**

DIRECTIONS    In each of the following sentences, choose the form of the word that would be considered appropriate in business and professional correspondence and reports. Cross out the incorrect choice; write the correct one in the blank. To help you decide which choice is correct, the word or words modified are underlined. (If you are uncertain about the part of speech of the underlined word or of the modifiers, consult your dictionary.)

EXAMPLE
(Almost, ~~Most~~) every employee must write business letters

each year.                                                           _____Almost_____

1. Writing one's first business letter can be an (~~awful,~~

   awfully) intimidating experience.                               _____awfully_____

2. Most people feel (reluctant, ~~reluctantly~~) about writing

   business letters.                                               _____reluctant_____

3. Procrastinating about writing a letter usually makes a

   writer's job more (difficult, ~~difficulter~~).                 _____difficult_____

4. You should (~~probable,~~ probably) write when an event is

   still current.                                                  _____probably_____

5. People who take the business of writing seriously

   (~~usual,~~ usually) try to make notes about what they want

   to say.                                                         _____usually_____

6. A (~~real,~~ really) clearly written letter means that its

   writer took the time to revise.                                _____really_____

Copyright © 1995 by Harcourt Brace & Company. All rights reserved.

7. A courteous business person <u>will</u> (~~careful~~, carefully) plan exactly what to say before writing.

    *carefully*

8. Letters from your customers (most, ~~mostly~~) <u>often</u> include questions they want answered.

    *most*

9. Delaying your response to an important letter can make a customer <u>react</u> (~~angry,~~ angrily).

    *angrily*

10. You are judged by employers as well as by customers according to how (~~quick~~, quickly) you <u>respond</u> to their requests.

    *quickly*

Copyright © 1995 by Harcourt Brace & Company. All rights reserved.

Deduct 3 1/3 for each incorrectly filled blank, 3 1/3 for each incorrectly circled word or words, and 3 1/3 for each incorrectly underlined word.

## Using Comparative and Superlative Modifiers                    Exercise 4–2

NAME _____ SCORE _____

**4c  Use the correct comparative and superlative forms of adjectives and adverbs.**
(See also **22c**.)

DIRECTIONS    In each of the following sentences, circle the correct form of the modifier within the parentheses and underline the word or words it modifies. In the blank, write whether you selected the comparative or the superlative form of the modifier. The word or words that the modifier refers to is underlined. (If you do not know how to form the comparative or superlative form of the modifier, consult your dictionary).

EXAMPLE
You will write letters (frequently, (more frequently)) than

reports.                                                      *comparative*

1. Convincing customers that they matter is one of the

   (expensivest, (most expensive)) goals a business has.      *superlative*

2. For that reason, it has become ((more important),

   importanter) than ever that you write effective letters.   *comparative*

3. Although a telephone call can take the place of some

   letters, many people still feel ((better), more better) hav-

   ing things put in writing.                                 *comparative*

4. These days, you'll probably "talk" to (more few, (fewer))

   customers in person than you do in letters.                *comparative*

5. A letter gives your reader the clearest, (exactest, (most

   exact)) record of what your company has agreed to do.      *superlative*

6. A letter will show a judge ((more precisely), preciselier)

   exactly what went on if your agreement is later called

   into question.                                             *comparative*

Copyright © 1995 by Harcourt Brace & Company. All rights reserved.

7.  You must use the (most clear, clearest) wording possible
    to prevent any misunderstandings from occurring later. _____superlative_____

8.  Most good writers think of clarity and conciseness as
    the two (more essential, essentialest, most essential)
    qualities of good business writing. _____superlative_____

9.  The three (importantest, most important, more impor-
    tant) things that a business letter must do are to get the
    reader to do what you want, to give the reader informa-
    tion, and to build goodwill. _____superlative_____

10. If you accomplish these goals, you can expect to be a
    (successfuller, more successful) business writer than
    those who forget to be considerate of their readers. _____comparative_____

Copyright © 1995 by Harcourt Brace & Company. All rights reserved.

Deduct 8 for each incorrectly filled blank and 2 for each incorrect underlining.

**Mastering Adjective and Adverb
Modifiers: A Review**                                    Exercise 4–3

NAME _____ SCORE _____

DIRECTIONS   In each of the following sentences cross out the inappropriate modifier within the parentheses and write the correct modifier in the blank. Then underline the word or words modified. (If you are uncertain about the parts of speech of the word or words you underline or about the proper form of the modifier, consult your dictionary.)

EXAMPLE
This letter is the most (~~skillful~~, skillfully) written piece of

correspondence I have seen.                              ___skillfully___

1. (Nearly, ~~Near~~) all good business letters follow the same

   general pattern.                                     ___Nearly___

2. Without being unpleasantly abrupt, the opening makes

   clear the purpose of the letter as (~~quick~~, quickly) as

   possible.                                            ___quickly___

3. The body of the letter then discusses (~~deeper~~, more

   deeply) what has been said in the opening.           ___more deeply___

4. Finally, the closing often tells the reader how to

   respond (~~easy~~, easily) to the writer's requests.  ___easily___

5. The closing may also emphasize a point that the writer

   considers to be the (~~more~~, most) important one.   ___most___

6. The so-called "bad-news" letter, however, opens

   (~~different~~, differently).                         ___differently___

7. It is the only (noticeable, ~~noticeably~~) exception to this

   general pattern.                                     ___noticeable___

Copyright © 1995 by Harcourt Brace & Company. All rights reserved.                    *115*

8. Bad news is (easier, ~~more easy~~) to bear if the writer begins the letter in a positive or neutral note.

_easier_

9. For example, rather than opening with "We refuse to fix your lawn mower," begin (~~pleasanter~~, more pleasantly) with "Thank you for writing to us about your lawn mower."

_more pleasantly_

10. In other words, the writer of the bad-news letter should be (~~real~~, really) careful to maintain the reader's goodwill by being as helpful and polite as possible.

_really_

Copyright © 1995 by Harcourt Brace & Company. All rights reserved.

## 5

**Choose the case form that shows the function of the nouns and pronouns in sentences.**

As you learned in Chapter **1**, a noun or pronoun may change form to indicate the way it works in a clause. The form of the noun or pronoun, referred to as its *case*, indicates its relationship to other words in the sentence. The case may be *subjective* (if it functions as a subject), *objective* (if it functions as an object), or *possessive* (if it shows ownership or possession). Nouns change their form for only one case—the possessive. (See also Chapter **15**.)

Certain pronouns change their form for each case; you must be aware of these various forms in order to make the function of these pronouns immediately clear in your writing.

| *Subjective* | *Objective* | *Possessive* |
|---|---|---|
| I | me | mine |
| we | us | our, ours |
| he, she | him, her | his, her, hers |
| they | them | their, theirs |
| who, whoever | whom, whomever | whose |

**Subjective Case**   The subjective case is used for subjects of verbs and for subject complements.

> *She* answers all letters of complaint.   [subject of verb]
> The best writer in the firm is *she*.   [subject complement]

**Note:**   You may sometimes find it more comfortable to avoid using the pronoun as a complement: "*She* is the best writer in the firm." OR "The best writer in the firm is *Mary*."

**Objective Case**   The objective case is used for both direct and indirect objects, for objects of prepositions, and for both subjects and objects of infinitives.

> The customer called *me* about his problem with our product.   [direct object]
> He gave *me* his opinion about what should be done to improve the product.   [indirect object]
> He sent the unused portion of the product to *me*.   [object of preposition]
> He asked *me* to refund his money.   [subject of infinitive *to refund*]
> He wanted to tell *me* about his difficulty in using the product.   [object of infinitive *to tell*]

**Possessive Case**   The possessive case is generally used before a gerund—a verbal that ends in *ing*—and acts as a noun. But a participle also sometimes has an *ing* ending. The possessive case is used before a gerund, which acts as a noun, but not before a participle, which acts as an adjective.

Copyright © 1995 by Harcourt Brace & Company. All rights reserved.

GERUND    I got tired of *his* criticizing my company's product. [*Criticizing* acts as a noun, the object of the preposition *of*.]

PARTICIPLE    I found *him* unrelenting in his attack on our product. [*Unrelenting* acts as an adjective, modifying *him*.]

Copyright © 1995 by Harcourt Brace & Company. All rights reserved.

Deduct 10 for each incorrectly filled blank.

## Case Forms of Pronouns

Exercise 5–1

NAME _____ SCORE _____

The subjective case (*I, we, he, she, they, who, whoever*) is used for subjects and subject complements; the objective case (*me, us, him, her, them, whom, whomever*) is used for objects of verbs and verbals, for objects of prepositions, and for both subjects and objects of infinitives (for example, *to go, to be*); the possessive case (*my, our, his, her, their, whose*) is generally used to modify a gerund.

SUBJECTIVE   OBJECTIVE   OBJECTIVE
*He* expected *us* to hire *him.*

SUBJECTIVE   POSSESSIVE   OBJECTIVE
*She* heard about *his* criticizing the product from *us.*

OBJECTIVE   POSSESSIVE   POSSESSIVE
*We* regret *their* not being able to attend *your* meeting.

DIRECTIONS   In the following sentences cross out the incorrect case form or forms within parentheses and write the correct form in the blank. List your reason for your choice in the space provided after the sentence. (After your answers have been checked, you may find it helpful to read them aloud several times to accustom your ear to the sound of the correct case forms.)

EXAMPLE
She showed (~~we~~, us) how the computer network made your office staff

more efficient.       *us*

Reason: *object of verb*

1. She explained to us about (you, your) developing a shared databank   *you or*

   all your employees could use.       *your*

   Reason: *object of preposition or possessive before*
   *a gerund*

2. A databank provides (them, ~~they~~) with easy-to-access resources

   created by many people.       *them*

   Reason: *indirect object of verb*

3. When we had studied this system for a day, we asked (~~she~~, her) how

   a network would help us.       *her*

   Reason: *object*

Copyright © 1995 by Harcourt Brace & Company. All rights reserved.      

4. With this new system, it would be necessary for (us, ~~we~~) to change
   the way we think about resource management in the office.      _us_

   Reason: *subject of infinitive, but give credit for object of preposition <u>for</u>*

5. John said that having access to forms for reports was enough to
   make (~~he~~, him) want to try out a databank system.      _him_

   Reason: *object of infinitive*

6. Because we learned that we could all easily access company records
   from the shared computer files, all of (~~we~~, us) immediately saw ways
   for the system to save us time.      _us_

   Reason: *object of preposition*

7. Our firm's employees no longer think that shared data will be a
   threat to (~~they~~, them).      _them_

   Reason: *object of preposition*

8. Now (we, ~~us~~) know how easy it can be to work cooperatively by
   retrieving computer files from linked storage banks.      _we_

   Reason: *subject*

9. When Harvey asked us if the system would be expensive, we told
   (~~he~~, him) that it was cheaper than everyone having their own stand-
   alone computer.      _him_

   Reason: *object of verb*

10. It was (he, ~~him~~) who had asked us to investigate this new system in
    the first place.      _he_

    Reason: *subject of complement*

 Copyright © 1995 by Harcourt Brace & Company. All rights reserved.

Deduct 10 for each incorrectly filled blank.

**Pronouns in Compounds and as Appositives**                    Exercise 5–2

NAME _____    SCORE _____

### 5a  Be aware of case forms for pronouns in compound constructions.

A pronoun has the same case form in a compound or an appositive construction as it would if it were used alone.

| | |
|---|---|
| COMPOUND CONSTRUCTIONS | Matthew and *I* took business writing courses taught by Mr. Rowe and *her*.  [Compare with "I took courses taught by *her*."] |
| APPOSITIVE CONSTRUCTIONS | *She*, the director of product information for a local firm, taught *us* students what we needed to know about business writing.  [Compare with "*She* taught *us* what we needed to know about business correspondence."] |

DIRECTIONS   In the following sentences cross out the incorrect case form within parentheses and write the correct form in the blank. (To decide which case form is correct, say aloud each part of the compound construction separately or say aloud the pronoun without the appositive that follows it, as illustrated in the examples.)

EXAMPLES

(We, ~~Us~~) employees now have access to computer "bulletin boards" where we can network with people from all over the country.   [*We now have access…*]

*We*

The most interested departments were (~~her and him~~, hers and his).   [*The most interested department was hers. The most interested department was his.*]

*hers and his*

1. Because we were interested in learning what other companies did, (the other employees and I, ~~the other employees and me~~) talked to colleagues across a computer network.

*the other employees and I*

2. (~~Sally and me~~, Sally and I) discovered a network that helps people get information about job discrimination questions.

*Sally and I*

Copyright © 1995 by Harcourt Brace & Company. All rights reserved.

3. Learning about an entire computer network of people who work with these problems gave (~~Sally and I~~, Sally and me) additional resources.

   _Sally and me_

4. Being able to ask questions that would be answered by dozens of people from all over the country within days made it possible for (~~the other managers and I~~, the other managers and me) to solve a pressing problem in our office quickly.

   _the other man-agers and me_

5. (We, ~~Us~~) managers decided that getting a variety of answers rapidly was definitely enhanced by our computer network contacts.

   _We_

6. Melissa, our computer expert, taught (us, ~~we~~) that computer networks are easy to use.

   _us_

7. Because Melissa and Jeff gained additional training at computer networking seminars, it became clear that (~~her and him~~, she and he) had valuable information to share with our co-workers.

   _she and he_

8. Furthermore, the seminars taught (~~Melissa and he~~, Melissa and him) that there were new computer options that made their jobs as managers easier.

   _Melissa and him_

9. (She, as well as he; ~~Her, as well as him~~) could see that once people got over their computer anxieties they would find computer bulletin board networks a source for discovering new management strategies quickly.

   _She, as well as he_

10. By the end of the workshop Jeff and Melissa held for us, it was clear that (~~Jeff and her~~, Jeff and she) had a lot they could teach us about computer networking.

    _Jeff and she_

Copyright © 1995 by Harcourt Brace & Company. All rights reserved.

Deduct 10 for each incorrectly filled blank.

**Pronouns in Subordinate Clauses and with *Self* Added**    Exercise 5–3

NAME _____ SCORE _____

**5b  Determine the case of each pronoun by its use in its *own* clause.**

> I think I know *who* should be chosen.    [Although *who* begins the clause that is the object of *I know*, in its own clause *who* is the subject of the verb *should be chosen*.]

> It is she *whom* we should choose.    [In its own clause, *whom* is the object of the verb *should choose*.]

*Self* is added to a pronoun only when a reflexive or an intensive pronoun is needed.

> I *myself* will answer the letter.    [intensive pronoun: intensifies *I*]
> I wrote a letter to *myself*.    [reflexive pronoun: reflects back to *I*]
> He wrote a letter to *me*.    [not *myself*; neither intensive nor reflexive]

**Note:**    *Hisself, theirselves, it self*, and *its self* are nonstandard forms of *himself, themselves*, and *itself*.

**5c  Use *whom* for all objects in formal written English.**

| NOT | They hired the person **who** they felt had the best qualifications. |
|-----|---------------------------------------------------------------------|
| BUT | They hired the person **whom** they felt had the best qualifications. [object of the verb *had*] |

DIRECTIONS    In the following sentences cross out the incorrect case form or forms within parentheses and write the correct form in the blank.

EXAMPLE
The employees asked her (~~who~~, whom) they should contact to

   learn more about desktop publishing skills.    _____whom_____

1.  Desktop publishing (~~it self~~, itself) is a cost-effective way

   to produce sophisticated documents in your own office.    _____itself_____

2.  People can learn to operate computer programs

   (~~themselfs~~, themselves, ~~theirselves~~) that allow them to

   include graphics and fancy type styles in their docu-

   ments.    _____themselves_____

3.  The technical writer in the office was one person (who,

   ~~whom~~) knew how to use this software.    _____who_____

Copyright © 1995 by Harcourt Brace & Company. All rights reserved.

4. It was this writer to (~~who~~, whom) they directed most of their questions about what desktop publishing could let them do with their office's newsletter.

_____whom_____

5. Well-designed newsletters and reports make (~~whomever~~, whoever) reads them view the company that sends them out as sophisticated and professional.

_____whoever_____

6. The writers for (whom, ~~who~~) desktop publishing is a skill can freelance for businesses needing such expertise but that cannot afford to hire someone full-time to design and produce their brochures, flyers, and reports.

_____whom_____

7. Mistakenly, these companies believe they are saving (~~them~~, themselves) money by not creating well-designed documents.

_____themselves_____

8. Our technical writer said that we could refer our desk-top project questions to (him, ~~himself~~) for suggestions.

_____him_____

9. We asked him (~~whom~~, who) could teach us how to use our new desktop publishing software.

_____who_____

10. He remarked that there were many self-instruction videos available that had been useful to (him, ~~himself~~, ~~hisself~~) as he began learning computer-assisted layout and design.

_____him_____

Copyright © 1995 by Harcourt Brace & Company. All rights reserved.

Deduct 10 for each incorrectly filled blank.

**Mastering Case: A Review**                                    Exercise 5–4

NAME _____ SCORE _____

DIRECTIONS    In the following sentences cross out the incorrect case form or forms within parentheses and write the correct form in the blank. Determine the use of the pronoun in its own clause before you choose the case form.

EXAMPLE
(~~Whoever~~, Whomever) a company wishes to contact quickly

would do well to consider purchasing a fax machine.          ____Whomever____

1. Our marketing director was the person to (~~who~~, whom)

   we looked for advice about how best to get ordering

   information to our customers within one working day.     ____whom____

2. She told us that clients (~~who~~, whom) our company

   wished to impress might value material that was sent to

   them via fax—a machine that sends photocopies over

   the telephone.                                           ____whom____

3. (~~They~~, Their, ~~Them~~) working over the telephone meant

   that we could get the material that a client requested to

   their office as soon as the phone call was completed.    ____Their____

4. Material sent on the fax contains a cover sheet that lets

   the operator at the other end of the line know to (~~who~~,

   whom) to give the material when it arrives.              ____whom____

5. The cover sheet should give clear delivery information:

   (whom, ~~who~~) the material is for, the sender's name,

   address, and return fax number, and a brief title

   describing the contents of the material.                 ____whom____

6. This cover sheet lets the person on whose fax machine

   it arrives know if (~~she~~, hers, ~~her~~) is the correct "address"

   and whom to contact if a mistake has been made.          ____hers____

Copyright © 1995 by Harcourt Brace & Company. All rights reserved.

7. Another way we found to send data almost instan-
taneously was via computer modems; (we, ~~us~~) at
Concept Marketing are very "high tech" when it comes
to communicating with our clients.                    *we*

8. When we arrange to do work for our clients, we let
them know what electronic media (~~them~~, they) can use
to contact our representatives.                       *they*

9. Being up-to-date with fax machines and computer
modems provides (us, ~~we~~) with the most efficient and
economical means of doing business in the
Information Age.                                      *us*

10. Being computer- and fax-accessible to customers for
(~~who~~, whom) these machines are a necessity has certainly increased our profits.                         *whom*

Copyright © 1995 by Harcourt Brace & Company. All rights reserved.

# 6

**Make a verb agree in number with its subject; make a pronoun agree in number with its antecedent.**

For your ideas to be clearly stated, it is essential that all subjects and verbs agree in number; a singular subject requires a singular verb, and a plural subject requires a plural verb. (Remember that an *s* ending shows *plural* number for the subject but *singular* number for the verb.)

SINGULAR     A good business letter makes clear the response that is expected from

the recipient of the letter.

PLURAL     Good business letters make clear the responses that are expected from

the recipients of the letters.

In the same way, a pronoun agrees in number with the noun (or the other pronoun) it refers to, called its *antecedent*.

SINGULAR     A good business *letter* makes *its* purpose clear.

PLURAL     Good business *letters* make *their* purpose clear.

Mastering agreement requires that you be able to do three things: (1) match up the simple subject or subjects with the verb or verbs; (2) know which nouns and pronouns are traditionally singular and which are traditionally plural; and (3) identify the antecedent of a pronoun (the noun the pronoun refers to) so that you can determine the number of the antecedent.

### 6a  Make a verb agree in number with its subject.

**Simple Subjects**    To make the subject and verb agree in number, you must be able to recognize the simple subject of a sentence as well as the verb. The simple subject is often surrounded by other words that are a part of the complete subject and that can easily be mistaken for the exact word or words that should agree in number with the verb.

SINGULAR     A device that encourages quick responses from recipients of request

letters is the stamped, addressed return envelope.   [The complete sub-

ject contains several plural nouns—*responses, recipients*, and *letters*—

that must not be mistaken for the simple subject, which is singular.]

Copyright © 1995 by Harcourt Brace & Company. All rights reserved.

PLURAL    Devices that encourage a quick response from the recipient of a request letter include the stamped, addressed return envelope, a reply card with answers to check, and free prizes or other rewards for a prompt response. [The complete subject contains several singular nouns—*response, recipient,* and *letter*—that must not be mistaken for the simple subject, which is plural.]

Be particularly careful about the subject-verb agreement in the following situations:

**(1) When the subject or the verb ends in *k* or *t*:**

Often a business writer talks directly to the reader.

Journalists write guided by a different set of criteria.

Do not be misled by subjects and verbs that have endings not clearly sounded in rapid speech.

**(2) When the subject is followed by a prepositional phrase or a subordinate clause:**
Make the subject and verb agree when words intervene between them. The grammatical number of the subject does not change with the addition of expressions beginning with such words as *accompanied by, along with, as well as, in addition to, including, no less than, not to mention, together with.*

The reason *for expecting* a response is obvious.

The reason *which was outlined in the correspondence* is obvious.

**(3) When the subject follows the verb:**

There are many daily *reports* from agencies of the government.

**(4) When singular subjects are joined by *or, either...or, neither...nor*:**

*Either* Jane *or* Martin goes to the workshops.

The verb is singular *unless* one subject is singular and one is plural, in which case the verb agrees with the nearer subject:

*Neither* the computers *nor* the fax machine is working today.

Copyright © 1995 by Harcourt Brace & Company. All rights reserved.

**(5) When the subject and subject complement do not have the same number** (Usually you should rewrite the sentence, without using a form of *be*, to avoid the conflict in number.):

AWKWARD  Reports are one way to monitor progress within a company.

BETTER  Reports serve as one monitor of progress within a company.

**Singular and Plural Nouns and Pronouns**  Some noun subjects are traditionally singular, while others are traditionally plural. Those subjects that are traditionally singular include

**(1) singular subjects joined by *or* and *nor* and subjects introduced by *many a*:**

Neither the letter *nor* the advertisement requires a response.

*Many a* letter goes unnoticed.

**(2) collective nouns regarded as a unit:**

The *number* of request letters amazes me.

The *committee* has made its recommendation.

**(3) nouns that are plural in form but singular in meaning:**

The *news* creates a stir on Wall Street.

One hundred miles means *a long commute*.

**(4) titles of works or words referred to as words:**

*Night Line* features some of the best interviews on television.

*Employee benefits* is a term we use to mean *fringe benefits*.

Those subjects that are traditionally plural include

**(1) subjects joined by *and*:**

A letter *and* this memo have the same tone.

**(2) a plural subject following *or* or *nor*:**

Neither the manager *nor* his employees neglect correspondence.   [The verb agrees with

*employees*, the part of the subject to which it is nearer.]

Copyright © 1995 by Harcourt Brace & Company. All rights reserved.

### (3) collective nouns that do not act as a unit:

A *number* of corporations encourage their employees to return to school.

Certain nouns and pronouns are sometimes singular and sometimes plural, depending on their contexts in their sentences.

|  |  |
|---|---|
| SINGULAR | A *group* of claim letters has been examined by management. [Here *group* is considered a unit.] |
| PLURAL | A *group* of employees are taking different actions in response to the company's latest stock option plan. [Here *group* refers to many individuals, not to a unit.] |
| SINGULAR | *Some* of this report is extremely well written. |
| PLURAL | *Some* of those reports are extremely well written. |

Pronouns such as *each, either, neither, one, everybody, everyone, someone,* and *anyone* are traditionally singular; pronouns such as *both, few, several,* and *many* are traditionally plural.

## 6b  Make a pronoun agree in number and gender with its antecedent.

A pronoun must agree in number and gender with the noun (or the pronoun) it refers to—that is, with its antecedent. (See also **19j**.)

|  |  |
|---|---|
| SINGULAR | A clearly stated *request* is the *one* most likely to get action. |
| PLURAL | Clearly stated *requests* are the *ones* most likely to get action. |

A pronoun agrees in number with its antecedent even when the antecedent is in a different clause. (Remember, however, that the *case* of a pronoun is determined entirely by its function in its own clause; see **5b**.)

Copyright © 1995 by Harcourt Brace & Company. All rights reserved.

| | |
|---|---|
| SINGULAR | A good business letter makes clear the *response that* is expected from the recipient of the letter.  [Notice that the verb *is expected* is singular because the antecedent of *that, response*, is singular.] |
| PLURAL | Good business letters make clear the *responses that* are expected from the recipients of the letters.  [Notice that the verb *are expected* is plural because the antecedent of *that, responses*, is plural.] |
| SINGULAR | A *request that* is clearly stated is usually answered.  [*Request*, the antecedent of *that*, is singular; therefore *that* is also singular.] |
| PLURAL | *Requests that* are clearly stated are usually answered.  [*Requests*, the antecedent of *that*, is plural; therefore *that* is also plural.] |
| MASCULINE | Emory represents *his* company well. |
| FEMININE | Juanita represents *her* company well. |

**Singular and Plural Antecedents**   Some pronouns (like some nouns) are traditionally considered singular, whereas others are considered plural.

Pronouns such as *everybody, one, anyone, each, either, neither, sort*, and *kind* are traditionally considered singular.

We try to give *each* of our products the promotion *it* deserves.

Naturally, *everyone* expects *his* own favorite to be the most popular.

[CONTRAST: *Many* expect *their* own favorites to be the most popular.]

*Each* of the one hundred women surveyed was asked to send *her* reply promptly.

**Note:**   Today most writers, and especially business writers, try to avoid sexism in the use of personal pronouns. Whereas most writers once wrote, "*Each* of us should do *his* best," they now try to avoid using the masculine pronoun to refer to both men and women. A careful writer avoids using pronouns that exclude either gender or that stereotype male and female roles.

Copyright © 1995 by Harcourt Brace & Company. All rights reserved.

| NOT | A chief executive officer represents *his* company's interests. [excludes females] |
|---|---|
| NOT | A chief executive officer represents *her* company's interests. [excludes males] |
| BUT | Chief executive officers represent *their* companies' interests. [includes both genders] |

In other instances, writers inadvertently stereotype male and female roles:

> A pilot flies only after completing *his* safety check.   [excludes female pilots]
> A secretary often produces reports for *her* boss.   [excludes male secretaries]

To avoid sexism, some writers give both masculine and feminine pronoun references.

> The negotiator represents the interests of *his or her* clients.

Other writers recast such sentences in the passive voice.

> Clients' interests *are represented* by the negotiator.

Finally, to avoid using the pronoun altogether, some writers recast the sentence entirely.

> The negotiator represents clients' interests.

The use of any of these options may change the meaning of your sentence; some work more smoothly than others. Many writers—and readers—consider the compound phrases *his or her* stylistically awkward; many also find the forms *his/her* and *he/she* ugly, impersonal, and bureaucratic.

Perhaps the easiest way to avoid sexism is to use plural pronouns and antecedents unless a feminine or a masculine pronoun is clearly called for, when *his* would definitely refer to a male employee or *her* to a female employee.

> Negotiators represent the interests of *their* clients.

The most effective revisions include recasting the sentence in the plural or avoiding the use of the pronoun altogether. Pronouns such as *both, several, many*, and *few* are considered plural.

> *Few* of the people surveyed said that *they* disliked the product.

Pronouns such as *all, any, half, most, none*, and *some* may be singular or plural, depending on their context (that is, depending on the rest of the sentence or paragraph in which they appear).

| SINGULAR | *All of the information has served its* purpose. |
|---|---|
| PLURAL | *All* of the people surveyed *have sent their* replies. |

Similarly, a collective noun, such as *staff, committee*, or *board*, may call for either a singular or plural pronoun, depending on whether—in its context—it signifies a unit or individual members.

   Copyright © 1995 by Harcourt Brace & Company. All rights reserved.

SINGULAR

The *committee has completed its* report.

PLURAL

The *committee have gone* back to *their* various departments.

**Caution:** Avoid confusing or awkward shifts between singular and plural pronouns that refer to the same collective noun.

CONFUSING

The *committee has completed its* report and *gone* back to *their* various

departments .

CORRECTED

The *committee has completed its* report, and the *members have gone*

back to *their* various departments.

Copyright © 1995 by Harcourt Brace & Company. All rights reserved.

Deduct 10 for each incorrectly filled blank.

## Subject and Verb Agreement

Exercise 6–1

NAME _____    SCORE _____

DIRECTIONS   In each of the following sentences underline the subject with one line (remember that a verbal may act as a subject); then match it with one of the verbs in parentheses. Cross out the verb that does not agree with the subject, and in the blank write the verb that does agree. (When all of your answers have been checked, read each sentence aloud, emphasizing the subject and verb.)

EXAMPLE

The purpose of persuasive letters (is, ~~are~~) to sell a product, an idea, or a service.

_____is_____

1. Persuasive writing (~~try~~, tries) to win over readers.

_____tries_____

2. One way to sway readers (is, ~~are~~) to touch on their emotions.

_____is_____

3. Such a "sales" letter, like persuasive essays, often (~~use~~, uses) emotional appeals.

_____uses_____

4. The successful writer generally (~~employ~~, employs) any emotional appeal that speaks to the readers' special interests.

_____employs_____

5. An exaggerated emotional appeal sometimes (~~make~~, makes) your readers grow irritated with your message.

_____makes_____

6. To be effective, however, such a tactic (is, ~~are~~) not obvious.

_____is_____

7. Facts, figures, and logic generally (work, ~~works~~) best to persuade skeptical readers.

_____work_____

8. The writer of persuasive letters (has, ~~have~~) to remember that uninvited mail can annoy people.

_____has_____

9. As soon as the reader loses interest, such letters usually (wind, ~~winds~~) up in the recycling bin.

_____wind_____

10. Therefore, the biggest challenge that a writer of persuasive letters must meet (is, ~~are~~) to make the reader want to keep reading.

_____is_____

Copyright © 1995 by Harcourt Brace & Company. All rights reserved.

Deduct 5 for each subject or verb incorrectly identified and 5 for each incorrect sentence.

**Subject and Verb Agreement—Continued**                    Exercise 6–2

NAME _____  SCORE _____

DIRECTIONS   In the sentences that follow, rewrite each sentence, replacing the plural subjects and verbs with singular ones and the singular subjects and verbs with plural ones. Underline the subject of the new sentence with one line and the verb of the new sentence with two lines. You will also need to change the articles (*a, an,* and *the*) to make the sentences correct.

EXAMPLES
A persuasive letter usually arrives uninvited.

Persuasive **letters** usually **arrive** uninvited.

Readers have not requested such letters.

A **reader has not requested** such letters.

1. A writer of effective persuasive letters convinces readers to look beyond the first few lines.

   Writers of effective persuasive letters convince readers to look beyond the first few lines.

2. The opening lines of a persuasive letter are extremely important.

   The opening line of a persuasive letter is extremely important.

3. A persuasive writer generally follows a definite plan to gain the reader's attention.

   Persuasive writers generally follow a definite plan to gain the reader's attention.

Copyright © 1995 by Harcourt Brace & Company. All rights reserved.                    *137*

4. Appeals to the reader's self-interest form the opening of persuasive letters.

An appeal to the reader's self-interest forms the opening of persuasive letters.

5. An opening promises certain rewards to the readers, like health, popularity, success, or some other personal benefit.

Openings promise certain rewards to the readers, like health, popularity, success, or some other personal benefit.

6. A successful advertisement suggests effective ways to open a persuasive letter.

Successful advertisements suggest effective ways to open a persuasive letter.

7. The headlines of an advertisement serve much the same purpose as the opening sentence of a persuasive letter.

The headline of an advertisement serves much the same purpose as the opening sentence of a persuasive letter.

8. A headline gets the audience to pay attention to the rest of the advertisement.

Headlines get the audience to pay attention to the rest of the advertisement.

9. In successful advertisements and in persuasive letters, the benefit promised the audience is specified.

In successful advertisements and in persuasive letters, the benefits promised the audience are specified.

10. A reader favorably impressed by persuasive letters or advertisements wants to buy the product they describe.

Readers favorably impressed by persuasive letters or advertisements want to buy the product they describe.

 Copyright © 1995 by Harcourt Brace & Company. All rights reserved.

Deduct 10 for each incorrectly filled blank.

## Singular and Plural Noun Subjects

Exercise 6–3

NAME _____   SCORE _____

DIRECTIONS   In each of the following sentences underline the subject (or subjects, if compound) with one line and match it (or them) with one of the verbs in parentheses. Circle any key word or words that affect the number of the subject. Then cross out the verb that does not agree with the subject and, in the blank, write the verb that does agree.

EXAMPLE

(A) number of strategies (is, are) available to the persuasive

writer.   _____are_____

1. (News) that benefits the reader (aim, aims) at gratifying

   the reader's secret wishes.   _____aims_____

2. (Either) "How will such products make my life better?"

   (or) "Why should I buy this product?" (is, are) the

   reader's main question.   _____is_____

3. Saving money (and) being a part of the "in crowd" (is, are)

   other benefits a skillful writer can offer to the reader.   _____are_____

4. (Either) pleasure (or) comfort (answer, answers) those

   questions.   _____answers_____

5. A promise of something good (or) a tip about finances

   favorably (impress, impresses) a reader.   _____impresses_____

6. Promises (and) tips, of course, also (get, gets) many

   readers' attention.   _____get_____

7. (A) variety of other tactics (is, are) used to gain the

   reader's attention.   _____is_____

Copyright © 1995 by Harcourt Brace & Company. All rights reserved.

8. Often new information and satisfaction of curiosity
   (act, ~~acts~~) as a "promise" made to the reader of a persuasive letter.                                          *act*

9. "Completely new!" or "You've been selected!" (~~attract~~,
   attracts) the reader's attention.                        *attracts*

10. The group of attention-getting words that persuasive
    writers typically rely on (is, ~~are~~) surprisingly small.   *is*

  Copyright © 1995 by Harcourt Brace & Company. All rights reserved.

Deduct 10 for each incorrectly filled blank.

## Singular and Plural Noun and Pronoun Subjects

Exercise 6–4

NAME _____ SCORE _____

DIRECTIONS   In the following sentences cross out the verb in parentheses that does not agree with its subject. Then enter the correct verb in the blank.

EXAMPLE
One of the most important things to do in persuasive letters

(~~are~~, is) to involve the reader quickly.

_____is_____

1. A person (~~hope~~, hopes) to receive the benefits promised in a persuasive letter's opening line.

_____hopes_____

2. Few of us (~~reads~~, read) far if we do not see how a product can be of value to us.

_____read_____

3. Successful persuasive letter writers generally (~~mentions~~, mention) the word *you* in the letter's first few sentences.

_____mention_____

4. A number of persuasive strategies (~~works~~, work) well to make readers see themselves enjoying the products they are reading about.

_____work_____

5. "Do your eyes sting during allergy season? Now you can put an end to your discomfort" are opening lines that immediately (~~gets~~, get) the reader into the picture.

_____get_____

6. Skilled writers (~~capitalizes~~, capitalize) on the fact that many people suffer from severe allergies.

_____capitalize_____

7. Reports of favorable results from chronic allergy sufferers (~~follows~~, follow) to support the claims.

_____follow_____

8. A person reading this letter (feels, ~~feel~~) included among the stories told by the people in the letter.

_____feels_____

9. Both those suffering severe allergies and those with only slight symptoms (~~wants~~, want) to gain relief from their distress.

_____want_____

Copyright © 1995 by Harcourt Brace & Company. All rights reserved.

10. Sales letters, if they are to be successful, (~~tells~~, tell) the
    reader how the product can help them solve a problem.  _____ *tell* _____

Copyright © 1995 by Harcourt Brace & Company. All rights reserved.

Deduct 3 1/3 for each incorrectly marked pronoun, 3 1/3 for each incorrectly filled blank, and 3 1/3 for each incorrect underlining.

## Pronoun and Antecedent Agreement

Exercise 6–5

NAME _____ SCORE _____

DIRECTIONS    In each of the following sentences, select the pronoun that agrees in number with its antecedent (**Note:** Sometimes the antecedent comes *after* the pronoun that refers to it); cross out the incorrect pronoun, and write in the blank whether the pronoun is singular or plural. Finally, underline the noun (or nouns) functioning as the antecedent (or antecedents) of the pronoun you selected.

EXAMPLE

The writer and the designer of an advertisement work

together to plan (~~their~~, its) contents.          ___singular___

1. These advertising specialists decide on the fundamen-

   tal persuasive strategy (~~she~~, they) will use.        ___plural___

2. The illustrations in an advertisement are very impor-

   tant; (~~it~~, they) will catch a reader's eye.        ___plural___

3. Even if the reader is not aware of (its, ~~their~~) effect, a

   well-drawn piece of artwork can attract attention to an

   advertisement.        ___singular___

4. Because the visual components of the advertisement

   attract the most attention, the writer and designer plan

   (~~it~~, them) very carefully.        ___plural___

5. The most important part of the advertisement should

   be placed where readers will notice (it, ~~them~~).        ___singular___

6. Generally, an advertisement will devote more space to

   pictures than to words in order to make (its, ~~their~~)

   point.        ___singular___

Copyright © 1995 by Harcourt Brace & Company. All rights reserved.

7. The pictures in the advertisement should not, however,

   distract the reader from (its, ~~their~~) text.          <u>*singular*</u>

8. If the ad's creators need to include such information as

   cost and specifications, (~~he, she,~~ it, ~~they~~) will usually

   appear in small print near the end of the advertisement.   <u>*singular*</u>

9. Of course, if price and other details about a company's

   products are selling points, then the ad's writers will

   emphasize (~~it,~~ them).                                  <u>*plural*</u>

10. Good letter writers wishing to sell products may use the

    same strategy: emphasize cost if (it, ~~they~~) helps them to

    sell the product.                                         <u>*singular*</u>

Copyright © 1995 by Harcourt Brace & Company. All rights reserved.

Deduct 5 for each incorrectly marked or missed pronoun and 5 for each incorrectly revised sentence.

## Avoiding Sexism in the Use of Personal Pronouns                    Exercise 6–6

NAME _____ SCORE _____

Make your writing inclusive, not sexist. Avoid the use of pronouns that exclude either gender or that stereotype male or female roles.

NOT        A busy *executive* should schedule *his* time carefully.   [excludes females]

NOT        A busy *executive* should schedule *her* time carefully.   [excludes males]

BUT        Busy *executives* should schedule *their* time carefully.   [includes both genders]

The following sentences also stereotype female and male roles:

A *secretary* understands *her* responsibilities.
A *supervisor* understands *his* responsibilities.

Include both genders by using one of the following options, which are listed in order of preference:

### Options to Avoid Stereotyping

1. Recast the sentence so the subject and verb are plural.

   *Supervisors* understand *their* responsibilities.

2. Recast the sentence in the passive voice (see also **29d**).

   The responsibilities *are understood* by the supervisor.

3. Avoid the pronoun altogether.

   A *supervisor* understands the responsibilities.

4. Substitute a compound phrase.

   A *supervisor* understands *his or her* responsibilities.

Be aware that any of these inclusive options may change your meaning; some work more effectively in a given situation than others. Choose carefully the option that makes your point most clearly.

   Many readers consider the compound phrase *his or her* to be stylistically awkward, so use it sparingly. Others will find the forms *his/her*, *he/she*, and *s/he* to be ugly and bureaucratic; rewrite your sentence to avoid them.

DIRECTIONS   In each of the following sentences, underline those pronouns that incorrectly exclude either gender or that stereotype male or female roles. In the space provided, rewrite each sentence to eliminate the problem. **Note:** Use whichever strategy seems most appropriate and that does not distort the original meaning of the sentence.

Copyright © 1995 by Harcourt Brace & Company. All rights reserved.

EXAMPLE

In advertising, a client may not always be right, but <u>his</u> opinions should always be listened to.

In advertising, a client may not always be right, but his or her opinions should always be listened to.*

1. An advertising executive must certainly be sensitive to <u>her</u> clients' wishes.

2. When someone designs material to sell a product, <u>he/she</u> must also think of the advertisement's potential readers.

3. Of course, the writer wants <u>his</u> advertisements to sell the readers on the product, but not if it means deceiving them.

4. An exercise equipment company's advertisements may promise the customer something that its product cannot give <u>him/her</u>.

5. If <u>he</u> is told that a company can do something, the reader has a legal right to expect that which the advertisement told <u>him</u> is true.

6. Losing a customer's goodwill is something that the conscientious writer wants to avoid, for <u>she</u> knows that lost customers mean lost revenue for <u>her</u> and <u>her</u> company.

*Answers for this exercise will vary depending on the strategy the student uses.

Copyright © 1995 by Harcourt Brace & Company. All rights reserved.

7. A successful writer of persuasive letters never forgets that <u>his</u> reader's satisfaction is <u>his</u> most important consideration.

8. A writer who looks at what <u>she</u> says through a reader's eyes will create effective persuasive letters.

9. The reader of the letter offering discounts on hiking boots must see how buying them will benefit <u>her</u> personally.

10. A writer who knows <u>his</u> products and audience can well motivate <u>his</u> readers to buy what <u>his</u> letter is selling.

Copyright © 1995 by Harcourt Brace & Company. All rights reserved.

Deduct 5 for each incorrectly filled blank.

## Mastering Agreement: A Review

Exercise 6–7

NAME _____ SCORE _____

DIRECTIONS   In the following sentences underline the subject; then cross out the verb or pronoun in parentheses that does not agree with its subject or antecedent. Write the correct pronoun or verb in the blank.

EXAMPLE
Most successful advertisements (~~appeals~~, appeal) to both our

reason and our emotions.                                                   *appeal*

1. Details (~~convinces~~, convince) our reason to buy what

   our hearts desire.                                                      *convince*

2. Everyone tries to rationalize (~~his, her~~, his or her)

   desires.                                                               *his or her*

3. The details provided in the persuasive letter (offer,

   ~~offers~~) the reader the needed rationalization.                     *offer*

4. If you (want, ~~wants~~) to buy a new car, then the ad must

   convince you that the car is really necessary.                        *want*

5. A tool for persuading readers (is, ~~are~~) the testimonial of

   a satisfied customer.                                                  *is*

6. Popular advertisements for health and diet products

   demonstrate another strategy: showing (~~it~~, them) in use.           *them*

7. Many an out-of-shape person buys an exercise bike

   hoping to see (~~himself, herself~~, himself or herself,

   ~~themselves~~) transformed into a slender, fit person like

   the one pictured.                                                      *himself or herself*

Copyright © 1995 by Harcourt Brace & Company. All rights reserved.

8. The facts the advertisement lists (~~offers~~, offer) the reader proof that the product is "the one."

          *offer*

9. Still other effective kinds of information (~~includes~~, include) physical features of the products, the reputation of the company, and the performance data.

          *include*

10. Of course, the claims that a writer makes must be (~~one~~, ones) the reader will believe to be true.

          *ones*

11. If a writer knows the facts, the legitimate promises that can be made about a product or service (~~is~~, are) usually many.

          *are*

12. A persuasive writer must emphasize the facts about (~~his/her, his~~, his or her) product that give it an edge over the competitor's.

          *his or her*

13. Successful persuasive letters usually (~~asks~~, ask) the reader to do something.

          *ask*

14. The closing of the letter (encourages, ~~encourage~~) the reader to send for more information or fill out a questionnaire or an application form.

          *encourages*

15. The writer of a persuasive letter must clearly state what action (~~he expects~~, he or she expects, ~~they expect~~) the reader to take.

          *he or she expects*

Copyright © 1995 by Harcourt Brace & Company. All rights reserved.

16. A persuasive letter usually (adheres, ~~adhere~~) to a set
    pattern: it captures a reader's attention, interests the
    reader in the product, and asks for some response.　　　adheres

17. Sentences and paragraphs in an effective persuasive
    letter are relatively short; (~~its,~~ their) vocabulary is
    simple but mature.　　　their

18. The company the writer represents must also never
    seem to be talking down to (its, ~~their~~) potential clients.　　　its

19. Both consideration and a courteous tone (~~wins,~~ win)
    customers.　　　win

20. As in any other kind of business letter, one of the main
    purposes of a persuasive one (is, ~~are~~) to build goodwill
    for the company.　　　is

Copyright © 1995 by Harcourt Brace & Company. All rights reserved.

## 7

**Use the appropriate forms of the verb and use them correctly and logically.**

**Regular Verbs**   Most verbs are called *regular verbs;* that is, the changes they under-go to show tense (or time) are predictable; *d* or *ed* is usually added to the end of the present tense to form the past tense and the past participle. All the tenses of verbs are formed from the three principal parts of the verb—present, past, and past participle—together with auxiliary (helping) verbs, such as *will* and *have.* Thus, a verb's ending (called its *inflection*) and/or the helping verb will allow you to determine that verb's tense. Although different systems are sometimes used to classify the number of verb tenses in English, the usual practice is to distinguish six tenses: present, past, future, present perfect, past perfect, and future perfect. In addition, these six tenses each has its progressive form.

| | |
|---|---|
| PRESENT | I prepare the report.   [denotes action (or occurrence) at the present time] |
| PROGRESSIVE | I am preparing…   [denotes action in progress at the present time] |
| PAST | I prepared the report yesterday.   [denotes action in the past] |
| PROGRESSIVE | I was preparing…   [denotes action in progress at a past time] |
| FUTURE | I will prepare the report tomorrow.   [denotes action in the future] |
| PROGRESSIVE | I will be preparing…   [denotes action in progress at a future time] |
| PRESENT PERFECT | I have prepared the report many times.   [emphasizes completion in the present of action previously begun] |
| PROGRESSIVE | I have been preparing…   [emphasizes progress to the present of action previously begun] |
| PAST PERFECT | I had prepared the report before the manager requested it. [emphasizes completion at a past time of action previously begun] |

Copyright © 1995 by Harcourt Brace & Company. All rights reserved.

| PROGRESSIVE | I <u>had been preparing</u>… [emphasizes progress until some past time of action previously begun] |
|---|---|
| FUTURE PERFECT | I <u>will have prepared</u> the report before the manager requests it. [emphasizes completion of an action by some future time] |
| PROGRESSIVE | I <u>will have been preparing</u>… [emphasizes progress of an action continuing until some future time] |

**Note:** You may have noticed that other words besides the main verb and its auxiliaries can express time—for example, *yesterday, tomorrow,* and *before.* The future is frequently expressed by a form of the present tense plus a word like *tomorrow* and/or an infinitive.

I *am preparing* the report *tomorrow.*

I *am going* to *prepare* the report *tomorrow.*

**Irregular Verbs**    Irregular verbs do not form the past and past participle in the usual way; instead, they undergo various kinds of changes or, in a few cases, no change at all. (See the chart of frequently used irregular verbs in the Appendix.)

*run, ran, run, running*
*choose, chose, chosen, choosing*
*burst, burst, burst, bursting*

The dictionary lists all four parts of irregular verbs, usually at the beginning of the entry. The dictionary also lists all forms of regular verbs that undergo a change in spelling for the past, the past participle, or the present participle. This change in spelling is most frequently the substituting of *i* for *y*, doubling of the last letter, or changing *y* to *id*.

*try, tried, tried, trying*
*occur, occurred, occurred, occurring*
*pay, paid, paid, paying*

**Auxiliary Verbs**    Auxiliary verbs are combined with the basic verb forms to indicate tense or voice (active or passive), to add emphasis, to ask questions, and to express the negative. The following words are commonly used as auxiliaries:

| | | | |
|---|---|---|---|
| have | be | will | may |
| has | am | | might |
| had | are | can | must |
| | is | | ought to |
| do | was | would | has to |
| does | were | should | have to |
| did | been | could | used to |

    Copyright © 1995 by Harcourt Brace & Company. All rights reserved.

For the purpose of this discussion of auxiliaries, consider the auxiliary verb *do*. The present tense *do* (or *does*) is used with the present tense form of a verb for questions, for the negative, and for special emphasis.

*Does* she *prepare* reports well?   [a question]

She *does* not (OR *doesn't*) *prepare* reports well.   [a negative]

She *does prepare* reports well.   [special emphasis]

When *did*, the past-tense form of *do*, is used as an auxiliary with a main verb, the writer emphasizes past time even though the main verb remains in the present-tense form. This *did* form is used mainly for questions, for the negative, and for special emphasis.

*Did* she *prepare* the report yesterday?   [a question]

She *did* not (OR *didn't*) *prepare* the report yesterday.   [a negative]

She *did prepare* the report yesterday.   [special emphasis]

**Learn the Uses of the Passive Voice.**   Most sentences use verbs in the active voice; that is, the verb expresses an action carried out by the subject. Sometimes, however, a writer reverses the pattern, in which case the subject does not act but is acted upon; such a verb is in the passive voice.

To form the passive voice, place a form of the verb *be* in front of the past participle form of the verb (for example—*is prepared, was prepared, has been prepared, will be prepared*).

ACTIVE VOICE      The executives often prepare reports.

PASSIVE VOICE      Reports are often prepared by the executives.

As you probably noticed from the above examples, the object of a sentence with an active verb becomes the subject of a sentence with a passive verb. In a passive verb construction, the actual person or thing doing or responsible for the action is often identified by the use of a prepositional phrase beginning with *by* (as in the example of the passive voice above). Sometimes this "agent" is left unstated in the sentence.

Writers use the passive voice when they do not know the doer of the action ("Mr. McDowell's store *was robbed* last night") or when they want to emphasize the verb or the receiver of the action of the verb ("A report *is* sometimes *rewritten* three times before it *is submitted* to upper management"). Writers employ the passive voice sparingly because it sounds highly impersonal, leads to repetitive patterns, and sometimes deprives writing of emphasis (see also Chapter **29**).

Copyright © 1995 by Harcourt Brace & Company. All rights reserved.

**Note:** Business writers find the passive voice most useful when they do not want to hurt the reader's feelings ("The motor *was left on*" instead of "You left the motor on") or when they do not wish to use the first person pronoun in formal report writing ("The cost *was estimated* to be $10,000" rather than "I estimated the cost to be $10,000").

Copyright © 1995 by Harcourt Brace & Company. All rights reserved.

Deduct 2 for each error in verb choice.

**Regular and Irregular Verbs**                                    Exercise 7–1

NAME _____    SCORE _____

DIRECTIONS   Mastering verb forms, especially irregular verb forms, requires memorizing them (just as you would memorize multiplication tables or chemical formulas) and accustoming your ear to the correct forms. The best way to learn verb forms, then, is through written and oral drill of the five forms of those verbs that cause difficulty: present, past, present or past perfect (both formed from the past participle), progressive, and the form with a word such as *do, does,* or *did* as an auxiliary.

Using the models given as your example, create short sentences for the verbs and objects or modifiers listed. Use either *he* or *she* for your subject. (Consult your dictionary if you are unsure of the way to form any of the tenses.)

EXAMPLE

draw/illustration

PRESENT

She draws an illustration.

PAST

She drew an illustration.

PRESENT PERFECT

She has drawn an illustration.

PROGRESSIVE PRESENT

She is drawing an illustration.

*did* FORM OF PAST AS A QUESTION

Did she draw an illustration?

1.  speak/about the new product line
    PRESENT
    She speaks about the new product line.

    PAST
    She spoke about the new product line.

    PRESENT PERFECT
    She has spoken about the new product line.

    PROGRESSIVE PRESENT
    She is speaking about the new product line.

    *did* FORM OF PRESENT IN THE NEGATIVE
    She does not speak about the new product line.

Copyright © 1995 by Harcourt Brace & Company. All rights reserved.

2. go/to the product demonstration

   PRESENT

   He goes to the product demonstration.

   PAST

   He went to the product demonstration.

   PAST PERFECT

   He had gone to the product demonstration.

   PROGRESSIVE PAST

   He was going to the product demonstration.

   *did* FORM OF PAST FOR EMPHASIS

   He did go to the product demonstration.

3. run/the product demonstration

   PRESENT

   She runs the product demonstration.

   PAST

   She ran the product demonstration.

   PRESENT PERFECT

   She has run the product demonstration.

   PROGRESSIVE FUTURE

   She will be running the product demonstration.

   *did* FORM OF PRESENT AS A QUESTION

   Does she run the product demonstration?

4. choose/a new sales territory

   PRESENT

   He chooses a new sales territory.

   PAST

   He chose a new sales territory.

   PAST PERFECT

   He had chosen a new sales territory.

   PROGRESSIVE PRESENT

   He is choosing a new sales territory.

   *did* FORM OF PAST IN THE NEGATIVE

   He did not choose a new sales territory.

Copyright © 1995 by Harcourt Brace & Company. All rights reserved.

5. cash/the travel reimbursement

   PRESENT
   She cashes the travel reimbursement.

   PAST
   She cashed the travel reimbursement.

   PRESENT PERFECT
   She has cashed the travel reimbursement.

   PROGRESSIVE PRESENT
   She is cashing the travel reimbursement.

   *did* FORM OF PAST AS A QUESTION
   Did she cash the travel reimbursement?

6. write/follow-up reports

   PRESENT
   He writes follow-up reports.

   PAST
   He wrote follow-up reports.

   PAST PERFECT
   He had written follow-up reports.

   PROGRESSIVE FUTURE
   He will be writing follow-up reports.

   *did* FORM OF PRESENT FOR EMPHASIS
   He does write follow-up reports.

7. bring/the employee evaluations

   PRESENT
   She brings the employee evaluations.

   PAST
   She brought the employee evaluations.

   PRESENT PERFECT
   She has brought the employee evaluations.

   PROGRESSIVE PRESENT
   She is bringing the employee evaluations.

   *did* FORM OF PAST AS A QUESTION
   Did she bring the employee evaluations?

Copyright © 1995 by Harcourt Brace & Company. All rights reserved.

8. begin/to collect data for the report

   PRESENT

   He begins to collect data for the report.

   PAST

   He began to collect data for the report.

   PAST PERFECT

   He had begun to collect data for the report.

   PROGRESSIVE FUTURE

   He will be beginning to collect data for the report.

   *did* FORM OF PRESENT IN THE NEGATIVE

   He does not begin to collect data for the report.

9. sit/on the interview committee

   PRESENT

   She sits on the interview committee.

   PAST

   She sat on the interview committee.

   PRESENT PERFECT

   She has sat on the interview committee.

   PROGRESSIVE PAST

   She was sitting on the interview committee.

   *did* FORM OF PRESENT AS A QUESTION

   Does she sit on the interview committee?

10. take/advice from the attorney

    PRESENT

    He takes advice from the attorney.

    PAST

    He took advice from the attorney.

    PAST PERFECT

    He had taken advice from the attorney.

    PROGRESSIVE PAST

    He was taking advice from the attorney.

    *did* FORM OF PAST IN THE NEGATIVE

    He did not take advice from the attorney.

Copyright © 1995 by Harcourt Brace & Company. All rights reserved.

Deduct 10 for each error in verb choice.

**Using Irregular Verbs**                                    Exercise 7–2

NAME _____ SCORE _____

DIRECTIONS    The questions below use either *past tense* or *future tense* verbs with the auxiliaries *did* and *will* (the verbs are underlined twice). Answer those questions having past tense verbs with statements that use the present perfect form of the verb with *already*. Answer those questions that have future tense verbs with statements that use the past tense. Consult your dictionary for the various forms of all verbs of which you are unsure.

> EXAMPLES
> Will the lack of a day care facility grow into a problem?
>
> Yes, the lack of a day care facility grew into a problem.
> Did the ice burst the waste water valve?
>
> Yes. the ice has already burst the waste water valve.

1. Will the account executive know of the client's change in plans?

   Yes, the account executive knew of the client's change in plans.

2. Did the marketing manager begin the meeting on time?

   Yes, the marketing manager has already begun the meeting on time.

3. Will the low profits last quarter shake our investors' confidence?

   Yes, the low profits last quarter shook our investors' confidence.

4. Did the company decide to pay the damages?

   Yes, the company has already decided to pay the damages.

5. Will the employees take the new stock purchase option?

   Yes, the employees took the new stock purchase option.

6. Did she speak with the negotiator?

   Yes, she has already spoken with the negotiator.

Copyright © 1995 by Harcourt Brace & Company. All rights reserved.

7.  Will prices fall because of the merger?

    Yes, the prices <u>fell</u> because of the merger.

8.  Did the lawyer give us a reason for the suit?

    Yes, the lawyer <u>has</u> already <u>given</u> us a reason for the suit.

9.  Will the new supervisor bring the contracts?

    Yes, the new supervisor <u>brought</u> the contracts.

10. Did the stock's value fall?

    Yes, the stock's value <u>has</u> already <u>fallen</u>.

Copyright © 1995 by Harcourt Brace & Company. All rights reserved.

There are four main points to be aware of when you write the tense of a verb.

**(1) Be sure to put *ed* on the end of all past tense regular verbs (unless they end in *e*—in which case simply add *d*).**

When the company developed problems, a troubleshooter was requested.

**Caution:** Do not omit a needed *d* or *ed* because of pronunciation.

NOT His presentation prejudice them against him.

BUT His presentation prejudiced them against him.

NOT She talk with her supervisor.

BUT She talked with her supervisor.

**(2) Be sure not to confuse the past tense with the past participle form.**

The troubleshooter was carefully chosen [NOT *chose*].

The troubleshooter began [NOT *begun*] his investigation.

**(3) Be sure not to give an irregular verb the *ed* ending.**

The whistle blew [NOT *blowed*] loudly at noon.

The employees knew [NOT *knowed*] what the whistle meant.

**(4) Be especially careful with troublesome verbs like *lie* and *lay*, *sit* and *set* and *rise* and *raise*.**

Notice that *lie* and *sit* are alike: they signify a *state* of resting and do not take objects. Notice also that *lay* and *set* are alike: they signify the *action* of placing, and they do take objects.

He lay [NOT *laid*] down on a couch in his office.

He had sat [NOT *had set*] too long on a hard chair.

Finally, notice that while *rise* does not take an object, *raise*, on the other hand, does.

Stock prices rose [NOT *raised*] during the last month.

The broker raised the clients' surcharge.

Copyright © 1995 by Harcourt Brace & Company. All rights reserved.

In numbers 1–10, deduct 6 2/3 for each incorrectly filled right-hand blank. In numbers 11–15, deduct 6 2/3 for each incorrect sentence.

## Verbs That Cause Difficulties

Exercise 7–3

NAME _____ SCORE _____

DIRECTIONS    After each of the following sentences the present form of a verb is given. In the blank within the sentence and also in the blank at the right, write the tense called for by the meaning of the sentence. Consult your dictionary if you are uncertain about the other forms of a verb.

EXAMPLE
Managers are frequently ___*required*___ to evaluate

written reports.   (require)                          ___*required*___

1. Once a report is ____*begun*____, careful writers

   consider their audience.   (begin)                ___*begun*___

2. The words the writer has ____*used*____ should be

   a part of the reader's familiar vocabulary.   (use)   ___*used*___

3. Successful word choice in technical writing does not

   ____*lie*____ in using technical jargon.   (lie)    ___*lie*___

4. Once you have ____*sat*____ down to write a

   report, select words that the reader is likely to

   understand.   (sit)                              ___*sat*___

5. A report that is ____*written*____ without much plan-

   ning will usually make a poor impression.   (write)   ___*written*___

6. A great deal of research has been ____*done*____ to

   determine what makes writing clear.   (do)       ___*done*___

7. Recommendations ____*given*____ in clear, precise

   sentences are easier to understand.   (give)     ___*given*___

Copyright © 1995 by Harcourt Brace & Company. All rights reserved.

8. The writer reports whatever has <u>happened</u> simply and concisely. (happen)

<u>happened</u>

9. No writer should use fifteen words to communicate an idea when only ten are <u>required</u>. (require)

<u>required</u>

10. A successful report has <u>brought</u> information to the reader's attention quickly. (bring)

<u>brought</u>

DIRECTIONS   In the following section, write sentences using the correct form of the verb.

EXAMPLE
past tense of *choose*

The writer chose her words with care.*

11. past perfect of *draw*

12. third person singular of *go*

13. past perfect of *fall*

14. past tense of *ask*

15. past tense of *break*

*Answers will vary.

Copyright © 1995 by Harcourt Brace & Company. All rights reserved.

Deduct 10 for each incorrectly filled blank.

**Special Problems with Verbs**                                    Exercise 7–4

NAME _____ SCORE _____

Make the tense of a verb in a subordinate clause or of a verbal relate logically to the tense of the verb in the main clause.

She rested for a few minutes after she *had finished* the year-end report.  [The action of

the subordinate verb, *had finished*, occurred before the action of the main verb, *rested*.]

*Having finished* the year-end report, she was able to begin other projects.  [The perfect

form of the verbal, *having finished*, shows action completed before the action of the

main verb, *was*.]

He would have wanted *to complete* the project.  [Use the present infinitive after a verb in

the perfect tense.]

He would want *to complete* the project.  [The present infinitive may be used after a verb

that is not in the present tense.]

**Caution:**  Avoid switching tenses needlessly in a sentence. (See also **27a**.)

Use the subjunctive mood to express a condition contrary to fact (often introduced by *if* ); to state a wish; and to express a demand, a recommendation, or a request in a *that* clause.

If we were given an extra week, we *might finish* this report on time.

They wished they *were* better report writers.

Your supervisor insisted that you *be given* this assignment.

Use the present tense to state facts or ideas that are generally regarded as being true.

A clearly presented report *shows* the reader the answers.

Haste *makes* waste.

Copyright © 1995 by Harcourt Brace & Company. All rights reserved.

DIRECTIONS   In the following sentences cross out the incorrect form of the subordinate verb or verbal in parentheses and write the correct form in the blank.

EXAMPLE
John Chee wanted (to communicate, ~~to have communicated~~)

his ideas clearly and concisely.                          *to communicate*

1. After John (~~studied,~~ had studied) his first draft, he found many words that he could omit.

    *had studied*

2. When he reread his draft, he saw that he (~~used,~~ had used) many unnecessary words.

    *had used*

3. "If I (were, ~~was~~) the reader of this report," John thought, "I wouldn't want to wade through these wordy paragraphs."

    *were*

4. After he (~~evaluates,~~ had evaluated) the report even more closely, John discovered many weak "there is" and "there are" sentences.

    *had evaluated*

5. Rereading to identify other useless words, Mr. Chee (crossed, ~~crosses~~) out "in regard to" and wrote "regarding."

    *crossed*

6. He also ought to (~~say,~~ have said), "since" instead of "in view of the fact that."

    *have said*

7. In one paragraph, John (~~wrote,~~ had written), "There is a product available," when he could have saved words by saying, "A product is available."

    *had written*

8. "My reader expects that my words (be, ~~are~~) carefully selected," John reminded himself.

    *be*

9. He realized that it is generally wise (to choose, ~~to have chosen~~) the shortest, most effective wording possible.

    *to choose*

10. (~~Concentrating,~~ Having concentrated) on eliminating wordiness, Mr. Chee was pleased when his boss complimented him on his report's clarity.

    *Having concentrated*

Copyright © 1995 by Harcourt Brace & Company. All rights reserved.

Deduct 5 for each incorrectly filled blank.

**Mastering Verbs: A Review**                    Exercise 7–5

NAME _____    SCORE _____

DIRECTIONS    In the following sentences cross out the incorrect form or forms of the verb in parentheses and write the correct form in the blank.

EXAMPLE
When I began writing business reports, I (use, used) to like

long sentences.                                   _____used_____

1. I was (advise, advised) to be concise, even with verbs.    _____advised_____

2. Many reports have been (written, wrote) that could
   have communicated the same point with fewer words.    _____written_____

3. I had (suppose, supposed) they made me sound intelli-
   gent, but they only made my writing wordy.    _____supposed_____

4. One place I (have got, get) into trouble is with word
   choice, especially verbs.    _____get_____

5. Like spelling errors, verb errors (will rise, will raise)
   doubts about a writer's accuracy.    _____will raise_____

6. When you have the choice, the simpler, clearer verbs
   should be (used, use).    _____used_____

7. One type of wordiness is (caused, cause) by the use of
   long verbal phrases.    _____caused_____

8. Some writers are (tempt, tempted) to use wordy verbal
   phrases such as *be in receipt of* instead of the less-stuffy
   *received*.    _____tempted_____

9. Using long verbal phrases has often (led, lead) to a
   reader misunderstanding the writer's message.    _____led_____

10. Writers who have (chose, choose, chosen) their words
    with care make their points clearly and effectively.    _____chosen_____

11. A passive verb is "slow" because it always (require,
    requires, required) an additional verb, a form of *be*, and
    often a *by* phrase.    _____requires_____

Copyright © 1995 by Harcourt Brace & Company. All rights reserved.    *169*

12. Because active verbs result in more concise, informative sentences, report writers generally (~~chosen~~, choose) them over passive verbs.

      *choose*

13. However, if the doer of the action is not (seen, ~~saw~~) as more important than the receiver of the action, then a passive verb is appropriate.

      *seen*

14. *The store gave each customer a ten-percent discount* emphasizes the store's action, whereas *Each customer was (~~gave~~, given) a ten-percent discount* emphasizes the customer.

      *given*

15. No definite rule can be (~~sit~~, set) for when it is appropriate to use the passive voice.

      *set*

16. However, a formula can be (~~lay~~, laid, ~~lain~~) out: passive verbs can be used when the doer of the action is not known.

      *laid*

17. Verbs such as *get* and *make* are also (used, ~~use~~) too frequently by poor writers.

      *used*

18. Many managers have (~~shook~~, shaken, ~~shaked~~) their heads at the number of *gets* they find in reports.

      *shaken*

19. One such report (~~begin, begun~~, began): "After we get our materials ordered, we will get the team together to build the prototype."

      *began*

20. One thing that a successful writer (~~say~~, said, ~~says~~) was important was to check all verb tenses carefully.

      *said*

Copyright © 1995 by Harcourt Brace & Company. All rights reserved.

# MANUSCRIPT FORM ms 8

## 8

**Prepare and proofread a neat, well-formatted manuscript.** (See also Chapters **33** and **35**).

Business letters, memorandums, and reports have definite formats, which are illustrated in Chapter **35**. The format for an essay written in college varies according to the length of the paper. The average college writing assignment usually requires no more than the essay itself and sometimes an outline and a title page. A research paper, on the other hand, may include a title page, an outline, the text, an endnote page or pages, and a bibliography.

Whether you are writing for college or a career, the most important advice to remember about format is to follow the directions given by your instructor or your supervisor. Many instructors and supervisors refuse to read papers that do not follow the format guidelines that they have specified.

Usually a college instructor's guidelines for manuscript preparation cover the points discussed in this section.

### 8a Use proper materials.

If you handwrite your papers, use wide-lined, $8\frac{1}{2}$ x 11-inch theme paper (not torn from a spiral notebook). Write in blue or black ink on one side of the paper only.

If you type your papers, use regular white $8\frac{1}{2}$ x 11-inch typing paper (neither erasable bond nor onion skin). Use a fresh black ribbon, double-space between lines, and type on one side of the paper only. Avoid fancy typefaces such as a script or all-capitals. Be sure that the keys are clean. If you make errors, correct them neatly with correction fluid, but avoid "painting out" entire lines since that gives the impression that your text and your reasoning are sloppy.

If you use a word processor to prepare your papers, select good quality, letter-size cut-sheet or pin-fed paper. Before handing in a finished text, be sure to separate the pages of continuous-feed paper and to remove any perforated edging. The printer's ribbon should be fresh enough to produce clear, dark characters. Ink-jet and laser print is always acceptable; if you are using a dot matrix printer, however, be sure to select the near-letter-quality option in your word processing program (or on the printer) since draft-mode print is fainter and difficult to read. In all cases, even if your printer or word processor allows you to select a variety of type sizes and styles (fonts), choose one that looks like a typewriter type (for example, Courier or Times Roman).

You can, however, make use of your word processing software's italics, underlining, and boldfacing options. If you are in doubt as to what a particular instructor finds acceptable, ask before completing your assignment.

**Note:** In business writing, handwritten documents are generally not acceptable.

Copyright © 1995 by Harcourt Brace & Company. All rights reserved.

## 8b Arrange your writing in a clear and orderly fashion on the page.

**(1) Legibility** Whether you handwrite, type, or word process your text, the final product should be easy on your reader's eye. For this reason, you will want to avoid flourishes, fancy letters, hard-to-read script, strikeovers, and tiny print. If your handwriting is particularly large, consider skipping every other line; if it is not easily legible, print.

**(2) Layout** Follow your instructor's guidelines about margins and other formatting concerns. In general, allow one-inch margins on all sides to give your instructor room to comment and to prevent your text from looking crowded on the page; margins wider than this make your work look insubstantial. Follow the ruled lines on notebook paper or set the margins on your typewriter or in the word processing program to conform to these guidelines.

Be certain to number your pages and divide words according to normal syllabication; most word processors will take care of these concerns for you if you set them to do so.

Double space all academic papers, except those you handwrite.

**(3) Indention** Indent the first lines of paragraphs uniformly: about an inch in handwritten copy and five spaces in typewritten or word-processed copy. Indent block quotations ten spaces.

**(4) Paging** Use Arabic numerals (1, 2, and so on)—without parentheses or periods—at the right margin, one-half inch from the top of each page. Put your last name immediately before the page number or, if your instructor prefers, give a short running title.

**(5) Title and heading** Instructors vary in what information they require and where they want this information placed. Usually papers carry the name of the student, the course title and number, the instructor's name, and the date. Often the number of the assignment is also included. This information should be placed one inch from the top and one inch from the left edge of the page, double-spacing after each line.

Center the title and double-space between the lines of a long title. Use neither quotation marks nor underlining with your title. Capitalize the first word of the title and all other words except articles, coordinating conjunctions, prepositions, and the *to* in infinitives. Leave one blank line between the title and the first paragraph. (Your instructor may ask you to make a title page. If so, you need not rewrite the title on the first page of the paper unless your instructor asks you to do so.)

**(6) Quoted lines** When you quote over four lines (or over forty words) of another's writing to explain or support your ideas, set off the entire quotation by indenting it ten spaces. Acknowledge the source of all quotations.

**(7) Punctuation** Never begin a line of your paper with a comma, a colon, a semicolon, a dash, or an end mark of punctuation; never end a line with the first of a pair of brackets, parentheses, or quotation marks.

Most word processing software automatically prevents these mistakes, but check to be sure you have set your program to print out correctly.

Copyright © 1995 by Harcourt Brace & Company. All rights reserved.

Leave one space after a comma, a semicolon, or a colon; leave two spaces after a period, a question mark, or an exclamation point. To indicate a dash, use two hyphens without spacing before, between or after. Use a pen to insert marks that are not on your machine or in your word processing program (such as accent marks or mathematical symbols).

**(8) Justification**  If you print your paper with word-processing software, do not justify (make straight vertically) the right-hand margin. Unless a printer has proportional spacing, justification inserts spacing between words so that every line is the same length; the irregular spacing within a line can be very distracting and sometimes will cause a reader to misunderstand you. For information about breaking a word at the end of a line, see **18f**.

**(9) Binding**  Unless directed to do otherwise, secure the pages of your paper with a paper clip; do not use staples, pins, or plastic folders.

**Note:**  Business reports are often punched and secured in a folder with prongs. Avoid plastic report covers having slide-on spines since pages easily pop out of this type of holder.

### 8c  Proofread your manuscript carefully before submitting it to readers.

Proofreading is different from revising or editing (see Chapter **33**). **Revising** requires you to consider and possibly to reorganize your ideas. **Editing** makes sure your prose is as clear, accurate, and stylistically consistent as possible. At this stage you should also pay close attention to the conventions of grammar, mechanics, punctuation, and spelling. **Proofreading** is the time to check for and correct typographical errors of layout, spelling, punctuation, and mechanics.

For papers written out of class, be sure to go over your rough draft and revise it carefully. It is helpful to set the paper aside for several hours or even a day before you begin reworking it. Doing so will give you greater objectivity and make it easier for you to spot places in need of extra work.

Few people create good papers without revising their first draft. A carefully revised piece of writing takes work and concentration, but the time you spend on this part of the writing process will pay off in a more clearly expressed, well organized final draft. When you need to make a change, draw a straight horizontal line through the part to be deleted and insert a caret (**∧**) at the point where the addition that is written above the line is to be made.

Proofread your text *after* you have revised and edited it. Make use of the Proofreading Checklist below whether you proofread manually or by means of a word processor. First, check the format of the paper as specified in the layout section. Next, check the items listed in each of the other three sections by reading your text one sentence at a time, starting with the *last* sentence and moving up the page. Read the words slowly, looking at and pronouncing each syllable carefully. If you find it difficult to look for each of the items simultaneously, repeat the process several times, looking for only one or two items each time. Keep a good dictionary handy...and use it. Refer also to the chapters and sections cross-referenced in this workbook.

Copyright © 1995 by Harcourt Brace & Company. All rights reserved.

**Proofreading Checklist**

**Layout**

1. Are all margins one inch wide or according to your instructor's specifications?
2. Is each page numbered?
3. Does the first page have the appropriate title and heading?
4. Is the first line of each paragraph indented five spaces (or one inch if handwritten)?
5. Is the type (or handwriting) dark, clean, clear, and legible?
6. Are the lines of typing or word processing double-spaced?
7. Are all listed items numbered sequentially?

**Spelling (18)**

1. Are all words spelled correctly?
2. Have you double-checked the words you frequently misspell?
3. Are any letters transposed (*form/from*)?
4. Are you consistent in spelling words that have more than one acceptable spelling (*theater/theatre*)?
5. Are all foreign words spelled correctly?

**Punctuation**

1. Do all sentences have appropriate closing punctuation (**17a–c**)?
2. Is all punctuation within sentences appropriately used and correctly placed (comma, **12–13**; semicolon, **14**; apostrophe, **15**; other internal marks of punctuation, **17d–i**; hyphen, **18f**)?
3. Are quotations carefully and correctly punctuated (**16**)?

**Capitalization and Italics**

1. Does each sentence begin with a capital letter (**9e**)?
2. Are all proper names, people's titles, and titles of published works correctly capitalized (**9a–d**)?
3. Are quotations properly capitalized (**16a**)?
4. Are italics used properly (**10**)?

**8d  Keep a record of your revisions to help you improve your writing.**

So that you can keep track of your progress and so that you will gain an understanding of what types of errors you routinely make and the problems that you frequently have, keep a list of the comments your instructor makes on your papers for future reference. Be sure to update your list frequently.

Copyright © 1995 by Harcourt Brace & Company. All rights reserved.

## 8e Use a word processor effectively.

A word processor can do much more for a writer than simply produce neatly formatted, typo-free printed pages—which is not such a small benefit in and of itself! But for a writer wanting to get the most out of drafting and revision work, the word processor is a real breakthrough since such machines enable you to insert and delete even large blocks of material with ease. Thus, a writer who works with a word processor can tinker with a text until it is clear and effective without having to recopy or retype passages in order to do so.

Furthermore, your word processor's search feature will allow you to check a draft for such things as a repetition, weak use of the passive voice, and inconsistencies in terminology. A style-check program can evaluate your paper for many kinds of grammatical problems and other mannerisms that may cause readers difficulties, including wordiness and the use of sexist language. A spelling checker can scan your text for typographical errors, but be aware that no program can identify *misused* words—*it's* for *its*, or *there* for *their* or *they're*, for instance. If you are a poor speller, however, over time such a program can actually help you to improve your spelling.

Word processors also allow their users to create sophisticated-looking texts. These programs will number pages automatically, space lines as you wish them to appear, alter the number of lines per page, produce a variety of different type styles (italic, boldface, to name two), underline words and phrases, and number notes. *Unless* your printer can produce proportional spacing, do not have your word processor justify (make even) the right margin, for the resulting lines contain added spaces between words that make reading difficult.

A word processor is a genuine writing tool, but one that you must learn to use to its best advantage. These computer programs will not do your thinking for you, and they will not catch oversights that result from making a series of rapid deletions and insertions that leaves parts of the old version in odd places on the page. Used as a means to manipulate the text you have written, the word processor will help you to develop and improve as a writer. But because computers *are* only machines, be sure to proofread all final drafts very carefully for inadvertent errors.

Copyright © 1995 by Harcourt Brace & Company. All rights reserved.

# CAPITALS

## 9

**Capitalize words according to standard conventions. Avoid unnecessary capitals.**

In general, capital letters are used for first words (the first word of a sentence, including a quoted sentence, a line of poetry, the salutation and complimentary close of a letter, and an item in an outline), and for names of specific persons, places, and things (in other words, proper nouns). A recently published dictionary is your best guide to current standards for capitalization and for the use of italics, abbreviations, and numbers.

The most important rules for capitalization are listed below, but you may find the style sheet on the next page as helpful as the rules.

**9a Capitalize words referring to persons, places, things, times, organizations, races (option: Blacks or blacks), and religions, but not words that refer to classes of persons, places, or things. Capitalize geographic locations only when they refer to specific areas of the country (*the West Coast*) or the world (*the Near East*).**

> Most of the **d**octors in the **E**ast attended the medical convention held in **A**tlanta, **G**eorgia, last **A**ugust.
> We are taking **B**usiness **E**nglish 201 and also a course in **r**eport **w**riting at the **U**niversity of **N**orth **C**arolina.

**9b Capitalize titles of persons that precede the name but not those that follow it.**

> My mother and her sister, my **A**unt **M**adge, met **P**rofessor **M**aya **A**ngelou, a member of the **E**nglish **D**epartment, as well as the heads of several **d**epartments at **W**ake **F**orest University.

**Note:** Usage varies with regard to capitalization of titles of high rank and titles of family members.

> **J**im **H**unt is governor (OR **G**overnor) of North Carolina.

**9c In titles and subtitles of books, plays, students' papers, and so on, capitalize the first word, the last word, and all other words except articles (*a, an,* and *the*), coordinating conjunctions, prepositions, or the *to* in infinitives.**

> I think that *How to Write for the World of Work* is an excellent reference book for all occupational writers.

**Exception:** Titles in an APA-style reference list.

**9d Capitalize the pronoun *I* and the interjection *O* but not *oh*, except when it begins a sentence.**

Copyright © 1995 by Harcourt Brace & Company. All rights reserved.

**9e  Capitalize the first word of every sentence (including a quoted sentence).**

**I** told my boss, "**T**he report will be in the mail tomorrow."

**Note:**  When only a part of a sentence is quoted, the first word is not capitalized.

Most experts agree that workers in the twenty-first century will demand "**a** bigger voice in decisions that affect their job performance."

---

*Style sheet for capitalization*

SPECIFIC PERSONS   Shakespeare, Buddha, Mr. Keogh, Mayor Koenig

SPECIFIC PLACES   Puerto Rico; Atlanta, Georgia; Western Avenue; the West (BUT "he lives west of here"); Broughton High School

SPECIFIC THINGS   the Statue of Liberty, the Bible, History 304 (BUT history class), the First World War, Parkinson's disease, Sanka coffee

SPECIFIC TIMES AND EVENTS   Wednesday, July (BUT winter, spring, summer, fall, autumn), Thanksgiving, the Age of Enlightenment, the Great Depression (BUT the twentieth century)

SPECIFIC ORGANIZATIONS   the Peace Corps, the Rotary Club, Phi Kappa Phi

SPECIFIC POLITICAL AND MILITARY BODIES   State Department, the United States Senate, Republican Party, United States Army (BUT the army)

RELIGIONS AND BELIEFS   Judaism, Methodists, Marxism (BUT capitalism, communism)

WORDS DERIVED FROM PROPER NAMES   Swedish, New Yorker, Oriental rugs, Labrador retriever

ESSENTIAL PARTS OF PROPER NAMES   the Bill of Rights, the Battle of the Bulge, the New Deal

PARTS OF A LETTER   Dear Mr. Jacobs, Very truly yours

ITEMS IN AN OUTLINE   I. Parts of a letter
        A. Date
        B. Inside address

---

   Copyright © 1995 by Harcourt Brace & Company. All rights reserved.

Deduct 5 3/4 for each incorrectly capitalized word or word group.

## Capitalization

Exercise 9–1

NAME _____ SCORE _____

DIRECTIONS   A word or words in one of each of the following pairs should be capitalized. Identify the group that needs capitalization by writing either *a* or *b* in the blank. Then revise the appropriate group of words.

EXAMPLE

(a)  a class in ecology at our college

(b)  ecology 1101 at washington state university         *b*

        E       W     S   U

1.  (a)  an army during the war

     (b)  the german army during world war II         *b*

       G     A        W    W

2.  (a)  reading an interesting industrial management case study

     (b)  reading the one minute manager         *b*

         T O M    M

3.  (a)  the mountains of our northwestern countries

     (b)  the blue ridge mountains         *b*

        B    R    M

4.  (a)  the age of reason

     (b)  the twentieth century         *a*

        A    R

5.  (a)  the gods of the ancient maya

     (b)  the goddess of the moon         *a*

             M

6.  (a)  president Lee Iacocca of chrysler corporation

     (b)  the president of the company         *a*

       P            C     C

7.  (a)  their branch campus in the south

     (b)  moving south to study business administration         *a*

                   S

8.  (a)  drove west for my vacation

     (b)  flew to north carolina during easter         *b*

            N    C          E

Copyright © 1995 by Harcourt Brace & Company. All rights reserved.

9. (a) a course in medical ethics

   (b) a course in ~~g~~german     *G*        _____b_____

10. (a) chickenpox

    (b) ~~h~~hodgkin's disease    *H*        _____b_____

11. (a) ~~r~~representative ~~c~~cowles speaking during assembly   *R*   *C*

    (b) the representative from our district        _____a_____

12. (a) bought a laptop computer for travelling

    (b) bought an ~~a~~apple computer    *A*        _____b_____

13. (a) told me that that is a great idea

    (b) said, "~~t~~that is a great idea!"    *T*        _____b_____

14. (a) spring flowers

    (b) the ~~s~~sunday paper    *S*        _____b_____

15. (a) an article in a popular magazine about business

    (b) "~~w~~what ~~y~~you ~~r~~really ~~w~~want from ~~y~~your ~~j~~job," in *~~b~~business ~~w~~week*     *W Y R W Y J B W*    _____b_____

Copyright © 1995 by Harcourt Brace & Company. All rights reserved.

Deduct 2 for each incorrectly capitalized word or word group.

**Capitalization—Continued** Exercise 9–2

NAME _____ SCORE _____

DIRECTIONS Each of the following sentences contains words and word groups that require capitalization. First, cross through the letters that should be capitalized and write the correct capital letters above them; then rewrite the sentences with the appropriate words or word groups capitalized.

EXAMPLE

N     A    P U

next summer we will travel to asia with faculty from purdue university and representatives

  I C

from intel corporation.

Next summer we will travel to Asia with faculty from Purdue
  University and representatives from Intel Corporation.

T    B  E     I

1. the professor in business economics 203 said, "i hope you finish your term project

during spring break."

The professor in Business Economics 203 said, "I hope you
  finish your term project during spring break."

T       S A     H  B

2. this fall we hope to visit the shedd aquarium and the hancock building while we

       M

are vacationing in the midwest.

This fall we hope to visit the Shedd Aquarium and the
  Hancock Building while we are vacationing in the Midwest.

T       P  K F    D  S

3. the president of our college and professor kathy fitzpatrick of the decision sciences

D        A  C  A

department spoke at a meeting of the academic computing association.

The president of our college and Professor Kathy Fitzpatrick
  of the Decision Sciences Department spoke at a meeting
  of the Academic Computing Association.

Copyright © 1995 by Harcourt Brace & Company. All rights reserved.

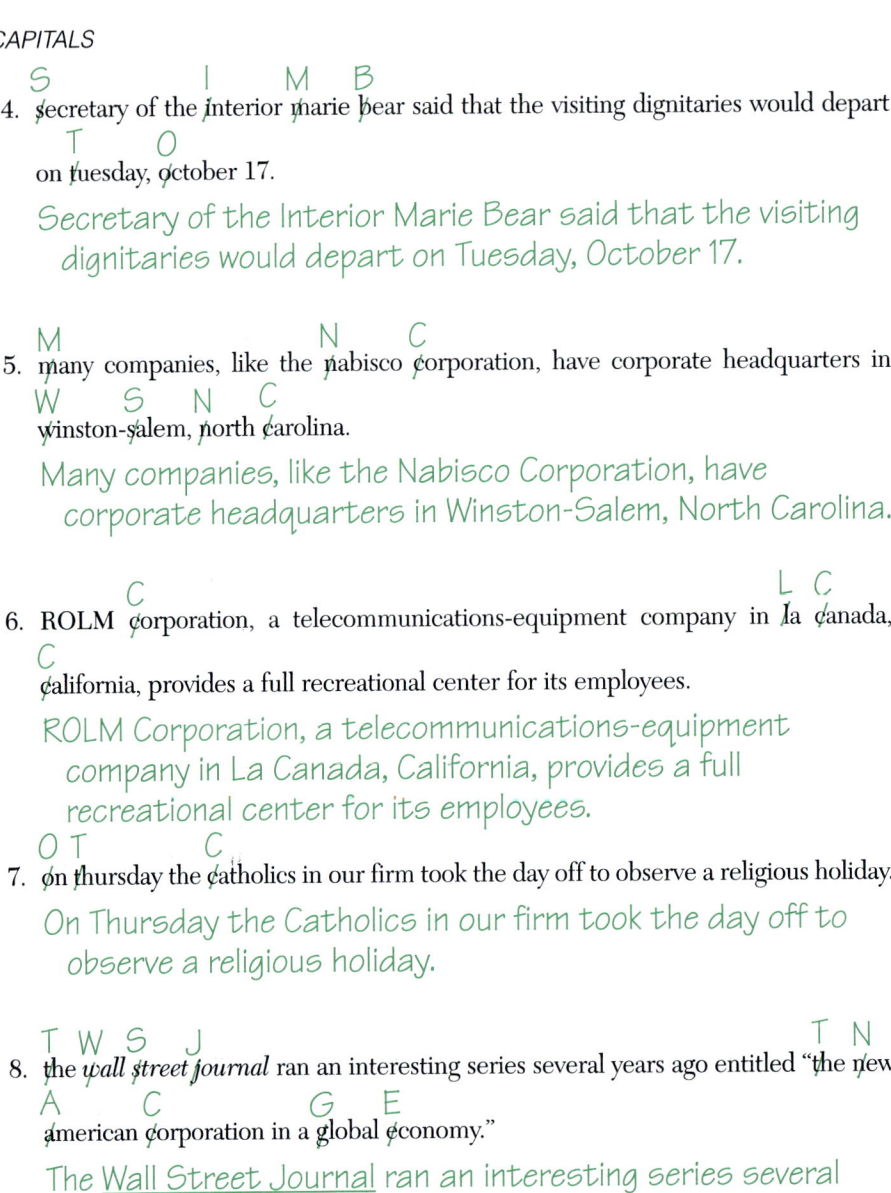

4. secretary of the interior marie bear said that the visiting dignitaries would depart
   <sup>S</sup>      <sup>I</sup>   <sup>M</sup> <sup>B</sup>

   on tuesday, october 17.
   <sup>T</sup>   <sup>O</sup>

   Secretary of the Interior Marie Bear said that the visiting
       dignitaries would depart on Tuesday, October 17.

5. many companies, like the nabisco corporation, have corporate headquarters in
   <sup>M</sup>            <sup>N</sup>    <sup>C</sup>

   winston-salem, north carolina.
   <sup>W</sup>    <sup>S</sup>   <sup>N</sup>   <sup>C</sup>

   Many companies, like the Nabisco Corporation, have
       corporate headquarters in Winston-Salem, North Carolina.

6. ROLM corporation, a telecommunications-equipment company in la canada,
         <sup>C</sup>                               <sup>L</sup> <sup>C</sup>

   california, provides a full recreational center for its employees.
   <sup>C</sup>

   ROLM Corporation, a telecommunications-equipment
       company in La Canada, California, provides a full
       recreational center for its employees.

7. on thursday the catholics in our firm took the day off to observe a religious holiday.
   <sup>O</sup> <sup>T</sup>      <sup>C</sup>

   On Thursday the Catholics in our firm took the day off to
       observe a religious holiday.

8. the wall street journal ran an interesting series several years ago entitled "the new
   <sup>T</sup> <sup>W</sup> <sup>S</sup> <sup>J</sup>                                      <sup>T</sup> <sup>N</sup>

   american corporation in a global economy."
   <sup>A</sup>     <sup>C</sup>       <sup>G</sup>   <sup>E</sup>

   The <u>Wall Street Journal</u> ran an interesting series several
       years ago entitled "The New American Corporation in a
       Global Economy."

Copyright © 1995 by Harcourt Brace & Company. All rights reserved.

# 10

**Use italics (underlining) according to conventional practices. Use italics (underlining) sparingly for emphasis.**

To show which words should be printed in italics, use underlining. If your composition were to be set in type by a printer, the words that you have underlined would then appear in italic type.

Since some of the rules for the use of quotations and italics overlap, you may want to study Chapter **16** together with this chapter. In general, italics are used for works that are contained under one cover, while quotation marks are used for works that are parts of a longer work.

> The article "Importing a Recession" appeared in a recent issue of *Newsweek*.
> Flannery O'Connor's short story "The Life You Save May Be Your Own" is part of the collection *A Good Man Is Hard to Find*.
> "The Imperial March" is from *The Empire Strikes Back*.

**10a Italicize (underline) the titles of separate publications (books, magazines, newspapers, pamphlets), and titles of plays, films, television and radio programs, entire recordings, works of art, long poems (several pages), comic strips, genera, species, and software programs.**

| | |
|---|---|
| BOOKS | A Room of One's Own OR *Backlash* |
| MAGAZINES | The Progressive OR *Utne Reader* |
| NEWSPAPERS | The Spokesman Review OR *The Charlotte Observer* |
| PLAYS, FILMS | 'Night, Mother OR *The Crying Game* |
| TV, RADIO SHOWS | Women Aloud OR *One in Ten* |
| RECORDINGS | The Chase OR *Never Enough* |
| WORKS OF ART | Michelangelo's David OR Judy Chicago's *The Dinner Party* |
| LONG POEMS | The Prelude OR *Howl* |
| COMIC STRIPS | Outland OR *Kudzu* |
| GENRE, SPECIES | Canus lupus OR *Felix domesticus* |
| SOFTWARE | PCWrite OR *Lotus* |

**Note:** Italicize legal citations.

> In 1973, the Supreme Court ruled in the case of *San Antonio Independent School District v. Rodriguez* that property taxes could be used to finance public education.

Copyright © 1995 by Harcourt Brace & Company. All rights reserved.

**10b Italicize (underline) foreign words and phrases in the context of an English sentence.**

> Most people would not think that wearing jeans, a sweatshirt, and tennis shoes to a job interview would be *très chic*. [In general, it is best to avoid a foreign term when an English equivalent is available.]

**Note:** Many words that were italicized as foreign—like *coup d'état* and *détente*—are now so frequently used that the italics have been dropped.

**10c Italicize (underline) the names of specific ships, satellites, and spacecraft.**

> The space shuttle *Discovery* returned to space in 1988.

**10d Italicize (underline) words, letters, and figures spoken of as such or used as illustrations, statistical symbols, or algebraic formulas.**

> $E=mc^2$
> Remember that *misspelled* has two *s*'s and two *l*'s.
> The word *petroleum* comes from two Latin words—*petra*, which means "rock," and *oleum*, which means "oil."

**Note:** Quotation marks may also be used to identify words used as such (see also **16c**).

 Copyright © 1995 by Harcourt Brace & Company. All rights reserved.

Deduct 4 for each incorrect underlining.

**Italics**                                                                                          Exercise 10–1

NAME _____ SCORE _____

DIRECTIONS   In the following sentences underline the words or word groups that should be printed in italics.

EXAMPLE
The movie Silkwood shows what happens when one person tries to fight the system.

1. Arthur Miller's play, Death of a Salesman, portrays a "little man" ground down by the system.

2. The* Atlanta Journal-Atlanta Constitution ran an interesting series of articles entitled "Working in the Year 2000."

3. Bruce Springsteen's album, Born in the USA, contains many songs about working women and men.

4. Some people would argue that the Pilgrims' Mayflower was the first "company car."

5. You might enjoy The Firm, a film about a corrupt law firm.

6. One spacecraft to visit Mars is named the Explorer.

7. Probably the most famous single ruling of the Supreme Court was handed down in 1954 in Brown v. Topeka Board of Education, which made segregation in the public schools unconstitutional.

8. The word advertise comes from the Middle English word advertisen, which means "to notify."

9. Saturday Night Live frequently shows TV audiences parodies of corporate life.

10. I used to forget that in receive the e comes before the i.

11. Megatrends 2000 is a very interesting book that projects what the working world will be like in the next decade.

12. Knowing how to run business software programs, like WordPerfect or dBase, is a definite plus for the job seeker.

13. The term ergonomics, which means "fitting the work to the worker," has an ics on the end, as do many of the names of other applied sciences.

14. Working Woman is a magazine read by many women wanting to keep up on trends and learn more about the workplace.

*The is also acceptable.

Copyright © 1995 by Harcourt Brace & Company. All rights reserved.

15. My English class is reading The Jungle, Upton Sinclair's exposé of the meat packing industry.

16. Zonker, a character in the comic strip Doonesbury, never seems to have a real job.

17. Many students read the* Wall Street Journal as a text for some of their business courses.

18. A popular rock and roll song of the 1950s, Get a Job, was aimed at an out-of-work teenager.

19. Some people would say that Homo sapiens can't stop working.

20. Many people forget that the possessive pronoun has no apostrophe, and so they write it's when they mean its.

*The is also acceptable.

Copyright © 1995 by Harcourt Brace & Company. All rights reserved.

## 11

**Use abbreviations only when appropriate for the audience, the purpose and the occasion. Spell out the first-time use of abbreviations and acronyms, and spell out numbers that can be expressed simply.**

Abbreviations are more common in business and technical writing than in other kinds of composition, but even there writers should take note of the following. First, a writer should only use those abbreviations that the reader is sure to understand. Second, a letter, memo, or report should never look as though it is overflowing with abbreviations. Finally, once an abbreviation has been introduced, the writer should use it consistently throughout the document.

Acronyms abound in almost any field; an acronym is a word made up of the first letters in a compound phrase—for instance, NASA, which stands for National Aeronautics and Space Administration. Few things are as annoying to a reader as an avalanche of these "invented" words. When you use an acronym, always write out the complete phrase or title the first time unless it is one that all your readers will understand.

Figures are commonly used in business and technical writing except when a number is the first word in a sentence or when the number to be used is ten or under. In other kinds of writing, figures are used only when the numbers could not be written out in one or two words (for example, 150; 2,300; $250.00) or when a series of numbers is being reported.

**11a In ordinary writing, designations preceding a proper name, such as *Miss*, *Ms.* (or *Ms*), *Mr.*, *Mrs.*, *Dr.*, and *St.* (for saint), and following a proper name, such as *Jr.*, *Sr.*, *II*, and *MD*, are commonly used.**

*Ms.* Elaine Freeman    *Mr.* Simon Liebowitz
*Dr.* Phillipe Asante    BUT Phillipe Asante, *MD*
E. T. Arnold, *III*    Harvey Lee, *Sr.*

**Caution:** Do not use redundant titles: Dr. H. U. Farr OR H. U. Farr, PhD    [NOT Dr. H. U. Farr, PhD]

**11b Spell out the names of states, countries, continents, months, days of the week, and units of measurement in formal writing.**

*Great Britain* (NOT *G.B.*), *New York* (NOT *N.Y.*)    [except for long names, like *USSR* for Union of Soviet Socialist Republics OR *DC* for District of Columbia]
*January* (NOT *Jan.*)
*Wednesday* (NOT *Wed.*)
nine *pounds* (NOT nine *lbs.*)

Copyright © 1995 by Harcourt Brace & Company. All rights reserved.

*Washington* (NOT *WA* OR *Wash.*) [It is appropriate to use the two-letter Post Office abbreviations for states on envelopes and in the heading and return address sections of business letters.]
*and* (NOT &)

**Note:** Do not use & (the ampersand) except in copying official titles or names of firms: AT&T.

**Note:** Use appropriate postal abbreviations on envelopes, and do not use periods:

| | | | | | |
|---|---|---|---|---|---|
| AL | Alabama | KY | Kentucky | ND | North Dakota |
| AK | Alaska | LA | Louisiana | OH | Ohio |
| AZ | Arizona | ME | Maine | OK | Oklahoma |
| AR | Arkansas | MD | Maryland | OR | Oregon |
| CA | California | MA | Massachusetts | PA | Pennsylvania |
| CO | Colorado | MI | Michigan | PR | Puerto Rico |
| CT | Connecticut | MN | Minnesota | RI | Rhode Island |
| DE | Delaware | MS | Mississippi | SC | South Carolina |
| DC | District of Columbia | MO | Missouri | SD | South Dakota |
| FL | Florida | MT | Montana | TN | Tennessee |
| GA | Georgia | NE | Nebraska | TX | Texas |
| HI | Hawaii | NV | Nevada | UT | Utah |
| ID | Idaho | NH | New Hampshire | VT | Vermont |
| IL | Illinois | NJ | New Jersey | VA | Virginia |
| IN | Indiana | NM | New Mexico | WA | Washington (state) |
| IA | Iowa | NY | New York | WV | West Virginia |
| KS | Kansas | NC | North Carolina | WI | Wisconsin |
| | | | | WY | Wyoming |

**11c Spell out *Street, Avenue, Road, Park, Mount, River, Company*, and other similar words used as a part of a proper name when used in formal writing.**

We used to live on Keller *Street*.

Writers often abbreviate such words when they form part of an address: 788 *N. Keller St.*

Abbreviations such as *Prof., Sen., 1st Lt.*, or *Capt.* should be used only before initials or full names (*Prof.* Rex H. Lankowski) and not before last names alone.

**11d Spell out the words *volume, chapter*, and *page* and the names of course of study.**

*chapter* 9 (NOT *ch.* 9)          *biology* (NOT *bio.*)

**Note:** *Volume, chapter*, and *page* are usually abbreviated in bibliographies.

Copyright © 1995 by Harcourt Brace & Company. All rights reserved.

### Special Usage Regarding Abbreviations

The following abbreviations and symbols are permissible, and, in fact, desirable (see also **11a**).

1. *Clipped forms of words*
   Some clipped forms, such as *info* for *information*, are avoided in formal writing. Others, such as *lab* for *laboratory* and *exam* for *examination*, are used so commonly that they are gaining in acceptance.

2. *Certain words used with dates or figures*
   1500 *BC*        *AD* 150        10:30 *a.m.* OR 10:30 *A.M.*
   10:30 *EST* or 10:30 *E.S.T.*    *No.* 5 or *no.* 5
   27.5 *MPG* or 27.5 *mpg*

3. *The* District of Columbia *and the* United States *used as adjectives*
   Washington, *D.C.*              the *U.S.* Army

4. *The names of organizations, agencies, countries, persons, or things usually referred to by their capitalized initials*
   *TVA, UNICEF, FBI, UK, JFK, VCR, IQ, MTV*

5. *Certain common Latin expressions* [the English equivalent is spelled out in brackets]
   *etc.* [and so forth]          *i.e.* [that is]
   *e.g.* [for example]           *cf.* [compare]
   *et al.* [and others]          *vs.* OR *v.* [versus]

**Note:** Today the English forms are generally preferred over their Latin equivalents.

**Caution:** Never write *and etc.,* and use the word *etc.* itself sparingly. Naming another item is more effective.

| | |
|---|---|
| NOT | Many business professionals are proficient in several languages: German, French, *etc.* |
| BUT | Many business professionals are proficient in several languages: *German, French, and Japanese.* |

The abbreviations *Inc.* and *Ltd.* are usually omitted in ordinary writing.
   Robarb    [NOT Robarb, Inc.]

   In documentation for reports and charts, certain abbreviations are commonly used: *p.* (page), *pp.* (pages), *col.* (column), *cols.* (columns), *no.* (number), *nos.* (numbers).
   In special circumstances—for instance, in tables or footnotes, where space is limited—any abbreviation listed in a standard dictionary is acceptable.

Copyright © 1995 by Harcourt Brace & Company. All rights reserved.

## ACRONYMS

### 11e Spell out the meaning of any acronym that may be unfamiliar to your reader the first time you use it.

The **R**ead **O**nly **M**emory (ROM) of the computer contains the routines that make it run. The ROM cannot be altered.

OR

The computer's ROM (Read Only Memory) is installed when it is manufactured.

## NUMBERS

### 11f Follow accepted practices for writing numbers; be consistent.

The *forty*-hour workweek may soon be changed to *thirty-five* hours.
In 1976 our country was *200* years old; our state, *187*; and our county, *125*.

#### Special Usage Regarding Numbers

1. *Specific time of day*
   2 a.m. or *2:00* a.m. OR *two* o'clock in the morning
   *4:30* p.m. OR *half-past four* in the afternoon

2. *Dates*
   November 9, *1909* OR 9 November *1909*   [NOT November *9th, 1909*]
   November *9th* OR *the ninth* of November OR November 9
   the *fifties* OR the *1950s*
   the *twentieth* century
   in *1914* OR in *1914–1918*
   from 1832 to 1855 OR *1832–1855*   [NOT from *1832–1855*]

3. *Addresses*
   *321* Harrison Street, Apartment *221*, Pullman, Washington *99163*   [OR *321* Harrison St., Apt. *221*, Pullman, WA *99163*]
   *1344* Seventh Street
   *666* West *225* Street OR *666* West *225th* Street

4. *Identification numbers*
   Interstate *40*   Elizabeth *II*   Room *308*   Channel *6*

5. Pages and divisions of books and plays
   page *234*   chapter *11*   part *5*
   in act *2*, scene *3* OR in Act *II*, Scene *iii*

6. *Decimals and percentages*
   a *3.87* average   *8¾* percent   *1.4* linear feet

7. *Large round numbers*
   *twenty million* dollars OR *$20 million* OR *$20,000,000*   [figures are used for emphasis only]

   Copyright © 1995 by Harcourt Brace & Company. All rights reserved.

8. *Repeated numbers* (in legal or commercial writing)

The teacher's salary will not break *thirty thousand (30,000)* dollars. OR The teacher's salary will not exceed *thirty thousand dollars ($30,000).*

**Note:** When numbers are used infrequently in a text, writers usually spell out those that can be expressed in one or two words and use figures for all others.

**Exception:** Business and technical writers generally use figures for all numbers above ten except when (1) a number occurs at the beginning of the sentence; (2) a fraction is used alone; or (3) the exact amount or number is not known.

The *40*-hour workweek may soon be changed to *35* hours.

*One hundred* years ago the average American worked about *fifty-five* hours a week, or *one-third* of the *168* hours in a week.

Copyright © 1995 by Harcourt Brace & Company. All rights reserved.

Deduct 5 for each incorrect answer.

**Abbreviations and Numbers** Exercise 11–1

NAME _____ SCORE _____

DIRECTIONS  Change any part of each of the following items to an abbreviation or a figure if the abbreviation or figure would be appropriate as a first reference in writing (not in tables or footnotes). Write your revision in the blank. If it would not be correct written as a number or figure, leave the answer line blank.

EXAMPLES
this Thursday morning

six o'clock in the morning
6 a.m. or 6 A.M.

1. Professor Lorton

2. Nan Chee, Master of Arts
   Nan Chee, MA

3. page eight of part two
   page 8 of part 2

4. eighty-eight percent
   88%

5. Rameses Road near Franklin Street

6. Doctor Brewster Langhorn
   Dr. Brewster Langhorn

7. twenty-two pounds, twelve ounces
   22 pounds, 12 ounces*

8. fifteen hundred years before Christ
   1500 BC

9. the advanced geology lab in Sanford Hall

10. five hundred twenty-four dollars and eighteen cents
    $524.18

*Writing out the numbers is also acceptable.

Copyright © 1995 by Harcourt Brace & Company. All rights reserved.

DIRECTIONS   Rewrite the following sentences to correct any errors in the use of abbreviations, acronyms, or numbers. If the sentence is correct, leave the answer line blank.

11.  1600 people walked on the picket lines in the twenty days of the strike.

*Sixteen hundred people walked on the picket lines in the twenty days of the strike.*

12.  We were told that an Ark. manufacturer wanted to buy computer chips from us.

*We were told that an Arkansas manufacturer wanted to buy computer chips from us.*

13.  The tax shelter we decided to look into was an IRA (Individual Retirement Account).

14.  When we went back over the report covering the last 6 months, we found errors in thirty-two percent of the prices listed on page 114.

*When we went back over the report covering the last six months, we found errors in 32 percent of the prices listed on page 114.*

15.  I think that Doctor Langley's report on IRAs (Individual Retirement Accounts) is long overdue.

*I think that Dr. Langley's report on IRAs (Individual Retirement Accounts) is long overdue.*

16.  You could send the request for materials to their home office at Seventy-five Moffit Dr. in Monte Vista, CO.

*You could send the request for materials to their home office at 75 Moffit Drive in Monte Vista, Colorado.*

Copyright © 1995 by Harcourt Brace & Company. All rights reserved.

17. When I told her that I wanted the reports on the 1st Tues. & third Fri. of April and Oct., she said it would be no problem.

    When I told her that I wanted the reports on the first Tuesday and third Friday of April and October, she said it would be no problem.

18. The sales force at IBM is quite different from what it was twenty-three years ago when he started on Aug. 29th, 1972.

    The sales force at IBM is quite different from what it was twenty-three years ago when he started on August 29, 1972.

19. My prof for my business writing class is Dr. Georgia Rhoades, PhD.

    My professor for my business writing class is Dr. Georgia Rhoades <u>or</u> Georgia Rhoades, PhD.

20. We decided that using disks & a hard drive would work, so we placed our orders and began revamping our documents.

    We decided that using disks and a hard drive would work, so we placed our orders and began revamping our documents.

Copyright © 1995 by Harcourt Brace & Company. All rights reserved.

Deduct 3 1/3 for each word or word group incorrectly revised.

## Capitalization, Italics, Abbreviations, Acronyms, and Numbers: A Review

Exercise 11–2

NAME _____ SCORE _____

DIRECTIONS   The following passages have been altered to include errors. Revise them to reflect the correct use of capital letters, italics, abbreviations, acronyms, and numbers. (In the scoring, a word group counts as a single change.) Apply the business writing principles discussed in **11f**.

Career decision-making, whether it involves choosing or changing one's job, is an

important process. ~~m~~[M]ost people spend more than 100,000 hours—one-sixth of their

lives—at work. As ~~Chas. f.~~ [Charles F.] Kettering, ~~bachelor of science~~ [B.S.], the ~~i~~[I]nventor and ~~e~~[E]ngineer,

once said, "~~t~~[T]he future is all we are interested in, because we are going to spend the rest

of our lives there." ~~o~~[O]bviously, anything that takes up so much of our lives should be care-

fully planned—to ensure a career directed by ~~c~~[C]hoice rather than ~~c~~[C]hance.

—DEAN L. HUMMEL, *"What Should I Be When I Grow Up?"*

Rangeley, ~~ME~~ [Maine], is the home of ~~Tranet~~ [TRANET] (~~t~~[T]ransnational ~~n~~[N]etwork for ~~a~~[A]ppropriate ~~a~~[A]lterna-

tive ~~t~~[T]echnologies)...TRANET's purpose is to link people, projects, ~~&~~ [and] resources in the

appropriate technical community. The network has ~~five hundred~~ [500] members worldwide,

publishes a quarterly newspaper, ... maintains files on some ~~fifteen hundred~~ [1,500]

~~A~~[a]ppropriate ~~T~~[t]echnology ~~P~~[p]rojects ~~&~~ [and] 10,000 individuals, has an extensive library, and is

able to arrange many successful linkages.

—JOHN NAISBITT, *Megatrends: Ten New Directions Transforming Our Lives*

Copyright © 1995 by Harcourt Brace & Company. All rights reserved.

T

/tests over the years show that the average sentence length in successful pulp maga-

12      15

zines has been kept between ~~twelve~~ and ~~fifteen~~ words. The Reader's Digest average is

and

consistently between 14 and 17, & that of Time 17 to 19.* Our count of 3-syllable words

3

shows the following averages for the same publications: True Confessions, ~~three~~ per-

9    10

cent; Reader's Digest, 8 to 9 percent; Time, ~~nine~~ to ~~ten~~ percent.

—ROBERT GUNNING, *The Technique of Clear Writing*

---

*Gunning writes out these numbers, but business writers would use figures.

Copyright © 1995 by Harcourt Brace & Company. All rights reserved.

# THE COMMA                                        ,/ 12 and ⊙ 13

## 12 and 13

### Apply basic principles governing comma usage and avoid superfluous commas.

In speaking, you use pauses and changes in voice pitch to make the meaning of your sentences clear. In writing, you use punctuation marks in a similar way, especially as you make additions to the basic pattern. As you will recall from Chapter **1**, the word order of a basic sentence follows a subject–verb–complement pattern:

SUBJECT          VERB          COMPLEMENT

The company president decided to fund the project.

Often, however, the sentences that you write will vary from this basic pattern.

PATTERN        *Addition,* subject–verb–complement.

After studying the report, the company president decided to fund the project.

PATTERN        Subject, *addition,* verb–complement

The company president, *after studying the report,* decided to fund the project.

PATTERN        Subject–verb–complement, *addition.*

The company president decided to fund the project, *after studying the report.*

Five main rules govern the use of the comma. In the exercises that follow, each of these rules is explained and illustrated (**12a, 12b,** and so forth). Cautions against the corresponding misuses are also provided (**13a, 13b,** and so forth).

### 12a  A comma ordinarily precedes a coordinating conjunction that links independent clauses.

A comma follows a main clause that is linked to another main clause by a coordinating conjunction—*and, but, or, nor for, so, yet.* This construction is called a *compound sentence.*

Copyright © 1995 by Harcourt Brace & Company. All rights reserved.

PATTERN    MAIN CLAUSE, coordinating conjunction MAIN CLAUSE.

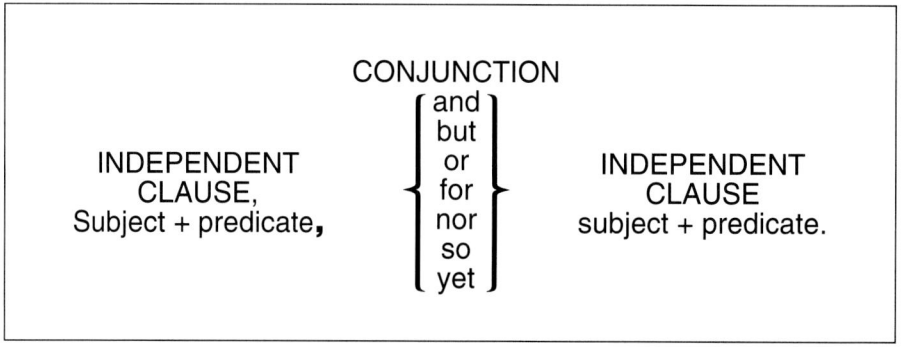

Businesses submit written proposals to gain new contracts, *and* experienced writers have the responsibility for producing them.

**Caution:** Do not place a comma after a coordinating conjunction linking main clauses.

(Throughout this chapter, a circled comma ⊚ indicates a misuse of the comma.)

NOT        Businesses submit written proposals to gain new contracts, and⊚ experienced writers have the responsibility for producing them.

**Note:** The semicolon may also be used when the two main clauses linked by the coordinating conjunction contain other commas.

Businesses, and sometimes private individuals, submit written proposals to gain new contracts; and experienced writers, or teams of writers and technicians, have the responsibility for producing them.

**13b(1)  A comma is not used *after* a coordinating conjunction.**

Businesses submit proposals for many purposes, and ⊚ these documents follow a variety of formats.    [The comma comes *before*, but not *after*, the coordinating conjunction.]

**13b(2)  Nor is a comma used *before* a coordinating conjunction when only words, phrases, or subordinate clauses (rather than main clauses) are being linked.**

TWO WORDS              Proposals vary in both length ⊚ and format.    [A comma is not used before a coordinating conjunction that links two words or phrases.]

TWO SUBORDINATE        Because proposals are time-consuming to write ⊚ and because
CLAUSES                they often treat complex problems, they require careful planning. [A comma is not used before a coordinating conjunction that links two subordinate clauses.]

Copyright © 1995 by Harcourt Brace & Company. All rights reserved.

In numbers 1–10, deduct 3 for each incorrectly placed or omitted comma and 3 for each incorrectly filled blank; in numbers 11–15, deduct 8 for each incorrect sentence.

## Commas and Coordinating Conjunctions  Exercise 12/13–1

NAME _____  SCORE _____

DIRECTIONS  In the following sentences insert an inverted caret (**V**) before coordinating conjunctions that connect main clauses. Then insert a comma after the first main clause and write a comma and the conjunction in the blank. If a sentence having no commas is correct as it stands, write *C* in the blank to indicate that no comma is needed. If a sentence contains a misused comma, circle the comma; then place a circled comma ( **☉** ) in the blank.

EXAMPLES

Written proposals explain what the company or person will do for someone and at what price. _____☉_____

Your company may have specific guidelines for proposal writing, and your document should conform to those requirements. _____, and_____

1. A good proposal convinces the reader that its writer understands the company's needs and offers a practical solution to the problem. _____☉_____

2. Many times proposals total hundreds of pages, but short proposals need to be thorough and specific too. _____, but_____

3. A company or a client may ask you to investigate a problem, and they will expect a written plan for solving it—the proposal. _____, and_____

4. The proposal must make clear what needs to be done and how to make the changes happen. _____☉_____

5. Details should be selected and logically organized so that they do not overwhelm the reader. _____☉_____

6. Such details are important, so the proposal should incorporate such information as time schedules and budgets. _____, so_____

7. One danger in writing persuasively is "information overload," but your proposal must include enough pertinent facts to be convincing. _____," but_____

8. Even personal qualifications may be a persuasive element in a proposal, so you may wish to include the résumés of key personnel. _____C_____

Copyright © 1995 by Harcourt Brace & Company. All rights reserved.

9. An *unsolicited* proposal alerts a company to a problem,<sup>V</sup>so this

   type of proposal must convince your reader that you are the one

   to solve it.        <u> , so </u>

10. An unsolicited proposal is more difficult to write,<sup>V</sup>for you must

    devise your own plan for presenting your material.     <u> , for </u>

DIRECTIONS   In the following section, write correctly punctuated sentences that follow the pattern described.

EXAMPLE

A sentence using *and* to join two prepositional phrases

She went around the corner and down the street.*

11. A sentence using *and* to connect two independent clauses

12. A sentence using *so* as a coordinating conjunction to join two independent clauses

13. A sentence using *and* to join two main verbs in the same independent clause

14. A sentence using the coordinating conjunction *but* to join two independent clauses

15. A sentence using *for* as a coordinating conjunction to join two independent clauses

*Answers will vary.

     Copyright © 1995 by Harcourt Brace & Company. All rights reserved.

In numbers 1–10, deduct 3 for each incorrectly placed comma and 3 for each incorrectly filled blank. In numbers 11–15, deduct 8 for each incorrect sentence.

## Commas and Introductory Additions                    Exercise 12/13–2

NAME _____     SCORE _____

### 12b  A comma usually follows introductory words, phrases, and clauses.

A comma often follows adverb clauses that precede main clauses. A comma often follows introductory phrases (especially verbal phrases) and transitional expressions. A comma follows an introductory interjection (such as *oh* or *well*) or an introductory *yes* or *no*.

---

**ADVERB CLAUSE, INDEPENDENT CLAUSE.**

---

**INTRODUCTORY PHRASE,**
**INTRODUCTORY WORD,** } **subject + predicate.**

---

> *When our company received a request for a proposal,* we asked our best writer to prepare it.   [introductory adverb clause (for a list of common adverb clause markers, see *Subordinators* in the Appendix)]
>
> *Following the guidelines suggested by the company,* the writer prepared an excellent proposal.   [introductory verbal phrase]

A comma is often omitted after introductory prepositional phrases when no misreading would result. When an adverb clause comes at the end of a sentence, it is not usually preceded by a comma unless the clause is introduced by *although*.

> *Not long after,* the company received a positive response from the company that solicited the proposal.   [The comma prevents misreading.]
>
> Our company was chosen ⊙ *because the writer of the proposal had prepared an excellent presentation.*   [concluding adverb clause]
>
> The writer of the proposal sold our company's product, *although more than twenty other companies also presented proposals.*   [concluding adverb clause introduced by *although*]

DIRECTIONS   After each introductory element in the sentences below, either write a *C* to indicate that the sentence is correct as it stands or insert an inverted caret (**V**) and a comma where one is needed. Then write the *C* or the comma in the blank.

EXAMPLES

When you write an unsolicited proposal**V** you generally may choose your

own format.                                                               ____**,**____

Quite often⊙an unsolicited proposal is presented in the form of a letter.     ____*C*____

*The zero marks the point where a student is likely to insert an unnecessary comma.

Copyright © 1995 by Harcourt Brace & Company. All rights reserved.

1. Even when the proposal takes the form of a letter,ᵛcaptions or headings still identify major sections.  
   *comma optional* \_\_\_\_\_,\_\_\_\_\_

2. In the abstract₀the writer usually provides a summary of the proposal's contents. \_\_\_\_\_C\_\_\_\_\_

3. By using the first section of the report to summarize or sketch the main points,ᵛthe writer tries to make the reader's job as easy as possible. \_\_\_\_\_,\_\_\_\_\_

4. Instead of having to read the entire document,ᵛthe reader can decide which sections of the report on which to concentrate. \_\_\_\_\_,\_\_\_\_\_

5. In many ways₀this abstract helps the reader to focus easily on the sections that follow. \_\_\_\_\_C\_\_\_\_\_

6. The key words in a section's first sentence often form the basis for a good heading,ᵛalthough that is not always the case. \_\_\_\_\_,\_\_\_\_\_

7. Remember,ᵛbecause you need to make the reports that you write easy to read,ᵛuse clear, helpful headings for all sections. \_\_\_\_\_,\_,\_\_\_\_\_

8. Producing an accurate proposal is extremely important₀because it may be interpreted as a legal document. \_\_\_\_\_C\_\_\_\_\_

9. In court₀you would be judged responsible for following through with everything promised in your proposal.  
   *comma optional* \_\_\_\_\_C\_\_\_\_\_

10. Legally,ᵛyou can be made to pay for the oversights in your proposal. \_\_\_\_\_,\_\_\_\_\_

Copyright © 1995 by Harcourt Brace & Company. All rights reserved.

DIRECTIONS   In the following section, write a sentence according to the pattern indicated.

EXAMPLE

A sentence containing a comma to prevent misreading

While it was running, the company booked seats at the new play.*

11. A sentence containing a concluding adverb clause starting with *after*

12. A sentence starting with the interjection *well*

13. A sentence containing an introductory verbal phrase

14. A sentence containing an introductory *no*

15. A sentence containing a concluding adverb clause introduced by *although*

*Answers will vary.

Copyright © 1995 by Harcourt Brace & Company. All rights reserved.   *205*

In numbers 1–10 deduct 4 for each series incorrectly marked and 4 for each incorrectly filled blank. In numbers 11–15, deduct 4 for each incorrect sentence.

## Commas and Items in a Series          Exercise 12/13–3

NAME _____ SCORE _____

**12c Commas are used to separate items in a series, including coordinate adjectives (in pairs or series).**

A series is a succession of three or more parallel elements. Note the commas:

      **1,**        **2,**      and     **3**

*English,* *mathematics,* and *psychology* are all disciplines with important applications

    to nearly any career.

              **1,**             **2,**      and         **3**

The office is *pleasant to work in,* *easy to get to,* and *inexpensive to maintain.*

Adjectives are coordinate when they describe the same noun (or noun substitute) in a parallel fashion—so that these adjectives could logically be joined by *and* or *or* and so that their order could be reversed without loss of sense. *Pleasant, easy,* and *inexpensive* in the preceding example are coordinate adjectives. Coordinate adjectives are also used in pairs:

        **1,**    **2**

They are *alert,* *energetic* employees.   [Note that the sequence could be reversed and the

    comma replaced by *and:* They are *energetic and alert* employees.]

In all the preceding examples notice that the commas are used where the coordinating conjunction *and* would otherwise appear. (In a series, the last comma usually is accompanied by the coordinating conjunction rather than replacing it.)

    **1**    and    **2**    and    **3**

English *and* mathematics *and* psychology

    **1,**       **2,**    and    **3**

English, mathematics, and psychology

       **1**      and   **2**    and      **3**

pleasant to work in *and* easy to get to *and* inexpensive to maintain

        **1**     **,**    **2**   **,and**      **3**

pleasant to work in, easy to get to, and inexpensive to maintain

   **1**   and    **2**

alert *and* energetic

    **1 ,**   **2**

alert, energetic

Copyright © 1995 by Harcourt Brace & Company. All rights reserved.

**13e Commas are not used between adjectives that are not coordinate (those that could not be linked by *and*), before the first item or after the last item in a series, or between *two* items linked by a coordinator.**

A modern ⊙ chrome ⊙ rocking chair stood in one corner.   [The adjectives are not coordinate: their sequence cannot be reversed, nor can they logically be joined by *and*.]

The office did not lack such necessary equipment as ⊙ desk, file cabinets, and typewriters. [No comma is used before the first item in the series.]

Yesterday a supply center delivered a photocopy machine, a calculator, and a cellular phone⊙ to the office.   [No comma is used after the last item in the series.]

DIRECTIONS   Identify each series (or pair) that needs commas by writing *1, 2* OR *1, 2, and 3* OR *1, 2, or 3* in the blanks. Insert an inverted caret (**V**) and commas where they belong in the sentence and also between the numbers in the blank to show the punctuation of the pattern. Write *C* after each sentence that has no items in a series that need punctuation.

EXAMPLES

Sometimes work needs to be done that involves people in the

home office͜people out in the field͜and clients.       _____1, 2, and 3_____

Many businesses make use of telephone conference calls to

get people together.       _____C_____

1. People who use this method report varying degrees of

   success, depending on several circumstances.       _____C_____

2. The person planning the call must find a time that is

   workable for all parties͜let them know the agenda for

   the phone meeting͜and provide them with the names of

   all the participants.       _____1, 2, and 3_____

3. Cordless speakerphones can be helpful.       _____C_____

4. Problems arise for conference participants, however,

   when fuzzy͜faint sound results from a weak microphone.       _____1, 2_____

5. Some people are uncomfortable talking into a micro-

   phone͜others are nervous about knowing when it is

   their turn to speak͜and still others are leery of not see-

   ing their counterparts' expressions.       _____1, 2, and 3_____

Copyright © 1995 by Harcourt Brace & Company. All rights reserved.

6. If you plan such a call, you should carefully consider your reasons for doing so, the personalities of the people who will be talking, and how well those people get along.  <u>1, 2, and 3</u>

7. One advantage of conference calls is that busy in-demand executives often can't go to another city, so talking on the phone to others working on a project may be the only way for you to get everyone together.  <u>1, 2</u>

8. These days businesses try to use time efficiently, cut costs, and keep expensive out-of-town travel to a minimum.  <u>1, 2, and 3</u>

9. Conference call meetings help people work together who need to share information or deal with common concerns "right now."  <u>C</u>

10. In terms of money, if such calls meet your needs, save valuable time, or both, they are probably a good investment.  <u>1, 2, or 3</u>

Copyright © 1995 by Harcourt Brace & Company. All rights reserved.

DIRECTIONS    In the following section write a correctly punctuated sentence containing the specified pattern.

EXAMPLE

a sentence using a series of three coordinate prepositional phrases

We talked with the client, with the ad executive, and with our supervisor.*

11.  a sentence using a series of three coordinate subjects

12.  a sentence using two coordinate adjectives with no *and* to join them

13.  a sentence using three coordinate direct objects

14.  a sentence using three main verbs

15.  a sentence using two coordinate adjectives joined by the word *and*

*Answers will vary.

   Copyright © 1995 by Harcourt Brace & Company. All rights reserved.

Deduct 10 for each incorrectly filled blank.

## Commas and Restrictive and Nonrestrictive Additions    Exercise 12/13–4

NAME _____    SCORE _____

### 12d Commas set off nonrestrictive clauses, phrases, and other parenthetical elements as well as contrasted elements, items in dates, and so on.

> The North Carolina Technical Writers' Workshop, *which was held in Raleigh during August,* attracted middle management personnel from all over the state.    [The *which* clause is not needed to identify *workshop.*]
>
> The organizer of the Workshop, *Leo Bernstein,* was pleased with the turnout.    [An appositive is usually nonrestrictive.]
>
> The new managers, *not to mention the experienced ones,* learned a great deal from the seminars.    [*Not to mention* introduces a parenthetical element.]

**Caution:**    Avoid the serious error of using only one comma to set off a nonrestrictive phrase or clause. When the second comma is not used, the writer seems to be separating the subject from the verb or the verb from the complement. (Remember that commas do not separate the parts of the basic sentence—subject–verb–complement—but rather show where additions that require punctuation have been made.)

> NOT    The workshop *which met in August* ⊙ led to an immediate improvement in the reports the managers wrote.
>
> NOT    The workshop ⊙ *which met in August* led to an immediate improvement in the reports that the managers wrote.
>
> BUT    The workshop, *which met in August,* led to an immediate improvement in the reports that the managers wrote.

Remember, then, to use two commas when a nonrestrictive or other parenthetical element appears in the middle of a sentence.

> The managers, fortunately for all concerned, praised the workshop's leaders.

When the explanatory phrase or clause ends a sentence, the second comma is replaced by the period.

> The managers praised the workshop's leaders, *I might add.*

When two sentences are joined, however, one of the two commas setting off a parenthetical element may be replaced by a semicolon.

> We were pleased with the training session; *I might add,* the managers praised the workshop's leaders.

### 13d Restrictive phrases and clauses (those that give information essential to the meaning of the terms they refer to) are not set off with commas.

The circled commas in the following examples are incorrect.

> The seminar ⊙ in technical writing ⊙ attracted participants from all over the country.    [The phrase identifies *seminar*]

Copyright © 1995 by Harcourt Brace & Company. All rights reserved.

The professor ⊙ *who planned the seminar* ⊙ was surprised by the number of applications received.   [The *who* clause identifies *professor*.]

Much of the writing *that was done as a result of the seminar* was published.   [*That* introduces a restrictive clause essential to identify *writing*.]

DIRECTIONS   In the sentences below, insert an inverted caret (**V**) and use commas to set off all nonrestrictive and parenthetical additions. Then in the blanks place (1) a dash followed by a comma (—**,**) if the nonrestrictive or parenthetical addition begins the sentence, (2) a comma followed by a dash (**,**—) if the addition ends the sentence, or (3) a dash enclosed within commas (**,**—**,**) if the addition comes within the sentence. Write *C* if there is no nonrestrictive or parenthetical addition to set off.

EXAMPLE

Fax machines, like other communication devices, can save a busy

professional time.                                                                                        _____,—,_____

1. Even when we plan ahead, sometimes unforeseen emergencies

   arise.                                                                                                       _____—,_____

2. Although a neatly prepared letter or report may look better in its

   original form, facsimile machines quickly get your material where it

   needs to go.                                                                                           _____—,_____

3. The fax machine, as it is called, transmits a photocopy of your docu-

   ment over the phone line.                                                                       _____,—,_____

4. The quality of the reproduction, even on expensive fax machines, can

   be fuzzy.                                                                                                _____,—,_____

5. On the other hand, a fax lets you react immediately to your client's

   request for data.                                                                                    _____—,_____

6. Sending material that someone needs "yesterday," it should be

   noted, is one way to make a client feel valued.                                   _____,—,_____

7. Most business persons, however, try to anticipate a client's needs in

   advance so they don't have to send things by fax or overnight mail.   _____,—,_____

8. Besides making things look rushed, these delivery systems can be

   very expensive.                                                                                      _____—,_____

9. Such conveniences can even allow us to procrastinate far too long

   or waste money because we're "too busy" to do things the old way.    _____C_____

10. I know some restaurants that, wasteful of paper as it may be, insist on

    faxes-only for all takeout orders.                                                       _____,—,_____

Copyright © 1995 by Harcourt Brace & Company. All rights reserved.

In numbers 1–10 deduct 3 1/3 for incorrect punctuation of a sentence and 3 1/3 for each incorrectly filled blank. In numbers 11–15, deduct 3 1/3 for each incorrect sentence.

## Conventional Uses of Commas

Exercise 12/13–5

NAME _____   SCORE _____

**12e  Commas are conventionally used to set off a variety of constructions: (1) negative or contrasted elements, (2) words in direct address, (3) words that explain who is speaking in a direct quotation, (4) items in dates, addresses, and geographic locations, and (5) a letter's complimentary close** (see Chapter **35**).

The most common kind of speech is extemporaneous, *not written or memorized.*
[A contrasted element is commonly introduced by *not*.]

*"Harold,* would you be in charge of the presentation for the board of directors next Friday," *the sales manager asked,* "that explains our new marketing program?"
[A comma is used after the name of someone addressed directly; commas set off expressions like *he said* or *she asked* (unless a question mark or exclamation point is called for). See also Chapter **16** for the placement of other punctuation in relationship to quotation marks.]

The annual convention of the Junior Chamber of Commerce was held at *Laguna Beach, California,* on *March 16, 1994.*

Official documents and reports sometimes arrange dates differently; the punctuation will then vary from the usual practice: *14 August 1994.* However, the usual form in business letters would be *August 14, 1994.*

**Note:**   If only the month and the year are given, no comma is necessary: *August 1994.*

**Caution:**   No comma is used before the zip code in a postal address: *New York, NY 10017.*

DIRECTIONS   Insert an inverted caret (**V**) and any needed commas in each of the following sentences. In the blank write the number that represents the reason you inserted the comma or commas: *1* for negative or contrasted elements, *2* for words in direct address, and *3* for words that explain who is speaking, and *4* for items in dates, addresses, or geographic locations. Some sentences require more than one comma.

EXAMPLE
Since June 1, 1994, this company has invited job finalists to make brief

presentations to a small group of supervisors.          __4__

1.  The company wanted Lynne to see the plant, not just meet with

interviewers on her college campus.          __1__

2.  "Lynne, could you come to our Spokane office for an interview?" the

personnel director asked.          __2__

Copyright © 1995 by Harcourt Brace & Company. All rights reserved.

3. The personnel director asked her to be ready to give a five-minute
   talk ͜ but not a formal speech.                                      1

4. "Please tell us something about your training as a technical writer,"
   the personnel director told Lynne.                                    3

5. "And, Lynne, could you please bring samples of your written
   work?" the personnel director asked.                                  2

6. "I had planned to bring copies of ads I wrote at IBM," Lynne told
   the personnel director.                                               3

7. "I think" she continued, "I will discuss the types of technical reports
   that I wrote on the job."                                             3

8. Lynne decided to emphasize her internship at IBM in Albuquerque,
   New Mexico, that ran from January to May 1994.                        4

9. Lynne said, "My technical communication course has also prepared
   me for working at your company."                                     3

10. On Thursday, September 21, 1994, Lynne flew from Corvallis,
    Oregon, to Spokane, confident that she was well-prepared for her
    interview.                                                           4

Copyright © 1995 by Harcourt Brace & Company. All rights reserved.

DIRECTIONS    In the following section, write sentences containing the required material; be sure to punctuate them correctly.

EXAMPLE

sentence that includes the date June 15 1994

On June 15, 1994, she will make her presentation to the client.*

11. sentence that includes a direct quotation

12. sentence that includes Wednesday November 24 1948

13. sentence that includes a direct quotation and an explanation of who is speaking

14. sentence that includes a question as a direct quotation

15. sentence that includes San Francisco California

*Answers will vary.

Copyright © 1995 by Harcourt Brace & Company. All rights reserved.

Deduct 3 for incorrect punctuation of a sentence and 2 for each incorrectly filled blank.

**Mastering Commas: A Review**                                    Exercise 12/13–6

NAME _____ SCORE _____

DIRECTIONS   Insert inverted carets (**V**) and commas as they are needed in the following sentences. (Not all sentences require commas.) Then in the blanks write the number representing the reason for the comma or commas that you add to a sentence: *1* for main clauses linked by a coordinator, *2* for introductory elements, *3* for items in a series, *4* for nonrestrictive clauses and phrases and other parenthetical elements, and *5* for any other conventional uses. If you do not need to add a comma to a sentence, write *O* in the blank.

EXAMPLE

When you are asked to prepare a report, find out as much as you can about

your audience.                                                               2

1. It is important to know who makes up your audience, and it helps to

   know how much understanding the audience has of the field about

   which you will be speaking.                                              1

2. If the audience is unfamiliar with your subject, you may need to give

   some background information.                                            2

3. It is wise to avoid technical vocabulary as much as possible when-

   ever you are writing for a group of people who are unfamiliar with

   your subject.                                                           O

4. People in your own field, on the other hand, will be able to follow a

   report that makes use of common technical words.                       4

5. Professionals in your own field, who are likely to know the technical

   vocabulary associated with your subject, must be treated with

   respect.                                                               4

6. You should not define simple technical terms, offer background

   information, or otherwise talk down to a reading audience that is

   already familiar with your subject.                                    3

7. If your reading audience is composed of friends and colleagues, your

   report can be less formal than if you are writing to strangers.        2

8. At the same time, writing for a group of friends and/or co-workers

   can be difficult.                                                      2 or 4

Copyright © 1995 by Harcourt Brace & Company. All rights reserved.

9. An old saying states, "A prophet is not without honor save in his own
   country."                                                         **5**

10. To a certain extent, this maxim applies whenever you must write for
    an audience that is familiar with you.                          **2 or 4**

11. It is often more difficult to convince friends than strangers that you
    know what you are talking about.                                **0**

12. You may need to use more evidence, not less, to convince an audi-
    ence made up of friends and co-workers.                         **4 or 5**

13. Since these readers know you quite well, they may not take your rec-
    ommendations seriously unless you support those ideas with details.  **2**

14. Of course, a reading audience that does not know you can also
    present difficulties.                                           **2 or 4**

15. Such an audience may make harsh, unjustified judgments about you
    even before finishing your report.                              **3**

16. These readers may, for example, decide that you are too inexpe-
    rienced to be an expert.                                        **4**

17. When writing for an audience that does not know you, you should
    prepare a rather formal report.                                 **2**

18. You will be more likely to write an effective report if you know the
    kind of audience you are addressing, but sometimes it is not possible
    to analyze an audience carefully.                               **1**

19. There are three suggestions, however, that can help you write to an
    audience.                                                       **4**

20. You should be clear, argue logically, and support your claims with
    facts and details.                                              **3**

Copyright © 1995 by Harcourt Brace & Company. All rights reserved.

## 14

**Use the semicolon between independent clauses not linked by a coordinating conjunction and between coordinate elements that already contain commas.**

A semicolon signals the completion of one part of a coordinate construction. It is a balancing point between sentence parts of equal grammatical rank.

**14a Use the semicolon to connect independent clauses not linked by a coordinating conjunction.**

A semicolon can be used instead of a coordinating conjunction to join two main clauses if they are closely related. Usually, one of the clauses explains the other or stands in contrast to it.

> A formal speech is written down and memorized; an extemporaneous speech is planned but not written down.    [The content of the second main clause contrasts with the idea in the first clause; the semicolon acts as the balancing point between the first and the second clause.]

If the second clause explains the first clause, often a colon is more appropriate. (See **17d**.)

> An impromptu speech is just what the term suggests: it is an unplanned speech that is delivered on the spur of the moment.

Often the semicolon between clauses is accompanied by a conjunctive adverb (such as *however*) or a transitional expression (such as *on the other hand*) that signals the exact relationship between the clauses.

> A written speech tends to be very formal; an extemporaneous speech sounds more natural and spontaneous.
> A written speech is suitable for many occasions; however, it is likely to be very boring when read on social occasions.

**Note:**    Remember that when a conjunctive adverb or a transitional expression is used *as an addition to* a main clause, it is often set off by commas.

> A written speech is suitable for some occasions; it is, *however*, likely to be very boring when read on social occasions.

Copyright © 1995 by Harcourt Brace & Company. All rights reserved.

This "addition" to the main clause can be moved to numerous places within the sentence.

> A written speech is suitable for some occasions; it is likely, *however,* to be very boring when read on social occasions.
>
> OR
>
> A written speech is suitable for some occasions; *however,* it is likely to be very boring when read on social occasions.    [Note that when the conjunctive adverb immediately follows the semicolon the semicolon absorbs the first comma.]

**Caution:**    Be especially careful to use a semicolon between two main clauses not joined by a coordinator when direct quotations are involved.

> "Prepare only an outline for a talk," the instructor suggested; "don't memorize a set of words."

#### 14b  Use the semicolon to separate elements which themselves contain commas.

> The four types of speeches we studied were the written speech, which is read to the audience; the memorized speech, which is first written down and then learned verbatim; the extemporaneous speech, in which a plan, but not the exact words, is often sketched out as a guide; and the impromptu speech, which is made without preparation or advance thought.

#### 14c  Use the semicolon to connect parts of equal grammatical rank, not between a clause and a phrase or between a subordinate clause or a main clause.

A semicolon should not be used between a clause and a phrase or between a main clause and a subordinate clause.

> NOT      He gave an extemporaneous speech; usually the most effective kind.
>
> BUT      He gave an extemporaneous speech, usually the most effective kind.
> [A comma, not a semicolon, is used between the clause and the phrase.]
>
> NOT      The speech sounded entirely natural; although it had been carefully planned.
>
> BUT      The speech sounded entirely natural, although it had been carefully planned.
> [A comma, not a semicolon, is appropriate between the main clause and the subordinate clause.]

    Copyright © 1995 by Harcourt Brace & Company. All rights reserved.

Deduct 5 for each caret incorrectly placed and 5 for each incorrectly filled blank.

**Semicolons Between Main Clauses**　　　　　　　　Exercise 14–1

NAME _____　SCORE _____

DIRECTIONS　In the following sentences insert an inverted caret (**V**) between main clauses and add the semicolon. In the blank, copy the semicolon and any conjunctive adverb or transitional expression that follows it. Be sure to include the comma with the expression if there is one. Write *C* if the sentence is correctly punctuated.

EXAMPLE

You may think that the application process ends when you

leave the interview;however, you still have more to do.　　**; however,**

1. At your interview, you thank the interviewer for talking

with you;you should also write a thank-you letter.　　**;**

2. Personnel directors are busy people;therefore, a letter

that rambles on can annoy your reader.　　**; therefore,**

3. Your thank-you letter shows that you are a considerate

person;employers find this an important trait.　　**;**

4. The thank-you letter provides you with an opportunity

to give more information;the company will never know

those additional facts about you unless you mention

them.　　**;**

5. Interviews always seem too short;for that reason, after

you get home, you will probably think of several points

that you wish you had made.　　**; for that reason,**

6. Your thank-you letter should not sound pushy;it should

not demand a response;it should not be "cute."　　**; ;**

7. However, your thank-you letter could remind the

reader who you are, would continue your contact with

the firm, and could allow you to give more details about

your qualifications.　　**C**

8. You want the company to think that you will be a com-

petent employee;therefore, use this letter to show how

your skills meet this particular company's needs.　　**; therefore,**

Copyright © 1995 by Harcourt Brace & Company. All rights reserved.

9. Once you mail your letter, sit back, wait patiently, and remember that no news is good news.    _____C_____

10. Six weeks may seem a long time to wait for the com-
    pany's response; nevertheless, companies often find it
    necessary to keep you waiting that long for a reply.    _; nevertheless,_

Copyright © 1995 by Harcourt Brace & Company. All rights reserved.

Deduct 2 1/2 for each caret incorrectly placed and 2 1/2 for each incorrectly filled blank.

## Semicolons and Commas

Exercise 14–2

NAME _____ SCORE _____

DIRECTIONS   In each sentence use an inverted caret (**V**) to mark the spot where a comma or a semicolon should go. Insert the correct punctuation mark in the sentence and also write it in the blank. (Some of the sentences will require two commas or semicolons.)

EXAMPLE

An on-site interview includes a visit to your prospective employer's place of
business;while there,you may be asked to give a short talk.   _____ ; , _____

1. Your extemporaneous talk is one you plan and rehearse,yet the actual
   wording of your talk will vary from presentation to presentation.   _____ , _____

2. Extemporaneous speakers generally prepare their presentations in
   advance,but an extemporaneous speech never has a final, unchang-
   ing set of words.   _____ , _____

3. This type of speech may not even be written down;it is,however,
   carefully thought out.   _____ ; , , _____

4. An extemporaneous speech can "instantly" be adapted to match the
   mood of the audience;for this reason,many people try to imagine a
   variety of possible audience responses as they prepare.   _____ ; , _____

5. The extemporaneous speech is a lifesaver if any of these conditions
   occur: the audience is enthusiastic,people look lost or puzzled,or
   someone interrupts by coming in late or asking a question.   _____ , , _____

6. Extemporaneous speakers generally use few notes for their presentations,so they can move about the lecture area more freely than
   they could when delivering a written speech.   _____ , _____

7. Because the speech's phrasing does vary with each presentation,you
   are less likely to sound monotonous,preachy,or uninvolved than you
   might when giving a memorized or written speech;yet the successful extemporaneous speaker still carefully plans and rehearses for
   each presentation beforehand.   _____ , , , ; _____

Copyright © 1995 by Harcourt Brace & Company. All rights reserved.

8. Speaking extemporaneously creates rapport with your listeners; thus, it is a skill that can benefit you as you interview.     _____ ; , _____

9. "What would you like to talk about in your presentation to the interview committee when you visit us," Ms. Getz asked; "what type of presentation do you plan to use?"     _____ , ; _____

10. "I'm going to give an extemporaneous speech that presents the challenges facing information technology in the next two years," I replied.     _____ , _____

Copyright © 1995 by Harcourt Brace & Company. All rights reserved.

## 15

**Use the apostrophe to show possession (except for personal pronouns), to mark omissions in contractions, and to form certain plurals.**

Remember that the apostrophe, in most of its uses, indicates that something has been omitted.

> Won't  [will not]
> We're  [we are]
> the class of '96  [the class of 1996]
> illustrator's drawings  [book *of* or *for* children]

**15a Use the apostrophe to show possession for nouns (including that of acronyms).**

Add either an *'s* or an *'* to form the possessive of nouns and some pronouns.

**(1) For singular nouns (including acronyms and indefinite pronouns), add the apostrophe and an s (*'s*).** (See the list of indefinite pronouns in the Appendix.)

> speaker's duty  [singular possessive; duty of one speaker]
> everyone's  [singular possessive of a pronoun]
> IBM's computer  [singular possessive of an acronym]

**Option:** Although most writers add *'s* to all proper names ending in *s*, some authorities permit adding only the apostrophe:

> Mars' terrain OR Mars's terrain  [singular possessive of a singular noun ending in *s*]

**(2) Add the apostrophe (') to all plural nouns that end in s to indicate the plural possessive case. Add the apostrophe and an s (*'s*) to all plural nouns not ending in s to indicate the plural possessive case.**

> speaker [singular]    speakers [plural]    speakers' [plural possessive]
> secretary [singular]    secretaries [plural]    secretaries' [plural possessive]

If the plural noun does not end in *s*, add the apostrophe and an *s* to show the possessive case.

> man [singular]    men [plural]    men's [plural possessive]
> woman [singular]    women [plural]    women's [plural possessive]
> Women's and men's issues were discussed at the meeting.

**(3) For compounds or to show joint ownership, add the apostrophe and an s only to the last word.**

> sister-in-law's office
> everyone else's raise
> chairman of the board's presentation
> Thelma and Harold's home office.

Copyright © 1995 by Harcourt Brace & Company. All rights reserved.

**(4) To indicate individual ownership, add the apostrophe and an *s* to each name.**

Sam**'**s and Jane**'**s offices   [Sam and Jane have different offices.]

**15b  Use an apostrophe to mark omissions in contractions and in numbers. Remember to place the apostrophe exactly where the omission occurs.**

*It***'***s* [it *is*] the duty of the president of the class of **'**95 [1995] to open the vault.

**Caution:**   The use of contractions is not common in writing unless a conversational tone is sought. For instance, contractions are often used in business letters to make the tone less formal; contractions would, however, not be used in formal business reports.

**15c  Use the apostrophe and *s* to form only certain plurals.**

final k**'**s or ks
1990**'**s or 1990s
V.F.W.**'**s or V.F.W.s
and**'**s or ands

**Caution:**   An apostrophe is never used for plural nouns that are not in the possessive case.

They put up *signs* to direct *visitors* to the right *buildings.*   [not *signs's, visitor's, building's*]

**15d  Personal pronouns and plural nouns that are not possessive do not take an apostrophe.**

Personal pronouns (*I, we, you, she, it, they*) have their own form to indicate possession (*my, our, your, his, hers, its, theirs*).

*Whose* project is this—*yours* or *theirs?*
The car lost *its* brakes.

Copyright © 1995 by Harcourt Brace & Company. All rights reserved.

Deduct 5 for each incorrectly filled blank.

**Making Nouns Possessive**                              Exercise 15–1

NAME _____ SCORE _____

DIRECTIONS   Rewrite each of the following word groups as a noun or a pronoun preceded by another noun or pronoun in the possessive case.

EXAMPLES
the salary of someone
someone's salary
the locations of the cities
the cities' locations

1. facilities belonging to IBM
   IBM's facilities

2. opinions held by people
   people's opinions

3. entries in the index
   the index's entries

4. the operating hours of the new wellness building
   the new wellness building's operating hours

5. the reunion of the Barths
   the Barths' reunion

6. the mailing address of your company
   your company's mailing address

7. the refunds of the customers
   the customers' refunds

8. problems of today
   today's problems

Copyright © 1995 by Harcourt Brace & Company. All rights reserved.

9.  the takeover of the two corporations
    the two corporations' takeover

10. the interpretations of the rule
    the rule's interpretations

11. the tax reports of Ms. Davis
    Ms. Davis's <u>or</u> Davis' tax reports

12. a statement from the ambassador from Mexico
    the ambassador from Mexico's statement

13. the record of the expert
    the expert's records

14. a patent belonging to Louise and Gene
    Louise and Gene's patent

16. the promotion of the men
    the men's promotion

17. concern of laboratory technologists
    the laboratory technologists' concern

18. bankruptcy of the business
    the business's or business' bankruptcy

19. software written by Helen Jones
    Helen Jones' or Jones's software

20. decisions made by us
    our decisions

Copyright © 1995 by Harcourt Brace & Company. All rights reserved.

Deduct 6 1/4 for each error.

## Mastering Apostrophes: A Review

Exercise 15–2

NAME _____ SCORE _____

DIRECTIONS   In the following sentences add all the apostrophes that are needed. Then in the blank enter each word, number, or letter to which you have added an apostrophe. Be careful not to add needless apostrophes.

EXAMPLE
Ms. Franklin, the state of North Carolina's chief conservation

advocate, spoke at the Boone town meeting last night.     _____Carolina's_____

1. Ms. Franklin's talk helped her audience understand its

   place in the conservation movement.     _____Franklin's_____

2. She pointed out that, in the 1990's, a city's inhabitants     1990's or 1990s

   must work together to solve the problem of waste.     _____city's_____

3. "It's not simply that the town's job becomes one of waste

   management," Franklin said; "residents have to be     It's

   involved, too."     _____town's_____

4. "Recycling's not easy, but, for most areas, there are no     Recycling's
   if's or if's
   ifs or when's about this problem," she went on.     when's or whens

5. "This area's landfills now are reaching capacity, and it     area's
   won't
   won't be long before they're full," Franklin warned.     they're

6. She pointed out that soon even towns with populations     100,000's

   below the 100,000's will face such difficulties.     or 100,000s

7. "All the Smiths and Jones of every town in the U.S.

   throw out tons of garbage each year; today's home

   owner is just as responsible for the problems as the

   large industries," she observed.     _____today's_____

8. In an effort to convince her listeners, she concluded

   with her best point: everyone's need to recycle

   materials.     _____everyone's_____

9. "Your hope—and your children's," Ms. Franklin said,

   "will be to make your homes small recycling centers."     _____children's_____

Copyright © 1995 by Harcourt Brace & Company. All rights reserved.

10. Ms. Franklin ended by repeating a timely slogan: "Think globally, act locally"; she hoped it would become her audience's motto as well.

*audience's*

Copyright © 1995 by Harcourt Brace & Company. All rights reserved.

## 16

**Use quotation marks for direct quotations (other than those in indented blocks), for some titles, and for words used in a special sense. Place other marks of punctuation in proper relation to the quotation marks.**

Quotation marks allow you to let your reader know that you are directly quoting (repeating word-for-word) what someone else has written, said, or thought.

> "The board will review the proposal on Tuesday," the memo said.
> "I'll be there," I told my co-worker. But I thought to myself, "With my luck, I'll probably have to be out of town."

**16a Use quotation marks (" ") for direct quotations and in all dialogue. Set off long quotations by indenting without quotation marks.**

**(1) Use double quotation marks (" ") for direct (but not indirect) quotations; use single quotation marks (' ') before and after a quotation within a quotation.**

| | |
|---|---|
| INDIRECT QUOTATION | He asked me if I would speak at the company's board meeting. [*If, whether,* and *that* frequently introduce indirect quotations.] |
| DIRECT QUOTATION | He asked me, "Will you speak at the company's board meeting?" [The indirect quotation is made a direct quotation.] |
| DIRECT QUOTATION | The program for the meeting noted that I was going to discuss "the effects of government regulations on the textile industry." [*The* is not capitalized because only a phrase is being quoted.] |

**Note:** Use single quotation marks (' ') for quotation marks that appear within other quotation marks.

> "The conference 'The Global Marketplace' is going on at the same time as our board meeting," Arnold told me.

**Caution:** In direct quotations, reproduce all quoted material *exactly* as it appears in the original, including capitalization and punctuation. If the material you are quoting contains an error, insert the word *sic* within brackets immediately after the error (See **17g**).

> The report went on to say, "the pipe busted [sic] under the excessive pressure."

**(2) Use quotation marks for dialogue (directly quoting conversation).**

In quoting dialogue (conversation), a new paragraph begins each time the speaker changes.

Copyright © 1995 by Harcourt Brace & Company. All rights reserved.

"I guess I'll have to miss the conference," I said.

"Had you planned to go before the board scheduled its meeting?" Arnold asked me, knowing that I have a deep interest in international business and would be sorry to miss such a meeting.

"Well," I responded, "I mailed in my registration fees and application to be a panel moderator two months ago."

**Note:**  When quoting more than one paragraph by one speaker, put quotation marks at the beginning of each new paragraph, but at the end of only the last paragraph.

**Note:**  Commas set off expressions like he said that introduce, interrupt, or follow direct quotations.

The secretary said, "Mr. Jones can't come to the meeting either."

"Mr. Jones can't come to the meeting either," the secretary said.

"Mr. Jones," the secretary said, "can't come to the meeting either."

**Caution:**  Remember that a divided quotation made up of two main clauses or two complete sentences must be punctuated with a semicolon or an end mark.

"Every time they try to convene the review board, this happens," she said; "I have to find someone to go in his place."

OR

"Every time they try to convene the review board, this happens," she said. "I have to find someone to go in his place."

**(3) Set off thoughts with double quotation marks, just as if they were stated.**

"I sure hope I get that account," I thought as I walked into their office.

**(4) Set off long quotations of prose and poetry by indention. Run short quotations into the text.**

**Prose**  If the material that you quote is one paragraph or less, all lines of a long quotation (more than four lines) are indented ten spaces from the left margin and are double-spaced. When you quote two or more paragraphs, indent the first line of each paragraph thirteen rather than ten spaces. Use quotation marks only if they appear in the original.

In <u>Communication for Management and Business</u>, Norman B. Sigband and Arthur H. Bell discuss the business meeting as an important means by which companies do such things as set long-range goals, plan marketing strategies, and consider policy changes.

> An effective meeting is a forum where knowledgeable individuals come together to solve organizational problems through open and participative communication. It is a place where the will to work

Copyright © 1995 by Harcourt Brace & Company. All rights reserved.

together is developed. It is also a group session that participants

find exciting and provocative; it's one where every member who

has something to say is heard; it's one where everyone is on an

equal level; it's one where decisions are reached (2).

**Poetry**   You may run fewer than four lines of poetry into the text. When run in, double quotation marks should begin and end the material, and a slash mark should be placed at the end of each line.

W. H. Auden's poem, "The Unknown Citizen," has to do with the common

working man: "And all the reports on his conduct agree / That, in the modern

sense of an old-fashioned word, he was a saint, / For in everything he did he

served the Greater Community."

More than four quoted lines of poetry are treated in the same manner as lengthy prose passages.

W. H. Auden's poem, "The Unknown Citizen," has to do with the common

working man:

He was found by the Bureau of Statistics to be

One against whom there was no official complaint,

And all the reports on his conduct agree

That, in the modern sense of an old-fashioned word, he was

a saint,

For in everything he did he served the Greater Community.

**16b  Use quotation marks for minor titles (short stories, short poems, essays, songs, articles in periodicals, and episodes of a radio or television series) and for subdivisions of books.**

The article "Speak Up for Success" appeared in a recent issue of Weekend Worker.

**Note:**   The title of the periodical, Weekend Worker, is italicized. (See also Chapter **10**.)

Copyright © 1995 by Harcourt Brace & Company. All rights reserved.

## 16c  Used sparingly, quotation marks may enclose words intended in a special or ironic sense.

**"**Work**"** for him means anything that he dislikes doing. (See also **10d**.)

**Note:**  Either quotation marks or italics may be used in definitions such as the following: **"**Jargon**"** means anything that a nontechnical reader is likely to find unclear or confusing.

**Caution:**  Avoid the tendency that some writers have of using quotation marks freely to call attention to clever phrasings. Many times what these writers consider to be clever ways of saying something are really only trite sayings, slang expressions, or colloquialisms that could best be stated in another way. (See also **20c**.)

| | |
|---|---|
| INEFFECTIVE | The sales representative thought he was a **"**hot shot,**"** but the rest of us knew that, if he kept acting irresponsibly, he'd be **"**given the pink slip**"** soon. |
| EFFECTIVE | The sales representative thought that he was very successful, but the rest of us knew that, if he kept acting irresponsibly, he'd be fired soon. |

## 16d  Do not overuse quotation marks.

Quotation marks are not used for titles of compositions, nor are they used to enclose a cliché or to mark a yes or no answer in indirect discourse.

| | |
|---|---|
| NOT | "No," he didn't feel that he had a "ghost of a chance." |
| BUT | No, he didn't feel that he had a ghost of a chance. |

## 16e  When using various marks of punctuation with quoted words, phrases, or sentences, follow the conventions of American printers.

**(1) Place the comma within the quotation marks. Place the period within the quotation marks if the quotation ends the sentence.**

"Well**,**" he said, "I'm ready to finish writing the report**.**"

**(2) Place the semicolon and the colon outside the quotation marks.**

The speaker pointed out that "big business is now beginning to speak out against over-regulation"**;** indeed, it is doing more than simply speaking out.
She looked at the folder marked "Confidential"**:** "Not to leave the Personnel Office."

**(3) Place the question mark, the exclamation point, and the dash within the quotation marks when they apply only to the quoted material. Place them outside when they do not.**

Have you read "Is Government Regulation Crippling Business**?**"  [The question mark applies to the quoted matter as well as to the entire sentence.]
Have you read "Arsenic and Old Factories"**?**  [The question mark does not apply to the quoted matter.]

Copyright © 1995 by Harcourt Brace & Company. All rights reserved.

Deduct 10 for each blank incorrectly filled.

**Quotation Marks** Exercise 16–1

NAME _____ SCORE _____

DIRECTIONS In the sentences below insert all needed quotation marks. In the blanks enter the quotation marks and the first and last word of each quoted part. Include other marks of punctuation used with the quotation marks, and place them in proper position—either inside or outside the quotation marks. Do not enclose an indirect quotation. Write C in the blank to indicate a sentence that is correct without quotation marks.

EXAMPLE

Gray Lanier's oral report entitled "How Much Regulation Is Too Much?" was of special interest to the business majors in the audience.

_____"How...much?"_____

1. Gray began her report with what she termed "essential background information."

"essential...information."
or
"essential background information."

2. She pointed out that seventy-five years ago business was concerned about the government's stand on monopolies.

_____C_____

3. "Then a decade or so later," Gray explained, "the main issue that disturbed business was unionism."

"Then...later," "the...unionism."

4. "What is the major concern of business today?" Gray asked.

"What...today?"

5. "Clearly, it is federal regulation," Gray responded to her rhetorical question.

"Clearly...regulation,"

6. For decades the public screamed, "Give us protection from big business!"

"Give...business!"

Copyright © 1995 by Harcourt Brace & Company. All rights reserved.

7. "After reading an article like 'Is Government Regulation Crippling Business?' one sees how strong big business's response has been," Gray stated.

      *"After...'Is...Business?'...been,"*

8. Gray went on to report that a bureaucracy of eighty thousand people was established to protect consumers and workers from injury.

      *C*

9. "The many agencies created by the government to act as the public's voice have had much success, especially in the area of pollution controls," Gray said.

      *"The...controls,"*

10. "But," Gray went on, "business also has its side, as exemplified in its complaint, 'The standards set by government agencies are too confusing and costly to result in significant benefits to the American consumer.' "

      *"But,"..."business...*
      *'The...consumer.' "*

Copyright © 1995 by Harcourt Brace & Company. All rights reserved.

## 17

**Use the end marks of punctuation—the period, the question mark, and the exclamation—and the internal marks of punctuation—the colon, the dash, parentheses, brackets, ellipsis points, and the slash—in accordance with conventional practices.** (For the use of the hyphen, see **18f**.)

Two spaces follow the period, question mark, exclamation point, and four-dot ellipsis points; one space follows the colon, the ending parenthesis and bracket, and each of the dots in three-space ellipsis points. No spaces follow the hyphen or dash.

End punctuation marks cause most writers little difficulty except when they must use these marks with direct quotations.

### 17a  Use the period as an end mark and with some abbreviations.

| | |
|---|---|
| DECLARATIVE SENTENCE | Samuel Foster, head of our Communication Arts Department, decided that it would be a good idea for students to learn how to use audio-visual equipment. |
| MILDLY IMPERATIVE SENTENCE | Learn how to use VCRs and projectors. |
| INDIRECT QUESTION | Foster asked Dr. Lee if he thought it would be a worthwhile workshop. |
| ABBREVIATION | Dr. Lee agreed to discuss integrating the use of visual equipment into an oral report. |

**Note:**  Declarative sentences may contain direct questions.

> Will the students already know this material? was a common question.  [No period follows the question mark and no quotation marks enclose the question.]

### 17b  Use the question mark after direct (but not indirect) questions.

What did Dr. Lee say?
She asked me what Dr. Lee said.

### 17c  Use the exclamation point after an emphatic interjection and after other expressions showing strong emotion, such as surprise or disbelief.

What an interesting presentation Dr. Lee made!
"Bravo!" some people in the audience responded.

**Caution:**  Do not use exclamation points to make your writing sound exciting or important. Rather, use exclamation points sparingly, and only to follow those sentences that do express strong emotion.

Copyright © 1995 by Harcourt Brace & Company. All rights reserved.

**Other Punctuation Marks**   Of the marks that do not appear at the end of a sentence (internal punctuation marks), the semicolon (see Chapter **14**), the colon, and the dash are closely related to the period because they cause the reader to stop—rather than to pause as they would at a comma.

**17d  Use the colon as a formal introducer to call attention to what follows and as a mark of separation in time and scriptural references and between titles and subtitles.**

**(1)  The colon directs attention to what follows: an explanation or summary, a series, or a quotation.**

>Dr. Lee explained the importance of visual aids in an oral presentation: either they are absolutely necessary to save words, or they add interest and variety to the speech.   [The second main clause explains the first one.]
>
>Dr. Lee named the purposes of adding visual aids to a speech: clarity, variety, and reinforcement.   [The list explains purposes.]
>
>Dr. Lee explained: "Visual aids save many words in an oral presentation. They often show in one picture or graph what could require fifteen minutes of speaking to explain." [The colon, rather than the comma, is used because the quotation runs for more than one sentence.]

**(2)  Use the colon between figures in time references and between titles and subtitles.**

>The presentation using visual aids is scheduled for 3:30 p.m.
>
>The book, *Working with Words, Teaching with Pictures: Presenting Your Ideas Clearly with Visual Aids*, is a helpful reference tool.

**Note:**   Many writers prefer to use the colon in scriptural references: She referred her friend to Psalms 3:5; however, MLA style recommends periods (Psalms 3.5) and recent Biblical scholarship uses this form.

**(3)  Do not use superfluous colons.**

In particular, avoid unnecessary colons, especially between verbs and their complements, prepositions and their objects, or after *such as*.

>NOT       Three reasons for using visual aids are: clarity, variety, and reinforcement.
>
>BUT       Three reasons for using visual aids are clarity, variety, and reinforcement.
>
>OR        Visual aids add three things to an oral report: clarity, variety, and reinforcement.

**17e  Use the dash to mark a break in thought, to set off a parenthetical element for emphasis or clarity, and to set off an introductory series.** (See also **17f.**)

>Clarity, variety, and reinforcement—these are three purposes of visual aids.   [The dash sets off an introductory series.]
>
>These three purposes—clarity, variety and reinforcement—are served by visual aids. [The list sets off a parenthetical element for emphasis.]

   Copyright © 1995 by Harcourt Brace & Company. All rights reserved.

Dr. Lee recommended—in fact, more than recommended—that we practice our oral presentations with the visual aids included.   [The dash marks an interruption or break in thought.]

**Caution:**   Use dashes sparingly and not as lazy substitutes for commas, semicolons, or end marks.

## 17f  Use parentheses to set of parenthetical, supplementary, or illustrative matter and to enclose figures or letters used for numbering.

Dr. Lee urged all of us to learn how to operate the various kinds of projectors (all available in our department) while we are studying oral reports.

We could use (1) opaque projectors, (2) filmstrip projectors, or (3) slide projectors.

**Note:**   Three marks of punctuation are used to set off matter which might be called parenthetical—that is, supplementary, incidental, or illustrative. The most commonly used are commas, which cause the reader only to pause and so see the parenthetical matter as closely related to the main idea of the sentence. Less frequently used are parentheses (which diminish the importance of the matter they set off). Dashes—which create a sharp visual break in the sentences—tend to emphasize what they set off. (Dashes or parentheses rather than commas may be necessary for clarity when the parenthetical matter itself includes commas.)

The computer, unlike any other labor-saving machine, affects every aspect of modern business practice.   [Commas would be used by most writers to set off this parenthetical matter because the information within commas is so closely related to the rest of the sentence.]

The computer (unlike any other labor-saving machine) affects every aspect of modern business practice.   [Parentheses minimize the importance of the parenthetical matter.]

The computer—unlike any other labor-saving device—affects every aspect of modern business practice.   [Dashes emphasize the parenthetical matter.]

Many factors—such as length of workday, time of shift, and occupational hazards—affect most people's attitudes toward their jobs.   [The dashes are needed for clarity to enclose the parenthetical matter that contains commas. Parentheses could also be used, but they would de-emphasize the list, whereas dashes emphasize it.]

### Punctuation of Parenthetical Matter

A writer may select a dash, parentheses, or commas to set off parenthetical material; each mark denotes a different degree of emphasis. Commas separate elements, usually without emphasizing them:

Computers help people generate a number of different graphics, including slides, overhead transparencies, and printed graphs.

Parentheses usually de-emphasize the material they enclose:

People who use visual aids (tables, charts, graphs) in their formal presentations usually practice incorporating them in their talk beforehand.

Copyright © 1995 by Harcourt Brace & Company. All rights reserved.

Dashes set off parenthetical elements and are used to emphasize such material:

> Not taking the time to practice talking from your visuals can have an effect on the quality of your presentation—often a disastrous one.

**17g  Brackets set off editorial comments, additions, or substitutions included within quoted matter. They may also serve as parentheses within parentheses.**

When you need to insert an explanation in a quotation, enclose your explanation in brackets to show that your words are not a part of the quoted matter.

> Dr. Lee explained, "They [visual aids] can cause difficulties if you have not practiced using them ahead of time."
>
> "Many insecure managers believe that [employees] should be constantly criticized to keep them on their toes."  [For clarity, the bracketed employees replaces the pronoun they which appeared in the original sentence.]
>
> A person in the audience yelled, "I seen [sic] it with my own eyes."  [Sic indicates something that was said or written which is not the standard word expected.]

**17h  Use the slash between terms to indicate that either term is applicable and to mark line divisions of quoted poetry.** (See also **16b**.)

> Most technical writing departments have an opaque and/or overhead projector available for classroom use.

**Note:**  No space precedes or follows the slash when indicating options.

> Those who believe in the necessity of work would disagree with Ezra Pound's lines "Sing we for love and idleness, / Naught else is worth the having."

**Note:**  One space precedes and follows the slash that marks breaks between lines of poetry.

> 11/24/48 MEANING November 24, 1948

**Note:**  No space precedes or follows the slashes in dates.

**Note:**  Extensive use of the slash to indicate that either of two terms is applicable (as in and/or or he/she) tends to make your writing choppy and should, therefore, be avoided.

**17i  Use ellipsis points (three equally spaced periods) to mark an omission from a quoted passage.**

> Dr. Lee explained, "Visual aids . . . often show in one picture or graph what would require fifteen minutes of speaking to explain."

 Copyright © 1995 by Harcourt Brace & Company. All rights reserved.

If ellipsis points are used to indicate that the end of a quoted sentence is being omitted, and if the part that is quoted forms a complete sentence itself, use the sentence period plus ellipsis points.

Dr. Lee asked if he would discuss ways to integrate visual equipment. . . .

**Note:** The ellipsis points are used in addition to the period; thus, you should leave no space after the last word in the sentence, as illustrated above.

Copyright © 1995 by Harcourt Brace & Company. All rights reserved.

Deduct 10 for each incorrect sentence.

**End Marks of Punctuation** Exercise 17–1

NAME _____ SCORE _____

DIRECTIONS   Write a sentence to illustrate each of the following uses of end marks and other of punctuation.

EXAMPLE
a quoted direct question
Kerry asked Dr. Lee, "Can I use a flip chart to illustrate this concept?"

1. a declarative sentence containing brackets

2. a sentence containing an abbreviation

3. an indirect question

4. an exclamation

5. a declarative sentence containing dashes

6. a mildly imperative sentence

Copyright © 1995 by Harcourt Brace & Company. All rights reserved.

7. a quotation that includes an ellipsis

8. a direct question

9. a declarative sentence containing a colon used to introduce a list

10. a declarative sentence containing parentheses

   Copyright © 1995 by Harcourt Brace & Company. All rights reserved.

Deduct 5 for each blank incorrectly filled.

**Internal Marks of Punctuation** Exercise 17–2

NAME _____ SCORE _____

DIRECTIONS    In each sentence use a caret (∧) to mark the spot where punctuation should be inserted. Then write the correct punctuation mark in the sentence at that spot and also in the blank. Some sentences will require punctuation in two places; in that case, write both marks of punctuation in the blank. This exercise includes not only the punctuation marks discussed in Chapter **17** but also the comma (Chapter **12**) and the semicolon (Chapter **14**).

EXAMPLE

Clarity, as well as visibility, is important in planning visual aids for an

oral report.                                                                    __,_,__

1.  Readers of a written report can study its visual aid as long as they

    need to, audiences have only a short time to understand a visual aid

    that is used in an oral report.                                            ___;___

2.  Since the audience has only a short time to study it, the visual should

    be kept simple.                                                            ___,___

3.  The speaker can simplify the visual aid in several ways, by eliminat-

    ing all but the absolutely necessary information, by using block

    diagrams, and by labeling graphs rather than using symbols or

    difficult abbreviations.                                                   _: or —_

4.  The speaker can also simplify by showing only trends, not exact

    numbers, in a graph.                                                       __,_,__

5.  A clear, simple table is far better in an oral presentation than is a

    table with many columns in small print.                                    ___,___

6.  Most visuals in books are too complex to be clear to an audience;

    therefore, you should resist the temptation to make transparencies

    of them just as they are.                                                  __;_,__

7.  To make a transparency based on a chart found in a book, you must

    eliminate a great deal of information and rewrite the remaining

    information in large letters.                                              ___,___

8.  One other criterion is important in creating good visual aids:

    audience control.                                                          _: or —_

Copyright © 1995 by Harcourt Brace & Company. All rights reserved.

9. Effective visual aids will help you to control an audience; on the other hand, poorly made ones will distract from your speech.  _____;_____

10. Even well-planned visuals can distract from your presentation if they are in front of an audience for the entire speech; consequently, they should be removed after, or covered before and after, you have made use of them.  _____;_____

11. Visual materials that are passed around the audience can, as you might guess, be especially distracting.  _____,  ,_____

12. You cannot control the visuals you pass around; the audience may examine them and ignore what you are saying.  ____: or ;____

13. Only a visual, then, that can be quickly removed when you are finished with it gives you audience control.  _____,  ,_____

14. If you can change or add to the material presented in a visual, you have even more control over the visual and, consequently, over the audience.  _____,_____

15. In addition to movies, slides, and transparencies, there are several simpler devices for displaying visual aids; for example, blackboards, posters, and flannel boards.  ____: or —____

16. Blackboards some people ignore such obvious kinds of visuals are a readily available visual aid.  ____— —____

17. Blackboards offer the speaker many advantages; they are easy to use; they do not require much preparation; and they hold the audience's attention as you write and draw on them.  _____:_____

18. They do have one major drawback; they may require a great deal of your time during the oral presentation.  _____:_____

19. Blackboards will present difficulties if you do not draw or write legibly, if you cannot draw and talk at the same time, or if you talk to the blackboard instead of to the audience.  __,  , or ; ;__

20. Still the blackboard, even in this technological age, is one of a speaker's best methods of presenting visual aids.  _____,  ,_____

Copyright © 1995 by Harcourt Brace & Company. All rights reserved.

Deduct 5 for misplaced punctuation and 5 for each blank incorrectly filled.

## Mastering Punctuation: A Review                    Exercise 17–3

NAME _____    SCORE _____

DIRECTIONS   In the sentences below use a caret (∧) to indicate where the correct end marks or internal punctuation marks—periods, question marks, exclamation points, colons, dashes, parentheses, brackets, and slashes—should go. Insert the punctuation mark in the correct place in the sentence and write it in the blank. In several sentences more than one kind of punctuation mark is possible.

EXAMPLE

According to Professor James Connally, there are certain criteria for

judging the value of visuals: visibility, simplicity, and control.        : or —

1. Visibility is an obvious criterion: if your audience cannot see your

   visual aid, they cannot gain anything from it.                          :

2. There are certain visuals, for example, a small photograph, a typed

   page, and a page from a book, that are too small to be seen beyond

   the first row.                                                          — —

3. Transparencies and large hand-lettered posters can be seen by the

   audience if the speaker prepares his/her visuals correctly.             /

4. There is a simple rule for lettering: letters should be at least 1 inch

   high for each 25 feet of distance between the visual and the

   audience.                                                               :

5. No rule for the size of other elements, drawings, photographs, and

   graphs, can be given.                                                   — —

6. The best advice that can be given is that you should set up the

   visuals (note the list in sentence 5) and move to the back row to see

   whether they are clearly visible from that distance.                    ( )

7. "Can you see your visuals from the back row?" I was asked by my

   instructor after I had set them up.                                     ?

8. "No!" I shouted back to her.                                            !

9. "Remember the instructions I gave you," she said. "If you cannot

   see the visuals, then the audience can't either."                       . .

Copyright © 1995 by Harcourt Brace & Company. All rights reserved.

10. In my self-evaluation I wrote, "I wonder what my audience would
    have thought if I had used the ones⎣visuals⎦I first prepared?"      _____ [ ] _____

Copyright © 1995 by Harcourt Brace & Company. All rights reserved.

Deduct 10 for each incorrect sentence.

**Mastering Punctuation: A Review**                    Exercise 17–4

NAME _____ SCORE _____

DIRECTIONS   For each of the following items, write a sentence using the punctuation that is needed to illustrate the item. If you need help punctuating your sentences, refer to the rule or rules indicated in parentheses.

EXAMPLE
a list in the middle of a sentence (**17e**)

Three main criteria—visibility, clarity, and control—
   determine the worth of a visual aid.

1.  a quotation of two or more sentences introduced by an expression like you said (**17d**)

2.  two main clauses not joined by a coordinating conjunction (**14a**)

3.  a break or interruption of the thought in the middle of a sentence (**17e**)

4.  a quotation with an editorial comment or explanation inserted (**17g**)

5.  a nonrestrictive clause (**12d**)

6.  supplementary or illustrative information in the middle of a sentence (**17f**)

7.  a declarative sentence with a quoted direct question (**16e, 17b**)

Copyright © 1995 by Harcourt Brace & Company. All rights reserved.

8.  a list or a series following a main clause (**17d**)

9.  an indirect quotation (**16a**)

10. a sentence that has a quotation within a quotation (**16a**)

Copyright © 1995 by Harcourt Brace & Company. All rights reserved.

# SPELLING AND HYPHENATION                    sp  18

## 18

**Spell every word according to established usage as shown by your dictionary. Hyphenate words in accordance with current usage.**

### Spelling

Misspelled words abound: a sign for the "Enterance" to a shopping mall or one marking "Handicap" parking. And, unfortunately, most people label the sign painter *and* the business owner as uneducated. No other mistake is so readily picked out and ridiculed as a spelling error. Moreover, in the business world, poor spelling can severely disadvantage otherwise talented people by making others view them as unprofessional, inaccurate, inconsiderate, and, at the worst extreme, illiterate. Since written communications are often the only contact that a businessperson may have with an associate or client, correcting bad spelling habits is a must. The same holds true for the college classroom.

If you are a poor speller, one who regularly misspells enough words to have your classwork or professional work graded down, you should begin a definite program for improving your spelling skills. There are many excellent spelling manuals available today that make use of the latest psychological studies to present words in a logical, easy-to-learn order. You may also find the following procedures helpful:

**(1)  Learn the rules of spelling that are presented in this chapter.**

**(2)  Proofread your papers carefully at least once for misspelled words only.**

As you write a rough draft, it is often difficult, and always distracting, to look up a great number of words; but you can put a check or some other identifying sign above those words you have any doubts about so that you can look up their spelling when you proofread.

If spelling is a particular problem for you, you may wish to slow down your proofreading by looking at your work a word at a time, pointing to each one with your pen or pencil. Placing a ruler or sheet of paper below the line you are reading also helps to focus your attention. And reading from bottom to top of the page or from right to left will also force you to pay attention to individual words, one by one. Finally, as you revise, be sure to write out a clean intermediate draft whenever possible since spotting spelling errors can be difficult in a text covered with corrections and cross-outs or one that is written in a hurried scrawl.

**(3)  Keep a list of the words you misspell.**

The words that you misspell on your writing assignments should be recorded in the Individual Spelling List at the end of this *Workbook*. Since most people have a tendency to misspell certain words repeatedly, you should update the list frequently as you revise.

Copyright © 1995 by Harcourt Brace & Company. All rights reserved.

**(4) Write by syllables the words you misspell; then write the definitions of the words; finally, use the words in sentences.**

e•nig•mat•ic     puzzling or baffling
The report was enigmatic until I looked up words whose meanings I did not know.

pro•pen•si•ty     a natural inclination or tendency
My supervisor has a propensity for making spot-checks.

**(5) Learn to spell these words, which are commonly used in business and professional writing.**

| | | | |
|---|---|---|---|
| absence | correspondence | influential | proceed |
| accommodate | correspondent | initiate | professional |
| accomplish | courteous | insistence | prominent |
| achievement | decision | interrupt | quantity |
| acquainted | defendant | judgment | questionnaire |
| address | dependent | OR judgement | receipt |
| annual | description | knowledge | receive |
| answer | desirable | labeled | recognize |
| apparatus | development | laboratory | recommend |
| apparent | difference | library | reference |
| appropriate | disadvantage | lien | referred |
| argument | dissatisfied | maintenance | repetition |
| arrangement | division | management | rescind |
| article | efficient | maneuver | resistance |
| attach | eligible | manual | respectfully |
| attendance | eliminate | medicine | restaurant |
| attorney | envelope | mortgage | salary |
| balance | equipment | necessary | schedule |
| basically | especially | noticeable | secretarial |
| beginning | essential | occasion | separate |
| brochure | excellent | occurred | serviceable |
| bureaucracy | experience | opinion | similar |
| business | familiar | opportunity | sincerely |
| calculator | February | original | stationary |
| calendar | financial | pamphlet | stationery |
| catalog | foreman | parallel | strategy |
| category | fundamental | possess | succeed |
| characteristic | generally | practical | superintendent |
| college | government | precede | technician |
| committee | guarantee | prefer | technique |
| competition | height | prepare | tendency |
| concede | identify | presence | thorough |
| congratulate | immediately | prevalent | unusual |
| consensus | incessant | probably | |
| convenience | indispensable | procedure | |

Copyright © 1995 by Harcourt Brace & Company. All rights reserved.

**(6) Learn the different meanings for these confusing words.**

accept, except
access, excess
adapt, adopt
advice, advise
affect, effect
aisles, isles
alley, ally
allude, elude
allusion, illusion
already, all ready
altar, alter
altogether, all together
always, all ways
angel, angle
ascent, assent
assistance, assistants
baring, barring, bearing
birth, berth
board, bored
born, borne
break, brake
breath, breathe
buy, by
canvas, canvass
capital, capitol
censor, censure, sensor
choose, chose
cite, sight, site
clothes, cloths
coarse, course
complement, compliment
conscience, conscious
council, counsel
credible, creditable
cursor, curser
dairy, diary
decent, descent, dissent
desert, dessert
detract, distract
device, devise
dominant, dominate
dual, duel
dyeing, dying
elicit, illicit
envelop, envelope
fair, fare
faze, phase
formerly, formally
forth, fourth
forward, foreword
gorilla, guerrilla
hear, here

heard, herd
heroin, heroine
hoarse, horse
hole, whole
holy, wholly
human, humane
instance, instants
its, it's
later, latter
led, lead
lessen, lesson
lightening, lightning
lose, loose
maybe, may be
minor, miner
moral, morale
of, off
passed, past
patience, patients
peace, piece
persecute, prosecute
personal, personnel
perspective, prospective
plain, plane
pray, prey
precede, proceed
predominant, predominate
presence, presents
principal, principle
prophecy, prophesy
purpose, propose
quiet, quit
respectfully, respectively
right, rite, write
road, rode
sense, since
shone, shown
stationary, stationery
statue, stature, statute
straight, strait
taut, taunt
than, then
their, there, they're
thorough, through
to, too, two
track, tract
waist, waste
weak, week
weather, whether
were, where
who's, whose
your, you're

Copyright © 1995 by Harcourt Brace & Company. All rights reserved.

**(7) Invest in a good spelling dictionary.**

A spelling dictionary is a small, inexpensive book that gives only the spelling and syllable breaks for each word. It will make looking up words faster and easier.

**(8) If you use a word processor, use its spelling checker.**

The spell-check feature of a word processing program will help you to catch many spelling errors (except for words that are misused rather than misspelled, for example, accept and except). If your word processor does not offer a spelling check option, you can still use your computer in this way by purchasing a compatible spell-check program, a software package that can evaluate texts written in a variety of word processing programs. Your spelling checker can help you learn to be a better speller simply because it will call your attention to the mistakes you are making and because such programs require you to select the correct word to replace the misspelling.

Copyright © 1995 by Harcourt Brace & Company. All rights reserved.

Deduct 2 1/2 for each incorrectly filled blank.

# Misspelling Caused by Mispronunciation

Exercise 18–1

NAME _____ SCORE _____

### 18a  Do not misspell a word because of mispronunciation.

To avoid omitting, adding, transposing, or changing a letter in a word, pronounce the word carefully according to the way your dictionary divides it into syllables.

The places where common mistakes are made in pronunciation—and spelling—are indicated in **boldface.**

| | |
|---|---|
| OMISSIONS | can**di**date, every**thing**, govern**m**ent, of**t**en |
| ADDITIONS | ath**l**ete, laun**d**ry, drown**e**d |
| TRANSPOSITIONS | per**f**orm, child**re**n, trag**ed**y |
| CHANGE | acc**u**rate, prej**u**dice, sep**a**rate |

DIRECTIONS    With the aid of your dictionary, write out each of the following words by syllables, indicate the position of the primary accent, and pronounce the word correctly and distinctly. (Different dictionaries vary in the way they divide words into syllables. You may find that in a few cases your word divisions differ from someone else's.) Avoid any careless omission, addition, transposition, or change in your pronunciation.

EXAMPLE
similar          sim´ • i • lar

| | | | |
|---|---|---|---|
| 1. privilege | priv´ • i • lege | 14. different | dif´ • fer • ent |
| 2. supposedly | sup • pos´ • ed • ly | 15. scissors | scis´ • sors |
| 3. knowledge | knowl´ • edge | 16. surprise | sur • prise´ |
| 4. asked | asked | 17. receipt | re • ceipt´ |
| 5. February | Feb´ • ru • ary | 18. accidentally | ac • ci • den´ • tal • ly |
| 6. especially | es • pe´ • cial • ly | 19. escape | es • cape´ |
| 7. sophomore | soph´ • o • more | 20. destruction | de • struc´ • tion |
| 8. used | used | 21. prisoner | pris´ • o • ner |
| 9. partner | part´ • ner | 22. perhaps | per • haps´ |
| 10. interest | in´ • ter • est | 23. represent | rep • re • sent´ |
| 11. family | fam´ • i • ly | 24. prepare | pre • pare´ |
| 12. pamphlet | pam´ • phlet | 25. environment | en • vi´ • ron • ment |
| 13. mirror | mir´ • ror | 26. library | li´ • brar • y |

Copyright © 1995 by Harcourt Brace & Company. All rights reserved.

27. describe     de • scribe′

28. congratulate     con • grat′ • u • late

29. candidate     can′ • di • date

30. recognize     rec′ • og • nize

31. interpret     in • ter′ • pret

32. athletic     ath • let′ • ic

33. hindrance     hin′ • drance

34. professor     pro • fes′ • sor

35. hungry     hun′ • gry

36. mischievous     mis′ • chie • vous

37. circumstance     cir′ • cum • stance

38. prescription     pre • scrip′ • tion

39. temperament     tem′ • per • a • ment

40. further     fur′ • ther

Copyright © 1995 by Harcourt Brace & Company. All rights reserved.

Deduct 4 for each incorrectly filled blank.

# Confusion of Words Similar in Sound and/or Spelling    Exercise 18–2

NAME _____ SCORE _____

**18b Distinguish between words that have a similar sound or spelling. Use the spelling required by the word's meaning in the context of the sentence.**

| | | |
|---|---|---|
| affect—effect | emigrate from— | principal—principle |
| a lot—allot |     immigrate to | quiet—quit—quite |
| already—all ready | eminent—imminent | raise—rise |
| altogether—all together | everyone—every one | respective—respectful |
| allusion—illusion | imply—infer | sensuous—sensual |
| anyone—any one | later—latter | someone—some one |
| awhile—a while | lay—lie | stationary—stationery |
| censor—censure | liable—likely | their—there—they're |
| complementary— | lose—loose | then—than |
|     complimentary | may be—maybe | to—too—two |
| conscious—conscience | morale—moral | your—you're |
| continual—continuous | off—of | |

(Make a note of words you misuse on the Individual Spelling List on page 458.)

DIRECTIONS   In the following sentences cross out the spelling or spellings in parentheses that do not fit the meaning, and write the correct spelling in the blank at the right. Consult your dictionary freely.

EXAMPLE
(Their, ~~There, They're~~) loan did not go through.     _____Their_____

1. With the growth of large corporations, the success rate of small businesses is bound to (~~altar~~, alter).     _____alter_____

2. Economic ups and downs have less of an (~~affect~~, effect) on diversified conglomerates.     _____effect_____

3. People find this change hard to (accept, ~~except~~).     _____accept_____

4. Today, managing a successful cottage industry (~~presence~~, presents) many potential problems.     _____presents_____

5. People who think they can make a living making and selling crafts are often in for (~~quiet, quit~~, quite) a surprise.     _____quite_____

Copyright © 1995 by Harcourt Brace & Company. All rights reserved.

6. The (principal, ~~principle~~) difficulty they encounter is
   finding a market for their goods.                                    _principal_

7. Many people are not (~~holey~~, wholly, ~~holy~~) convinced
   that individually crafted goods are worth the higher
   prices their makers charge.                                          _wholly_

8. A pessimist might (prophesy, ~~prophecy~~) the eventual
   death of handmade goods.                                             _prophesy_

9. Others find this forecast (~~to~~, too, ~~two~~) gloomy.              _too_

10. Some theorists think that greedy consumerism often
    (precedes, ~~proceeds~~) an economic recession.                     _precedes_

11. Too much credit card buying can signal a (~~week~~, weak)
    economy.                                                            _weak_

12. But most consumers are not (~~conscience~~, conscious) of
    these early warning signals.                                        _conscious_

13. Is there any (~~advise~~, advice) to offer the average
    businessperson?                                                     _advice_

14. Traditional theories (passed, ~~past~~) over some factors
    that contributed to the most recent recession.                     _passed_

15. This represents one (~~instants~~, instance) of the complex
    nature of a global economy.                                        _instance_

16. By the time experts could evaluate all the data, the
    deadline had (~~all ready~~, already) passed.                       _already_

17. But an economy never becomes truly (~~stationery~~,
    stationary).                                                        _stationary_

18. Even so, the reasons for its shifts continue to (elude,
    ~~allude~~) analysts and investors.                                 _elude_

19. (It's, ~~Its~~) one thing to talk about economic instability
    and quite another to pinpoint its causes.                          _It's_

20. Some people would rather complain (~~then~~, than) try to
    find solutions to the problems.                                    _than_

Copyright © 1995 by Harcourt Brace & Company. All rights reserved.

21. Everyone seems to have (~~ideals,~~ ideas) about how to improve the economy.

      ideas

22. But ideas do little to lift the (morale, ~~moral~~) of people whose businesses collapse.

      morale

23. (Whether, ~~Weather~~) one runs a cottage industry or a large corporation, profits still matter.

      Whether

24. The desire to compete can (~~led,~~ lead) people into new business ventures.

      lead

25. Those who do not overestimate their potential for success will be the ones who do not (~~loose,~~ lose).

      lose

Copyright © 1995 by Harcourt Brace & Company. All rights reserved.

Deduct 3 for each incorrectly filled blank.

## Addition of Prefixes

Exercise 18–3

NAME _____ SCORE _____

### 18c  Distinguish between the prefix and the root.

The root is the base word to which a prefix or a suffix is added.

| | | | | | | | |
|---|---|---|---|---|---|---|---|
| dis- | + | agree | = disagree | over- | + | active | = overactive |
| im- | + | mortal | = immortal | re- | + | place | = replace |
| ir- | + | responsible | = irresponsible | un- | + | necessary | = unnecessary |
| mis- | + | spent | = misspent | under- | + | developed | = underdeveloped |

DIRECTIONS   In the blank at the right enter the correct spelling of each word with the prefix added. Consult your dictionary freely. Some dictionaries may hyphenate some of the following words. (See also **18f(3)**.)

EXAMPLES

| | | | |
|---|---|---|---|
| mis- + | | quote | *misquote* |
| pre- + | | eminent | *preeminent* |
| 1. mis- | + | state | *misstate* |
| 2. re- | + | consider | *reconsider* |
| 3. dis- | + | credit | *discredit* |
| 4. im- | + | material | *immaterial* |
| 5. under- | + | nourish | *undernourish* |
| 6. re- | + | organize | *reorganize* |
| 7. un- | + | natural | *unnatural* |
| 8. mis- | + | appropriate | *misappropriate* |
| 9. over- | + | ride | *override* |
| 10. dis- | + | service | *disservice* |
| 11. pre- | + | caution | *precaution* |
| 12. mis- | + | step | *misstep* |
| 13. in- | + | continent | *incontinent* |
| 14. dis- | + | satisfied | *dissatisfied* |
| 15. pre- | + | sorted | *presorted* |
| 16. un- | + | earthly | *unearthly* |
| 17. under- | + | represented | *underrepresented* |

Copyright © 1995 by Harcourt Brace & Company. All rights reserved.

| | | | |
|---|---|---|---|
| 18. dis- | + | embark | disembark |
| 19. re- | + | constitute | reconstitute |
| 20. over- | + | react | overreact |
| 21. dis- | + | inherit | disinherit |
| 22. mis- | + | spell | misspell |
| 23. pre- | + | dominate | predominate |
| 24. im- | + | mature | immature |
| 25. un- | + | noticed | unnoticed |
| 26. re- | + | activate | reactivate |
| 27. over- | + | rated | overrated |
| 28. para- | + | normal | paranormal |
| 29. under- | + | achiever | underachiever |
| 30. extra- | + | ordinary | extraordinary |
| 31. dis- | + | appear | disappear |
| 32. mis- | + | pronounce | mispronounce |
| 33. pre- | + | existing | preexisting |
| 34. re- | + | examine | reexamine |
| 35. dis- | + | place | displace |

Copyright © 1995 by Harcourt Brace & Company. All rights reserved.

Deduct 5 for each incorrectly filled blank.

## Adding Suffixes—Final *e*

Exercise 18–4

NAME _____ SCORE _____

**18d(1)  Drop the final *e* before a suffix beginning with a vowel but not before a suffix beginning with a consonant.**

| | | | | | |
|---|---|---|---|---|---|
| bride | + -al | = bridal | entire | + -ly | = entirely |
| care | + -ful | = careful | fame | + -ous | = famous |

**Exceptions:**  awe, awful; due, duly; hoe, hoeing; singe, singeing. After c or g the final e is retained before suffixes beginning with a or o: notice, noticeable; courage, courageous.

DIRECTIONS   Write the correct spelling of each word with the suffix added. Consult your dictionary freely. Write (ex) after each answer that is an exception to rule **18d(1)**.

EXAMPLES

| | | | |
|---|---|---|---|
| argue | + | -ing | *arguing* |
| dye | + | -ing | *dyeing (ex)* |
| 1. like | + | -ly | *likely* |
| 2. arrange | + | -ment | *arrangement* |
| 3. resource | + | -ful | *resourceful* |
| 4. outrage | + | -ous | *outrageous (ex)* |
| 5. manage | + | -ment | *management* |
| 6. value | + | -able | *valuable* |
| 7. extreme | + | -ly | *extremely* |
| 8. use | + | -age | *usage* |
| 9. become | + | -ing | *becoming* |
| 10. reverse | + | -ible | *reversible* |
| 11. advise | + | -able | *advisable* |
| 12. judge | + | -ment | *judgement or judgment* |
| 13. sure | + | -ly | *surely* |
| 14. knowledge | + | -able | *knowledgeable (ex)* |
| 15. live | + | -ing | *living* |
| 16. acre | + | -age | *acreage (ex)* |

Copyright © 1995 by Harcourt Brace & Company. All rights reserved.

263

17. sincere    +    -ly      _____sincerely_____

18. excite     +    -able    _____excitable_____

19. write      +    -ing     _____writing_____

20. argue      +    -ment    _____argument (ex)_____

Copyright © 1995 by Harcourt Brace & Company. All rights reserved.

Deduct 3 1/3 for each incorrectly filled blank.

## Adding Suffixes—Doubling the Consonant

Exercise 18–5

NAME _____  SCORE _____

**18d(2)  When the suffix begins with a vowel (*ing, ed, ence, ance, able*), double a final single consonant if it is preceded by a single vowel that is in an accented syllable.** (A one-syllable word, of course, is always accented.)

> mop, mopped   [Compare with mope, moped]
> mop, mop•ping   [Compare with mope, mop•ing]
> con•fer′, con•fer′•red   [Final consonant in the accented syllable]
> ben′•e•fit; ben′•e•fited   [Final consonant not in the accented syllable]
> need, need•ed   [Final consonant not preceded by a single vowel]

DIRECTIONS   In the blank at the right enter the correct spelling of each word with the suffix added. Consult your dictionary freely.

EXAMPLE

| | | | |
|---|---|---|---|
| mirror | + | -ed | _mirrored_ |
| 1. regret | + | -ed | _regretted_ |
| 2. refer | + | -ed | _referred_ |
| 3. transmit | + | -er | _transmitter_ |
| 4. untap | + | -ed | _untapped_ |
| 5. attach | + | -ed | _attached_ |
| 6. permit | + | -ing | _permitting_ |
| 7. pour | + | -ing | _pouring_ |
| 8. proceed | + | -ed | _proceeded_ |
| 9. rot | + | -en | _rotten_ |
| 10. jar | + | -ing | _jarring_ |
| 11. label | + | -ed | _labeled_ |
| 12. witch | + | -es | _witches_ |
| 13. control | + | -able | _controllable_ |
| 14. abhor | + | -ent | _abhorrent_ |
| 15. equip | + | -ed | _equipped_ |
| 16. prefer | + | -ence | _preference_ |
| 17. top | + | -ed | _topped_ |

Copyright © 1995 by Harcourt Brace & Company. All rights reserved.

| | | | |
|---|---|---|---|
| 18. scissor | + | -ed | scissored |
| 19. notch | + | -es | notches |
| 20. cut | + | -er | cutter |
| 21. begin | + | -ing | beginning |
| 22. forgot | + | -en | forgotten |
| 23. stop | + | -er | stopper |
| 24. fat | + | -en | fatten |
| 25. omit | + | -ing | omitting |
| 26. occur | + | -ence | occurrence |
| 27. big | + | -est | biggest |
| 28. greet | + | -ing | greeting |
| 29. quiet | + | -ed | quieted |
| 30. travel | + | -er | traveler |

Copyright © 1995 by Harcourt Brace & Company. All rights reserved.

Deduct 10 for each incorrectly filled blank.

## Adding Suffixes—Final *y*

Exercise 18–6

NAME _____   SCORE _____

**18d(3)  Change the *y* to *i* before a suffix except -*ing*.**

| | | | | | | | |
|---|---|---|---|---|---|---|---|
| defy | + | -ance | = | defiance | happy | + | -ness | = | happiness |
| modify | + | -er | = | modifier | modify | + | -ing | = | modifying |
| heavy | + | -er | = | heavier | pretty | + | cr | = | prettier |

   To make a noun plural or a verb singular, the final y preceded by a consonant is changed to i and es is added.

| | | | | | | | | | |
|---|---|---|---|---|---|---|---|---|---|
| duty | + | -es | = | duties | deny | + | -es | = | denies |
| ally | + | -es | = | allies | copy | + | -es | = | copies |

A final y preceded by a vowel is usually not changed before a suffix.

| | | | | | | | | | |
|---|---|---|---|---|---|---|---|---|---|
| annoy | + | -ed | = | annoyed | turkey | + | -s | = | turkeys |

**Exceptions:**   pay, paid; lay, laid; say, said; day, daily.

DIRECTIONS   Enter the correct spelling of each word with the suffix added. Consult your dictionary freely. Write (ex) after each word that is an exception to rule **18d(3)**.

| EXAMPLES | | | |
|---|---|---|---|
| boundary | + | -es | *boundaries* |
| pay | + | -ed | *paid (ex)* |
| 1. lonely | + | -ness | *loneliness* |
| 2. bury | + | -ed | *buried* |
| 3. monkey | + | -s | *monkeys* |
| 4. chimney | + | -s | *chimneys* |
| 5. hungry | + | -ly | *hungrily* |
| 6. fallacy | + | -es | *fallacies* |
| 7. donkey | + | -s | *donkeys* |
| 8. lay | + | -ed | *laid (ex)* |
| 9. try | + | -es | *tries* |
| 10. accompany | + | -es | *accompanies* |

Copyright © 1995 by Harcourt Brace & Company. All rights reserved.

Deduct 3 1/3 for each incorrectly filled blank.

## Forming the Plural

Exercise 18–7

NAME _____  SCORE _____

**18d(4)  Form the plural of most nouns by (1) adding *s* to the singular form of the noun, (2) adding *es* to singular nouns that end in *s, ch, sh,* or *x*, or (3) changing the final *y* to *i* and adding *es* if the noun ends in a *y* and is preceded by a consonant** (see also **18d(3)**).

| | | |
|---|---|---|
| boy→boys | fox→foxes | mystery→mysteries |
| cupful→cupfuls | Harris→Harrises | beauty→beauties |
| Brown→Browns | wolf→wolves | reply→replies |
| | [ f changed to v] | |

A few nouns change their form for the plural: woman→women; child→children. And a few nouns ending in o take the es plural: tomato→tomatoes; hero→heroes.

Others do not change at all: deer→deer; sheep→sheep.

DIRECTIONS    In the blank enter the plural form of each word. Consult you dictionary freely.

EXAMPLES

ray          _rays_

batch        _batches_

| | | | | |
|---|---|---|---|---|
| 1. | elf | _elves_ | 16. witch | _witches_ |
| 2. | company | _companies_ | 17. switch | _switches_ |
| 3. | box | _boxes_ | 18. leech | _leeches_ |
| 4. | negotiator | _negotiators_ | 19. business | _businesses_ |
| 5. | man | _men_ | 20. leaf | _leaves_ |
| 6. | policy | _policies_ | 21. pencil | _pencils_ |
| 7. | moose | _moose_ | 22. notation | _notations_ |
| 8. | beach | _beaches_ | 23. commando | _commandos or -does_ |
| 9. | genius | _geniuses_ | 24. knife | _knives_ |
| 10. | guarantee | _guarantees_ | 25. sandwich | _sandwiches_ |
| 11. | Davis | _Davises_ | 26. dress | _dresses_ |
| 12. | calf | _calves_ | 27. industry | _industries_ |
| 13. | loaf | _loaves_ | 28. handful | _handfuls_ |
| 14. | alloy | _alloys_ | 29. geologist | _geologists_ |
| 15. | navy | _navies_ | 30. potato | _potatoes_ |

Copyright © 1995 by Harcourt Brace & Company. All rights reserved.

Deduct 5 for each incorrectly filled blank.

## Confusion of *ei* and *ie*

Exercise 18–8

NAME _____     SCORE _____

**18e  Apply the rules to avoid confusion of *ei* and *ie*.**

When the sound is ee (as in see), write ei after c (receipt, ceiling), and ie after any other letter (relieve, priest); when the sound is other than ee, usually write ei (eight, their, reign).

**Exceptions:**   either, neither, financier, leisure, seize, species, weird.

**Note:**   This rule does not apply when ei or ie is not pronounced as one simple sound (alien, audience, fiery) or when cie stands for shə (conscience, ancient, efficient).

DIRECTIONS   Fill in the blanks in the following words by writing ei or ie. Consult your dictionary freely. Write (ex) after any word that is an exception to rule **18e**.

EXAMPLES
dec_ei_ve

_ei_ther (ex)

1.  misch_ie_f (ex)

2.  conc_ei_ted

3.  rec_ei_ve

4.  spec_ie_s (ex)

5.  w_ei_ght

6.  w_ei_rd (ex)

7.  h_ei_ght

8.  gr_ie_ve

9.  l_ei_sure (ex)

10.  s_ie_ge

11.  y_ei_ld

12.  ch_ie_f

13.  f_ie_nd

14.  c_ei_ling

15.  sl_ei_gh

16.  gr_ie_f

17.  bel_ie_f

18.  n_ei_ther (ex)

19.  rel_ie_ve

20.  th_ie_f

Copyright © 1995 by Harcourt Brace & Company. All rights reserved.

Deduct 3 1/3 for each incorrect item.

**Hyphenated Words**                                   Exercise 18–9

NAME _____     SCORE _____

**18f Hyphenate words to express the idea of a unit, to avoid ambiguity, and to divide words at the end of a line.**

In general, use the hyphen (1) between two or more words serving as a single word (except when the first word is an adverb ending in -ly), (2) with compound numbers from twenty-one to ninety-nine and with fractions, (3) with prefixes or suffixes for clarity, (4) with the prefixes ex-, self-, all-, and great- and with the suffix -elect, (5) between a prefix and a proper name, (6) never after an adverb ending in -ly, (7) a compound using a comparative or superlative, (8) in chemical terms, (9) or in a modifier using a letter or numeral as the second element.

    (1)  The twenty-year mortgage   [adjective]
           Ronnie's ex-wife   [noun]
    (2)  forty-five, one-fifth
    (3)  re-collect the surplus   [to distinguish from recollect an event]
    (4)  ex-husband, self-help, all-knowing, great-grandmother, mayor-elect
    (5)  mid-July, un-American
    (6)  fondly remembered teacher, quickly forgotten mishap
    (7)  a better-made plan
    (8)  hydrogen-chloride molecule
    (9)  Type-III virus

DIRECTIONS   Supply hyphens where they are needed in the following list. Not all items require hyphens.

    EXAMPLES
    a well-earned vacation

    a vacation well spent

1. western-style jeans

2. The series had four parts.

3. an all-inclusive study

4. book-lined shelves

5. The music appeals to teenage audiences.

6. a one-third return rate

7. The implications are far reaching.

8. Councilwoman-elect Miller

9. poorly constructed building

Copyright © 1995 by Harcourt Brace & Company. All rights reserved.    *273*

10.  a fifty-eight year old woman

11.  a long-distance call

12.  a four-part series

13.  The guard re-searched the car.

14.  employees who are goal oriented

15.  the all-knowing attitude of the chairman

16.  far-reaching results

17.  chocolate-covered caterpillars

18.  a six-foot python

19.  self-sufficient

20.  a frequently misspelled last name

21.  the up-and-down pattern of the stock market

22.  He is my great-uncle.

23.  She feels all right now.

24.  One-eighth of those surveyed liked the idea.

25.  the inadequately labeled package

26.  the self-monitored workout schedule

27.  a low-interest loan

28.  mid-October

29.  She is eighty-four.

30.  ex-President Bush

Copyright © 1995 by Harcourt Brace & Company. All rights reserved.

## 19

**Choose words appropriate to the audience, the purpose, and the occasion. Use a good, up-to-date dictionary to select words that express your ideas exactly.**

An up-to-date desk dictionary is a necessary reference tool for any student or professional person. (A desk dictionary is based on one of the unabridged—complete, unshortened—dictionaries, such as *Webster's Third New International*, usually found on a stand in the reference area of the library.) An up-to-date dictionary not only will show you how words are spelled and hyphenated, but it also provides other information. For example, (1) it shows you how to pronounce a word like *harass*; (2) it gives information about a word's origin and gives the various meanings of the word as it is used today; (3) it lists the forms and possible uses of a verb like *sing*; (4) it gives the synonyms and antonyms of a word like *oppose*; and (5) it may provide usage labels for words like *poke, nowhere*, and *irregardless*. A desk dictionary may also supply you with miscellaneous information such as a brief history of the English language, the dates and identities of famous people, geographical facts, and lists of colleges and universities in the United States and Canada. A current desk dictionary is one of the best investments that you can make.

### 19a Use a good dictionary intelligently.

Study the introductory matter to find out what your dictionary's guides to abbreviations and pronunciation are; to know what plural and tense forms your dictionary lists; to learn what attitude your dictionary takes toward usage labels (dictionaries vary in the kinds of labels they use, and some dictionaries label more words than others do); and to understand the order in which the meanings of words are listed—that is, in order of common usage or of historical development.

Your dictionary will provide you with information about the following things:

(1) Spelling, syllabication (word division), and pronunciation
(2) Parts of speech and inflected forms
(3) Definitions and examples of usage
(4) Synonyms and antonyms
(5) Etymologies (origin and development of a word)

Most words (and most meanings of words) in dictionaries are unlabeled; that is, they are appropriate on any occasion because they are in general use in the English-speaking world.

Avoid choosing words with the labels discussed in **19b–g** unless you are certain that they are appropriate to your chosen reading audience and your purpose.

Copyright © 1995 by Harcourt Brace & Company. All rights reserved.     

**19b  Use informal words only when appropriate to the audience, the purpose, and the occasion.**

There is one class of words—labeled Informal or sometimes Colloquial—that is commonly used and understood by most writers and speakers. Words in this class are appropriate in speaking and in informal writing and are usually necessary in recording dialogue, since most people speak less formally than they write. In most of your college and professional writing, however, you should generally avoid words labeled Informal or Colloquial.

| | |
|---|---|
| INFORMAL | The writer lifted the passage from a report he was studying. |
| STANDARD OR FORMAL | The writer plagiarized the passage from a report he was studying. |

Except in dialogue, contractions are usually not appropriate in formal writing, though they may be used (in moderation) in business letters when a conversational tone is sought.

| | |
|---|---|
| INFORMAL | There's hardly anyone who doesn't respond to a good oral presentation. |
| STANDARD OR FORMAL | There is hardly anyone who does not respond to a good oral presentation. |

**19c  Use newly coined words or slang only when appropriate to the audience, the purpose, and the occasion.**

Slang words are popular expressions that either change their meanings rapidly or pass out of use quickly. (Labeled Slang in the dictionary.)

| | |
|---|---|
| SLANG | She was uptight about the interview. |
| APPROPRIATE | She was nervous about the interview. |

Newly coined words can be slang expressions, but they also include words created to cover new situations, concepts, and so on. Because of the newness of the concept itself, many readers may remain unfamiliar with the term used to label it. For example, until the1988 presidential campaign, few people had heard of spin doctors or sound bites. If you are unsure whether your reader will understand the new word that you intend to use, define it or find a substitute.

| | |
|---|---|
| NEWLY COINED WORD | Last night's news offered two sound bites from the candidate's speech. |
| APPROPRIATE | Last night's news offered two excerpts from the candidate's speech. |

**19d  Use regional words only when appropriate to the audience.**

These are words used by people in one section of the country; consequently, readers outside the region where a given word is current may misunderstand their meaning. (Labeled Dialectical, Regional, or Colloquial in the dictionary.)

Copyright © 1995 by Harcourt Brace & Company. All rights reserved.

| | |
|---|---|
| REGIONAL | The company's car is right nice. |
| APPROPRIATE | The company's car is very nice. |

## 19e  Avoid nonstandard words and usages.

Including nonstandard words or phrases in your writing may lead your reader to think of you as uneducated. (Labeled Nonstandard or Illiterate in the dictionary or omitted entirely.)

| | |
|---|---|
| NONSTANDARD | He busted the computer. |
| APPROPRIATE | He broke the computer. |

## 19f  Avoid archaic and obsolete words.

These words are no longer used in ordinary writing and tend to mark the writer as being pretentious or a snob. (Labeled Archaic, Obsolete, Obsolescent, or Rare in the dictionary.)

| | |
|---|---|
| OBSOLETE | The eldritch computer no longer served their purpose. |
| APPROPRIATE | The ancient computer no longer served their purpose. |

## 19g  Use technical words and jargon only when appropriate to the audience, the purpose, and the occasion.

These words are appropriate only for a specialized audience. When the occasion demands the use of a word that is labeled as belonging to a particular profession or trade—for example, an address to a medical convention might call for technical language or even jargon—the word may be judged appropriate because the audience will understand it. But in general speaking and writing you should depend on the multitude of unlabeled words that most audiences or readers can be expected to understand.

## 19h  Use a simple, straight forward style. Avoid overwriting.

A poetic style is generally not appropriate in college essays or professional reports. Usually such writing seems wordy, vague, and even ridiculous.

| | |
|---|---|
| FLOWERY | He was a tower of power in our community, a blazing meteor in a prosperous enterprise. |
| PLAIN BUT CLEAR | He was a powerful man in our community, a remarkably successful businessman. |

## 19i  Avoid sexist language. (See also **6b**.)

To avoid sexist usage, make your language inclusive; always give equal treatment to both women and men. Avoid the generic use of man to refer to both men and women, and do not stereotype sex roles—for example, assuming that all nurses are women and all doctors are men.

Copyright © 1995 by Harcourt Brace & Company. All rights reserved.

| INAPPROPRIATE | APPROPRIATE |
| --- | --- |
| poetess | poet |
| the common man | the average person, ordinary people |
| lady doctor | doctor |
| male nurse | nurse |
| mankind | humanity, people |
| policeman | police officer |
| weatherman | meteorologist, weather forecaster |
| The manual should indicate how an operator saves his data. | The manual should indicate how an operator saves the data. |
| My girl will set up the meeting. | My assistant will set up the meeting. |
| The executives and their wives attended the dinner. | The executives and their spouses attended the dinner. |

Copyright © 1995 by Harcourt Brace & Company. All rights reserved.

Deduct 1 1/2 for every incorrectly filled blank.

**Using the Dictionary**                                           Exercise 19–1

NAME _____ SCORE _____

The full title, the edition, and the date of publication of my dictionary are as follows:

_(Answers will vary here and throughout this exercise_

_depending on the student's dictionary.)_

**1. Abbreviations**   Where does the dictionary explain the abbreviations it uses?

_at the bottom of each page_

Write out the meaning of each of the abbreviations that follow these entries:

nohow, adv., Dial. _adverb, Dialect_

para-, pref.       _prefix_

woozy, adj.        _adjective_

incarcerate, tr. v. _transitive verb_

**2. Spelling and pronunciation**   Using your dictionary as a guide, write out by syllables each of the following words, and place the accent where it belongs. With the help of the diacritical marks (the accent marks and symbols), the phonetic respelling of the word (in parentheses or slashes immediately after the word), and the key at the bottom of the page, determine the preferred pronunciation (the first pronunciation given). Then pronounce each word correctly several times.

privilege     _priv´•i•lege_

clarion       _clar´•i•on_

mischievous   _mis´•chie•vous_

tambourine    _tam´•bou•rine_

Rewrite whichever of the following words that needs a hyphen:

multinational  _____

extraordinary  _____

selftaught     _self-taught_

Copyright © 1995 by Harcourt Brace & Company. All rights reserved.

Write the plurals of the following words:

appendix     *appendices or appendixes*

mouse     *mice*

datum     *data*

sheep     *sheep*

ox     *oxen*

**3. Derivations**    The derivation, or origin, of a word (given in brackets) often furnishes a literal meaning that helps you to remember the word. For each of the following words, give (a) the source—the language from which it is derived, (b) the original word or words, and (c) the original meaning.

| | Source | Original word(s) and meaning |
|---|---|---|
| fallow | *Old English* | *fealg*    *plowed land* |
| negate | *Latin* | *negare*    *to deny* |
| anodyne | *Greek* | *anōdunos*   *free from pain* <br> *an (without) + odune (pain)* |

**4. Meanings**    Usually words develop several different meanings. How many meanings are listed in your dictionary for the following words?

home, n.   *10*      run, v. tr.   *27*      round, adj.   *17*

out, adv.   *13*      with, prep.   *28*      catch, n.   *11*

Does your dictionary list meanings in order of historical development or in order of common usage? *common usage*

**5. Special labels**    Some words have technical, or field, labels. These words are likely to be understood by people involved in a particular field of study or occupation, but their definitions may be unknown to people outside the field. Based on your dictionary's label of the word, what field would be likely to use each of the following words? (If the label is abbreviated and you are unfamiliar with it, consult your dictionary's list of abbreviations.)

Mesozoic     *geology*

duodenum     *medicine*

iamb     *poetry*

 Copyright © 1995 by Harcourt Brace & Company. All rights reserved.

| white dwarf | astronomy |
|---|---|
| googolplex | mathematics |

**6. Usage labels**   For each italicized word in the items below, consult your dictionary to see if the meaning of the word as it is used here has a usage label (such as Slang or Informal). If it does, enter the label in the blank and rewrite the entire expression in standard English. If it does not, leave the blanks empty.

| | Usage label | Standard English usage |
|---|---|---|
| most everyone | Informal | almost everyone |
| suspicion nothing | Nonstandard (as verb) | suspect nothing |
| speaker don't see | Nonstandard | speaker doesn't see |
| he reckons so | Dialect | he thinks so |
| tardiness bugs me | Slang | tardiness bothers me |
| bust the window | Informal | break the window |
| a bad looking man | Slang | a good looking man |
| finalized the contract | | |
| tough luck | Slang | bad luck |

**7. Synonyms**   Even among words with essentially the same meaning (synonyms), one word usually fits a given context more exactly than any other. To differentiate precise shades of meaning, some dictionaries include special paragraphs showing groups of closely related words. What synonyms are specially differentiated in your dictionary for the following words?

suggest, v.   imply, hint, intimate, insinuate

talkative, adj.   loquacious, wordy, garrulous, voluble, effusive, verbose, glib

**8. Capitalization**   Check your dictionary; then rewrite any of the following words that may be capitalized.

| | | | |
|---|---|---|---|
| french | French | misogynist | |
| biology | | achilles | Achilles |
| humanism | Humanism | el salvador | El Salvador |

Copyright © 1995 by Harcourt Brace & Company. All rights reserved.

**9. Grammatical information**   Note that many words may serve as two or more parts of speech. List the parts of speech—vt., vi., n., adj., adv., prep., conj., interj., pro.—that each of the following words may be.

what            *pro., adj., adv., interj., conj.*

clear           *adj., vt., vi.*

mission         *n., vt.*

in              *prep., adv., adj., n.*

low             *adj., adv., n., vi.*

Note the grammatical information supplied by your dictionary for verbs, adjectives, and pronouns.

List the principal parts of the adjective dry:   *dry, drier, driest or dry, dryer, dryest*

List the principal parts of the verb lie:   *lie, lay, lain, lying*

List the principal parts of go:   *go, went, gone, going*

List the comparative and superlative degrees of the adjective good   *better, best*

List the comparative and superlative degrees of the adjective tall   *taller, tallest*

Should which be used to refer to people?   *no*

What is the distinction between the relative pronouns that and which?

*That introduces restrictive clauses; which introduces non-restrictive clauses.*

**10. Miscellaneous information**   Answer the following questions by referring to your dictionary, and be prepared to tell in what part of the dictionary the information is located.

Who was Alice Paul?   *An American social reformer*

Where is Tlalnepantla?   *South central Mexico, near Mexico City*

What is the AAUP?   *American Association of University Professors*

Does your dictionary give a history of the English language?   *yes*

Does your dictionary have a manual of style?   *yes*

   Copyright © 1995 by Harcourt Brace & Company. All rights reserved.

Deduct 10 for each blank incorrectly filled.

**Appropriate Usage**                                    Exercise 19–2

NAME _____ SCORE _____

DIRECTIONS    If the italicized word, with the meaning it has in its particular sentence, is labeled in your dictionary in any way, enter the label (such as nonstandard or informal) in the blank. If the word is not labeled, write standard in the blank. Discuss your answers in class to compare the usage labels of various dictionaries.

EXAMPLE
Juanita has been bothered alot by a pain in her wrists for some
time.                                                    *nonstandard*

1. She wasn't gonna talk with the plant nurse practitioner, but decided she should when the pain grew more intense.                                            *nonstandard*

2. I think it's creepy that typing made her wrists and hands ache.                                              *slang*

3. The physical therapist told Juanita that she could of developed carpal tunnel syndrome from typing.         *nonstandard*

4. We sort of wondered if it was the same thing as the repetitive motion injury we'd read about.              *informal*

5. Juanita didn't want to rat on her supervisor who had insisted that she continue her 8-hour data entry work even through her hands pained her to do so.          *slang*

6. I am kinda wondering how many people who work with their hands typing or assembling components have Juanita's injury.                                       *nonstandard*

7. It's easy to get into learning about workplace hazards after you've known someone who's been injured on the job.                                                *slang*

8. Her friend said that he ain't never heard of such a thing happening at our office before.                     *informal*

Copyright © 1995 by Harcourt Brace & Company. All rights reserved.

9. But Juanita and me know of at least two women and one man who've had hand surgery to relieve their pain.    *nonstandard*

10. Juanita is worried that she'll get nowhere's with her request for reassignment when she returns from her disability leave.    *nonstandard*

Copyright © 1995 by Harcourt Brace & Company. All rights reserved.

Deduct 10 for each blank incorrectly filled.

**Appropriate Usage—Continued**                    Exercise 19–3

NAME _____    SCORE _____

DIRECTIONS   In each sentence, select the proper word or words from the pairs in parentheses. Cross out the incorrect word or words and write the correct one in the blank. Rely on your dictionary to help you choose the word with the correct meaning or the word that is appropriate in formal writing.

EXAMPLE
Our office is (all ready, ~~already~~) to implement our company's

new smoking policy.                                 _____all ready_____

1. Through in-service education programs, we've learned
   that smoking (affects, ~~effects~~) other people besides the
   smoker.                                          _____affects_____

2. All of our employees had been discussing this issue for
   quite (~~awhile~~, a while).                     _____a while_____

3. Some of us were concerned that banning smoking
   would hurt employee (~~moral~~, morale).         _____morale_____

4. But we agreed that the guiding (~~principal~~, principle)
   should be how to safeguard everyone's health.    _____principle_____

5. (~~May be~~, Maybe) what we really needed to determine
   was how to accommodate those people who wanted to
   smoke without compromising those of us who didn't.   _____Maybe_____

6. Some companies are even considering whether they
   would be (~~likely~~, liable) for damages should someone
   prove they'd contracted an illness from second-hand
   smoke at work.                                   _____liable_____

7. Our health coordinator informed us that our old policy
   was too (~~lose~~, loose) to be effective.       _____loose_____

8. (~~Irregardless~~, Regardless) of the smokers' needs, she
   said we had to make it clear where people could and
   could not smoke.                                 _____Regardless_____

Copyright © 1995 by Harcourt Brace & Company. All rights reserved.                    285

9. (~~Less~~, Fewer) of us smoke than in the past, but there are still some employees who insist on doing so. _____Fewer_____

10. We finally decided that the company had to (accept, ~~except~~) the responsibility for making our working space smoke-free with the exception of several designated areas. _____accept_____

Copyright © 1995 by Harcourt Brace & Company. All rights reserved.

## 20

**Choose words that are exact, idiomatic, and fresh.**

To communicate clearly, you must choose your words carefully, using words that express your ideas and feelings *exactly*.

As you learned in **18b** and in Chapter **19**, there is a great difference in meaning between two words like *accept* and *except*, even though they sound nearly the same. There is also a great difference in meaning between *famous* and *notorious*—two words that suggest fame but in very different senses. Imagine how few products your company would sell if you used *notorious* for *famous* in your advertising copy:

> Our styling spray is *notorious* the world over for its effects on men's hair.

Obviously, the audience for your advertisement would envision undesirable results from using your company's product.

To be exact requires more than choosing words that are correct. You must also choose words that are specific enough to be clear and that are appropriate for the audience you are addressing. If you say that your company's styling spray makes hair "look nice," you may know what you mean, but such a general description is not likely to give your audience a clear picture of your product's effect. And if you say that the styling spray "imparts aesthetic enhancements to one's coiffure," you will probably lose your audience midway through your first sentence. Exactness, then, means that your words are correct, specific, and appropriate for your audience and purpose.

### 20a Select the words that exactly express your ideas.

#### 20a(1) Choose words that denote precisely what you mean. Avoid inaccurate, inexact, or ambiguous usage.

Inexact words can confuse readers or cause them to make associations that you had not intended. Often these problems arise because a writer has neglected to take into account a word's denotation (its explicit, dictionary meaning) or has ignored its connotation (what the word can suggest or imply). Practiced writers make sure that they choose the words they use with care to avoid unintentionally offending, alienating, or confusing their readers.

| | |
|---|---|
| DENOTATION PROBLEM | I urge you to *adapt* my proposal in its *entity*. |
| CORRECT DENOTATION | I urge you to *adopt* my proposal in its *entirety*. |
| CONNOTATION PROBLEM | I *beseech* you to adopt my proposal. |
| CORRECT CONNOTATION | I *urge* you to adopt my proposal. |

Remember that a wrong word is very noticeable to your reader and may, like a misspelled word, discredit your entire letter, report, or essay.

Copyright © 1995 by Harcourt Brace & Company. All rights reserved.

### 20a(2) Choose appropriate words.

Technical terminology that is appropriate for a reader familiar with your field may be meaningless to others. Technical jargon, or field talk, should be confined to presentations made to people within your own specialized area. When writing or speaking to a general audience, always clearly define any technical terms that you use, and use only those technical terms for which no ordinary word or explanation is available.

TECHNICAL    Our word processor uses diskettes that can store 130,000 bytes of information.

CLEAR        Our word processor uses diskettes that can contain 75 typed pages of information.

Appropriate words, then, are words with which your audience is likely to be familiar. Never use a fancy term like "ocular enhancers" when you simply mean glasses. Avoid other heavy, ornate language unless you want to be considered snobbish and pretentious. In short, choose the simple and familiar word or phrase whenever possible.

### 20a(3) Choose a specific and concrete word rather than a general and abstract one.

Words like big, interesting, exciting, wonderful, and good are too general to communicate an idea clearly to your reader. Giving exact details is essential in technical-report and business-letter writing—think how disastrous it would be if a doctor told a patient to take a couple of sleeping pills every now and then. Whenever possible choose the specific word or phrase that communicates the exact quality you have in mind.

GENERAL      Mr. Chomsky's report was interesting.

SPECIFIC     Mr. Chomsky's report explained the government regulations that apply to the labeling of drugs.

GENERAL      Learning to be a sales representative requires a lot of things.

SPECIFIC     Learning to be a sales representative requires that you get to know the product well, understand its main selling points, and determine the specific needs of your customers.

## 20b  Use idiomatic expressions correctly.

Exactness also includes the choice of idiomatic language. Idioms are expressions whose meanings differ from what the meanings of the individual words would lead you to expect. Native speakers are able to use idioms without thinking, but for someone unfamiliar with an expression such as kick the bucket, idioms can be confusing.

You use many idiomatic expressions every day without considering their meanings, especially phrasal verbs—for example, "I ran into an old friend" and "She played down the importance of money." In these examples and in other such expressions, the choice of the particle (into, down) accounts for the expression's being idiomatic. While most of us would not make the error of writing "I ran over an old friend" when we mean that we met an old friend, we might slip and use the unidiomatic comply to rather than the idiomatic comply with.

Copyright © 1995 by Harcourt Brace & Company. All rights reserved.

| UNIDIOMATIC | The product did not comply to the company's standards. |
|---|---|
| IDIOMATIC | The product did not comply with the company's standards. |

## 20c Choose fresh expressions instead of trite, worn-out ones.

Trite expressions, or clichés, are idiomatic expressions that have been used so often that they have become meaningless. At one time readers would have thought the expression "tried and true" was effective, a fresh and exact choice of words. Today, readers have seen and heard the expression so often that they hardly notice it, except perhaps to be bored or amused by it. In your reader's eyes, clichés can also mark you as a lazy, uncaring writer, one who will not make the effort to find a fresh way of saying something. Although clichés are common in most people's speech and may even occur at times in the work of professional writers, such words and phrases should generally be avoided because they no longer convey ideas exactly.

| TRITE | Last but not least, our salespeople will have to put their shoulders to the wheel or our competitors will blow us away in the next quarter. |
|---|---|
| EXACT | Last, our sales people will have to work hard or our competitors will outdistance us in the next quarter. |

Copyright © 1995 by Harcourt Brace & Company. All rights reserved.

Deduct 5 for each incorrectly filled blank.

**Exactness**                                    Exercise 20–1

NAME _____ SCORE _____

DIRECTIONS   In the following sentences cross out the word choice in parentheses that would be incorrect, trite, or inappropriate in an essay written for a general audience. Write the exact or appropriate word choice in the blank. Consult your dictionary freely.

EXAMPLE
Most businesspersons dress (appropriately for, ~~appropriately of~~) the occasion.

*appropriately for*

1. It is (~~plain as day~~, clear) that first impressions do make a difference.

   *clear*

2. Our skills, not our wardrobe, are the (predominant, ~~predominate~~) thing we want business associates to remember.

   *predominant*

3. If your clothes look too trendy, they (~~deflect~~, distract) your customers and may even offend them.

   *distract*

4. Inappropriate dress can be a (principal, ~~principle~~) reason that a customer reacts negatively to a salesperson.

   *principal*

5. Looking professional is the (essential element, ~~sine qua non~~) in winning a customer's confidence.

   *essential element*

6. Furthermore, a neat, well-groomed appearance (~~attributes~~, contributes) to your own confidence.

   *contributes*

7. While jeans and a sweatshirt may not be out of place at a play rehearsal, they would (alienate, ~~turn off~~) the clients of a real estate agent.

   *alienate*

8. The way you talk can also (~~infer~~, imply) things to your customer.

   *imply*

9. You should be (conscious, ~~conscience~~) of the impact that your way of speaking has on your clients.

   *conscious*

Copyright © 1995 by Harcourt Brace & Company. All rights reserved.

10. You should not appear to be excessively (enthusiastic, ~~enthused~~), or your customer may think you are insincere.

   *enthusiastic*

11. In some (~~instants~~, instances), you can offend your customer if you use inappropriate language.

   *instances*

12. People often feel talked down to when someone uses (too many, ~~a bunch of~~) technical terms.

   *too many*

13. (~~Obfuscating~~, Clouding) the issue with big words impresses few people, even experts.

   *Clouding*

14. Too many jargon terms can (~~blow~~, undermine) your chance of making a good impression.

   *undermine*

15. You should also be (aware, ~~cognizant~~) that slang makes some people think you do not take them seriously.

   *aware*

16. The (~~less~~, fewer) distractions you give your customers, the more successful you will be in your job.

   *fewer*

17. Taking your customers' needs into account is actually a way of paying them a (~~complement~~, compliment).

   *compliment*

18. Mannerisms such as gum chewing, hair twisting, and nail biting can also (irritate, ~~tick off~~) your customers.

   *irritate*

19. Of course, being considerate should also (affect, ~~effect~~) your customers' good opinion of you.

   *affect*

20. The truly (~~great~~, effective) businessperson is the one who puts the customers' needs first.

   *effective*

Copyright © 1995 by Harcourt Brace & Company. All rights reserved.

## 21

**Be concise. Repeat a word or phrase only when it is needed for emphasis, clarity, or coherence.**

Wordiness results from inexact word choice (see also Chapter **20**). Few writers, in their first drafts, are likely to make the best choices in phrasing. Therefore, to insure exactness and to eliminate wordiness, writers must carefully proofread and then revise their first drafts.

~~In today's society~~ *Today* workers are concerned not only with protection from hazardous

working conditions ~~and situations~~ but ~~they are~~ also ~~concerned~~ with the quality of the

workplace. They ~~ask and~~ demand that work be more than safe; they also want ~~work~~ *it* to

be interesting.

### 21a Make every word count; omit words or phrases that add nothing to the meaning.

Most wordiness in composition results from a writer's attempt to achieve an elevated style, to write sentences that sound impressive. Many unnecessary phrases inevitably show up in the compositions of writers who never use one exact word when they can instead write a long, impressive-sounding phrase. The temptation to use impressive words leads to monster sentences. Readers, however, are likely to spot the pretentiousness and may dismiss the content of the writing as foolish even when it is not.

No one wants her or his ideas to be laughed at, but the quickest way to get that response is to write something like "Immediately if not sooner it would be prudent when in the presence of combusting materials for all employees and staff to exit and leave the nearby premises by the most expeditious means possible as soon as they are physically able to do so." What did the writer want to say? "In case of fire, immediately leave the building by the nearest exit." By the time the reader finishes the first sentence, the paper (and the reader) might well be ashes. In other words, be direct.

Here is a sampling of verbose phrases and pretentious words, along with their briefer, more straightforward counterparts.

| *Wordy* | *Concise* |
|---|---|
| in today's society | now OR today |
| to be desirous of | want OR desire |
| to have a preference for | prefer |
| to be in agreement with | agree |
| due to the fact that | because OR since |

Copyright © 1995 by Harcourt Brace & Company. All rights reserved.

| | |
|---|---|
| in view of the fact that | because OR since |
| in order to | to |
| at this point in time | now |
| in this day and age | today |
| with reference to | about |
| prior to | before |
| in the event of | if |
| subsequent | after |
| substantial | big, large |
| inadvertency | error |
| promulgate | issue |
| domicile | home, house |
| remuneration | pay |
| disclose | show, uncover |
| utilize | use |
| circa | about |
| sequent | following |
| i.e. | that is |
| e.g. | for example |
| along the line of | about |
| consensus of opinion | consensus |
| during the time that | while |
| for the purpose of | for |
| have the need for | need |
| in due course | soon |
| in many cases | often, frequently |
| few and far between | seldom |
| under the circumstances | because |
| in some cases | sometimes |
| in most cases | usually |
| in spite of the fact that | although |

Another source of wordiness, particularly in student compositions, is the writer's lack of confidence in his or her opinions. Expressions such as "I think," "it seems to me," "in my opinion," and "would be" (for is) may be appropriate in writing about issues that are genuinely controversial, but more often they can be omitted. If you do not express your ideas confidently, your reader's confidence in them will be diminished, too.

WORDY    It seems to me that one reason for boredom among workers would be their mistaken belief that a job, to be satisfying, must be free of routine tasks.

CONCISE    One reason for boredom among workers is their mistaken belief that a job, to be satisfying, must be free of routine tasks.

Finally, you should work to eliminate unnecessary expletive constructions from your writing. This type of sentence uses there plus a form of to be and places the subject after the verb. An expletive construction generally weakens a sentence by removing the subject from the position of strong emphasis—the beginning.

Copyright © 1995 by Harcourt Brace & Company. All rights reserved.

WORDY     There are many causes of worker dissatisfaction.

CONCISE   Worker dissatisfaction has many causes.

It is also an expletive when it lacks an antecedent and is followed by a form of to be.

WORDY     It was tedious listening to the report.

CONCISE   Listening to the report was tedious.

**Note:**   In a few cases, no logical subject exists, and the it expletive construction is necessary: It is going to rain.

### 21b  Combine sentences or simplify phrases and clauses to eliminate needless words.

Often you can combine two main clauses through subordination (see **1e** and **24a**) to avoid wordiness.

WORDY     Many people feel that everyone except them has escaped routine chores, and as a result of this feeling they become dissatisfied with their work.

CONCISE   Many people become dissatisfied with their work because they feel that everyone except them has escaped routine chores.

### 21c  Repeat words and phrases only when necessary for emphasis, clarity, or coherence.

Repetition of the same word in several sentences, unless done to achieve emphasis (see Chapters **26b**, **29e**, and **32b**), results in monotonous writing. The use of pronouns and synonyms helps to avoid excessive repetition.

REPETITIOUS   Even creative writers face a number of routine chores. Writers must sit down at their desks each day and work a certain number of hours at their writing. Writers must revise the same piece of writing again and again.

BETTER        Even creative writers face a number of routine chores. They must sit down at their desks each day and work a certain number of hours at their writing. They must revise the same text again and again.

Combining sentences, using a colon if appropriate, can also eliminate needless repetition.

REPETITIOUS   There are two major causes of wordiness in writing. These two causes are needless repetition and the use of meaningless words and phrases.

CONCISE       There are two major causes of wordiness in writing: needless repetition and the use of meaningless words and phrases.

OR

The two major causes of wordiness in writing are needless repetition and the use of meaningless words and phrases.

Copyright © 1995 by Harcourt Brace & Company. All rights reserved.

Several popular expressions are always repetitious: each and every, any and all, various and sundry, if and when, combine together, return back. Other similar expressions include purple in color, triangular in shape, and City of Key West.

REPETITIOUS    Each and every job involves a certain amount of routine.

CONCISE    Every [OR Each] job involves a certain amount of routine.

REPETITIOUS    A total of three people complained about boredom.

CONCISE    Three people complained about boredom.

In introducing quotations, many inexperienced writers tend to overwork forms of the verb say. Remember that verbs besides say can introduce quotations effectively—for example, explain, point out, note, describe, observe, believe, feel, and think.

REPETITIOUS    Albert S. Glickman, a researcher on work and leisure, says, "Work and leisure are part of one life." Glickman also says that "we need to improve the net quality of life." He says we are inexperienced in handling our leisure time by saying: "So far we haven't had much experience in the use of free time."

BETTER    Albert S. Glickman, a researcher on work and leisure, believes that "work and leisure are part of one life." Glickman says, "We need to improve the net quality of life." He feels that we are inexperienced in handling the leisure part of our lives: "So far," Glickman points out, "we haven't had much experience in the use of free time."

Copyright © 1995 by Harcourt Brace & Company. All rights reserved.

Deduct 4 for each incorrect revision and 2 2/3 for each incorrectly filled blank.

## Avoiding Wordiness and Needless Repetition    Exercise 21–1

NAME _____    SCORE _____

DIRECTIONS    Cross out needless words in each of the following sentences. For each sentence that requires no further revision other than capitalization, punctuation, or deletion only, write 1 in the blank; for sentences that require additional changes in wording, write 2 in the blank and make the needed revision.

EXAMPLE

Probably
~~Most likely the reason why~~ Kevin believed he could work ~~by himself~~ alone

~~was~~ because he had never written collaboratively ~~before.~~*          2

1.  It seems clear and obvious that businesspersons need to ~~think about~~
    Obviously

    ~~and~~ understand the importance of ~~working and~~ cooperating with

    people on writing projects.          2

2.  ~~There are~~ distinct advantages ~~to writing collaboratively, and these~~
    Collaborative writing has

    ~~are~~ the time it saves and the useful, ~~helpful~~ knowledge each ~~and~~

    ~~every~~ person brings to such a project.          2

3.  Listening ~~to and~~ hearing what other people have to say on the sub-
                  H

    ject can generate ~~new and~~ fresh approaches.          1

4.  ~~It is clear that~~ most of us learn to write "alone" and perhaps are
    Clearly

    leery of collaboration, mistakenly seeing it as cheating.          2

5.  A successful group of people ~~working successfully together~~ requires

    ~~and needs~~ some patience and good listening skills on everyone's

    part.          1

6.  ~~In many cases and quite~~ often, you will not have the ~~luxury and~~
                              O

    good fortune to write with a ~~collaborative writing~~ group.          1

*Students may find ways to eliminate wordiness other than those shown here, in which case they should be given credit.

Copyright © 1995 by Harcourt Brace & Company. All rights reserved.

7. But more often than not on the job ~~where you~~ work, you will be
   ~~asked and~~ required to collaborate.  [*Usually* written above "often"; *at* written above "where"]     **2**

8. ~~Big, large,~~ complex projects must call on the skills ~~and knowledge~~
   of many, ~~numerous~~ people so that all ~~of the multitudinous aspects~~
   ~~and~~ sides of the problem ~~at hand~~ can be addressed.  [*C* written above "complex"]     **1**

9. In writing groups, you can ~~call on and~~ ask for the collective wisdom
   of your peers.     **1**

10. This wisdom also extends to ~~and reaches out to~~ everyone's skills as
    editors ~~as well~~.     **1**

11. ~~In the event that~~ one member of the team's ~~population~~ makes sug-
    gestions to improve ~~and make~~ something you wrote ~~better,~~ listen to
    what they have to say.  [*If* written above "In the event that"]     **2**

12. ~~At these times the reason why~~ listening skills are crucial ~~is~~ because
    you are all working for the same goal: a well-written document.  [*Then* written above]     **2**

13. Experienced writers ~~who have been writing for a long time over the
    years~~ learn not to take personally ~~or be hurt by~~ what a co-writer
    says.     **1**

14. ~~Due to the fact that~~ people working in groups get a lot of feedback
    about their writing, they can see their writing actually improve ~~and
    get better~~.  [*Because* written above "Due to the fact that"]     **2**

15. ~~It is recommended that~~ a business writer be open to the idea ~~and
    concept~~ of collaborative writing.  [*A* written above "a"; *should* written above "be"]     **2**

Copyright © 1995 by Harcourt Brace & Company. All rights reserved.

# 22

**Include all words or phrases necessary to complete the meaning of the sentence.**

**Note:** Since writers often omit words that are needed to complete a parallel construction, Chapter **22** may profitably be studied together with Chapter **26**.

**22a Include all articles, pronouns, conjunctions, and prepositions necessary for completeness.** (See also **26b**.)

**Note:** Use a caret (∧) to mark the place *below* the line where an omitted word, phrase, or mark of punctuation is to be inserted. Write the insertion *above* the line.

DIRECT QUOTATION     My speech teacher pointed out, "Your body language often communicates as much as your words do."

INDIRECT QUOTATION   My speech teacher pointed out ‸*that* body language often communicates as much as words do.   [The relative pronoun *that* generally introduces an indirect quotation; without *that*, *body language*, rather than the entire clause, seems to be the object of *pointed out*.]

Avoid using intensifiers like *so* and *such* without a completing *that* clause; do not write *The speaker was* **so** *tense* or *The speaker was* **such** *an interesting person*. Either omit the *so* or *such* or explain the meaning of the intensifier with a *that* clause.

The speaker was so tense/‸*that he made his audience uncomfortable.*

**Note:** The word *that* may be omitted when the meaning of the sentence would be clear at first reading without it.

The speaker was so tense he made his audience uncomfortable.

Omitting a preposition can result in unidiomatic phrasing.

The speaker believed ‸*in* and made use of gestures during oral presentations.   [*Believed in* (an idiom) means something quite different from *believed*. Without *in*, the sentence says that the speaker *believed gestures*—not what the writer intended.]

The type ‸*of* gestures used by the speaker emphasized certain points. [Without *of*, the word *type* seems to be an adjective modifying *gestures*.]

Do not omit an article from a list of items that requires both *a*'s and *an*'s in order for it to make sense.

Effective body language includes *a* use of gestures, *a* movement on stage whenever appropriate, and ‸*an* expressive face.

Copyright © 1995 by Harcourt Brace & Company. All rights reserved.

## 22b  Include necessary verbs and auxiliaries.

*used*

Speakers have always⋀and will continue to use gestures during their presentations. [Without the used the sentence would mean "Speakers have always continue and will continue to use gestures during their presentations." Have continue is an error in tense form.]

## 22c  Form complete comparisons.

*as,*            *, those of*

The speaker's gestures were as good⋀if not better than⋀any other speaker I had observed.

*other*

Body language is as important as any⋀part of the speech.

Copyright © 1995 by Harcourt Brace & Company. All rights reserved.

Deduct 10 for each incorrectly filled blank.

**Avoiding Omissions**                                    Exercise 22–1

NAME _____ SCORE _____

DIRECTIONS    In the following sentences insert the words that are needed to complete the sense; then write those words in the blanks.

EXAMPLE        *that*
We are not aware⌃oral presentations are a part of many people's

routine job activities.                                    _____*that*_____

1.  We are more nervous about giving an oral presentation than

    *about*
    we are⌃preparing a written one.                        _____*about*_____

    *Making successful*
2.  ⌃~~Successful~~ oral presentations may be somewhat intimidating

    at first, but talking to groups is a skill you will need to develop.    _____*Making*_____

                                                           *but*
3.  We know the importance of an organized piece of writing,⌃we

    forget that an oral presentation requires the same careful

    attention.                                             _____*but*_____

                          *a*
4.  Using an outline and⌃list of your visuals will help you keep

    your presentation on track.                            _____*a*_____

              *that*
5.  Remember⌃your audience generally is made up of people

    who share your interests.                              _____*that*_____

                                          *of*
6.  Good speakers understand the importance⌃and know how to

    use gestures to keep their audience's attention.       _____*of*_____

              *that*
7.  You will find⌃the gestures you use in ordinary conversation

    will be the most convincing in an oral presentation.   _____*that*_____

Copyright © 1995 by Harcourt Brace & Company. All rights reserved.

8. The speed at which you deliver your talk and the rate <sub>∧</sub> you *at which*

   breathe also affect your audience's ability to understand what

   you are saying.                                                    _at which_

9. Remember <sub>∧</sub> deep breathing will help you relax and speak *that*

   distinctly.                                                        _that_

10. The best way for you to convince your audience you're

    sincere has <sub>∧</sub> and always will be eye contact.  *been*   _been_

Copyright © 1995 by Harcourt Brace & Company. All rights reserved.

# SENTENCE UNITY　　　　　　　　　　su 23

## 23

### Write unified sentences.

Make sure that all parts of a sentence are clearly related and that the subject, or central focus, of the sentence is clear. Errors in unity are so common and so varied that it is impossible to show more than a sampling of them. (Often the instructor marks this type of mistake with a *K* or an *awk*, indicating that the sentence is awkward and needs to be entirely rewritten.) Most mistakes of this type stem from (1) a failure to establish a clear relationship between clauses in a sentence or (2) a tendency to overcrowd a sentence with adjectives and adverbs, thereby losing focus and confusing the reader.

### 23a Make the relationship of ideas in a sentence immediately clear to the reader.

Establish a clear relationship between main clauses in a sentence: develop unrelated ideas in separate sentences. (See also Chapter **24**.)

UNCLEAR　　Creighton Alexander lost his audience after only three minutes of speaking, and his face never showed a change of expression.

CLEAR　　Because his face never showed a change of expression, Creighton Alexander lost his audience after only three minutes of speaking.

OR

Creighton Alexander's face never showed a change of expression even though he lost his audience after only three minutes of speaking.

OR

Creighton Alexander lost his audience after only three minutes of speaking. His face never showed a change of expression.

### 23b Avoid excessive or poorly ordered detail.

Keep the central focus of the sentence clear. Adding too many phrases or clauses to the base sentence (*subject–verb–complement*) will make the focus of the sentence unclear.

UNCLEAR　　Creighton Alexander, with his shifting eyes and rigid body, which showed his nervousness all too clearly, while he stood as if planted behind the lectern, failed to establish any rapport with his audience. [The focus of the sentence—*Creighton Alexander*—has been lost.]

CLEAR　　Creighton Alexander, with his shifting eyes and rigid body, failed to establish any rapport with his audience.

Copyright © 1995 by Harcourt Brace & Company. All rights reserved.　　　*303*

## 23c  Revise mixed metaphors and mixed constructions.

MIXED     When speakers ramble and stumble causes their audience to lose the thread of the argument.   [adverb clause + predicate]

REVISED     When speakers ramble and stumble, they cause their audience to lose the thread of the argument.   [adverb clause, main clause]

MIXED     It was a long speech but which was quite interesting.

REVISED     It was a long speech, but it was quite interesting.

OR

It was a long speech which was quite interesting.   [noun + adjective clause]

MIXED     Locating the lost file was like trying to find a grain of sand in the forest.

REVISED     Locating the lost file was like trying to find a needle in a haystack.

**Note:**   Sometimes a sentence is flawed by the use of a singular noun instead of a plural one: "Many who attended the sales meeting brought their own cars."   [NOT car]

## 23d  Avoid faulty predication.

Faulty predication occurs when the subject and predicate do not fit each other logically.

ILLOGICAL     Because the speaker was enthusiastic kept the audience interested. [A because clause is not a noun or a pronoun and thus cannot function as a subject.]

LOGICAL     The speaker's enthusiasm kept the audience interested.   [Enthusiasm is a noun and can serve as the subject.]

OR

Because the speaker was enthusiastic, the audience stayed interested.

## 23e  Define words or expressions precisely.

### (1)  Avoid faulty *is–when, is–where,* and *is–because* definitions.

Combining is with the adverbs when, where or because often creates an illogical statement since forms of to be indicate identity or equality between the subject and what follows.

ILLOGICAL     Gesturing is when a speaker uses his or her hands to clarify or emphasize certain points.   [Gesturing is an act, not a time.]

LOGICAL     Gesturing is the speaker's use of his or her hands to explain or emphasize certain points.

Copyright © 1995 by Harcourt Brace & Company. All rights reserved.

**(2) Write clear, precise definitions.** (See also **32d7**.)

Define terms with which your reader is unfamiliar. Often a short dictionary definition will do.

> When referring to the volume of the speaker's voice, the term means "loudness."

Including one or two synonyms is also helpful; they are often listed as appositives.

> The volume of your voice is its loudness.

Examples can help your reader understand your terms as well.

> Some gestures (pointing or nodding) help your listener follow your most important points.

Be sure to make certain that you let your reader know which meaning of the word you are using.

> In this discussion, I will use the word tone to refer to the emotional color of a speaker's voice.

Copyright © 1995 by Harcourt Brace & Company. All rights reserved.

Deduct 7 for each incorrect revision and 3 for each incorrectly filled blank.

**Unity of Sentence Structure**                                  Exercise 23–1

NAME _____  SCORE _____

DIRECTIONS    In the blanks enter 1 or 2 to indicate whether the chief difficulty in each sentence is (1) the linking of unrelated ideas or (2) unnecessary or excessive additions to the base sentence. Then revise the sentences to make them unified.

> EXAMPLE
>
> ~~When you take the time to look,~~ If people are not paying attention to your
>
> talk, you should, ~~and probably would want to~~ change your manner of
>
> presentation.*                                                        2

1. Look closely at the people you are addressing; ~~and~~ the pitch, rate of
   speech, and volume of your voice also help to establish rapport with
   your audience.                                                        1

2. If your audience seems not to be listening to you, the problem
   may be that you are speaking too softly so ~~or~~ that the audience cannot
   hear you.                                                             1

3. ~~Sometimes, besides talking too softly, another reason~~ People also
   cannot follow ~~is~~ when you are speaking indistinctly.              2

4. Sometimes people have trouble understanding you if you talk too
   rapidly. ~~and~~ Sometimes a high-pitched voice can also irritate the
   audience.                                                            1

5. The audience's attention drifted, because ~~and~~ the speaker's voice was so low
   that what he had to say sounded boring.                              1

*Students may find ways to achieve unity other than those shown here, in which case they should be given credit.

Copyright © 1995 by Harcourt Brace & Company. All rights reserved.

6. ~~One of the least excusable errors in oral presentation,~~ *S* ~~s~~lurred

   speech, which can be described as a lazy way of talking that suggests

   *your audience*

   ~~to your audience that~~ you are not really concerned about ~~them~~, can

   make it very difficult for your listeners to understand what you have

   to say.                                                                  2

7. Many speakers ruin the conclusion of their speeches by belaboring

   the issue, making their listeners think that they are finished when

   they are not ~~so~~ all speakers should keep their concluding remarks

   concise and relevant.                                                    2

   *occurs*

8. One of the most common problems in speeches ~~is~~ when the speaker

   continues for many minutes after he has indicated that his speech is

   about to end.                                                            2

9. Finally, a speaker should not hurry from the rostrum once the

   *since*

   speech is completed, ~~and~~ the audience may want to applaud.            1

10. Applause, ~~which is not expected in certain situations, such as a com-~~

    ~~pany briefing, and~~ which usually follows a few seconds of silent eye

    contact with the audience, should be accepted from the rostrum,

    not from your seat.                                                     2

Copyright © 1995 by Harcourt Brace & Company. All rights reserved.

## 24

**Use subordination to relate ideas concisely and effectively. Use coordination to give ideas equal emphasis.** (See also **1e** and **2b**.)

In Chapter **1** you learned that short, choppy sentences may often be combined. When one of the short sentences is made into a sentence addition or modifier, the writer is using subordination. A writer uses subordination, or sentence combining, not only to improve style but also to show more clearly the relationships between ideas.

**24a  Use subordination to combine a series of related short sentences into longer, more effective units.**

Instead of writing a series of short, choppy sentences, combine the sentences by expressing the main idea in the main or base clause and the less important ideas in subordinate clauses or phrase additions.

While a short sentence used among others of varying length can have an impact on a reader and make the idea it contains stand out, a paragraph composed of nothing but short sentences will seem fragmented with no controlling central point. Most readers rapidly grow bored by such writing.

| | |
|---|---|
| CHOPPY | A question-and-answer period may follow your speech. Be sure to be courteous and correct in your responses. |
| SUBORDINATION | *If a question-and-answer period follows your speech,* be sure to be courteous and correct in your responses. |
| CHOPPY | Repeat the question. Answer it concisely and carefully. |
| SUBORDINATION | *After repeating the question,* answer it concisely and carefully. |
| CHOPPY | Andrea Joseph accepted questions from many people. The people were seated in various parts of the room. |
| SUBORDINATION | Andrea Joseph accepted questions from many people *who were seated in various parts of the room.* |

**24b  To avoid stringing main clauses together, relate them by using subordination and coordination.**

Instead of writing loose, strung-out compound sentences, express the main idea in a main clause and make the less important ideas subordinate. Use coordination to give ideas equal emphasis.

| | |
|---|---|
| STRUNG-OUT | A hostile person in the audience tried to harass Andrea with questions she was not qualified to answer, so Andrea replied simply, "I do not have the information to answer your questions at this time." |

Copyright © 1995 by Harcourt Brace & Company. All rights reserved.

SUBORDINATED   When a hostile person in the audience tried to harass her with questions she was not qualified to answer, Andrea replied simply, "I do not have information to answer your questions at this time." [The writer emphasizes Andrea's reply.]

COORDINATED   A hostile person in the audience tried to harass Andrea with questions she was not qualified to answer, and she replied simply, "I do not have the information to answer your questions at this time." [The writer gives equal emphasis to the harassment of Andrea and her reply.]

## 24c  Avoid faulty or excessive subordination.

Too many subordinate clauses in a sentence can make the focus of the sentence unclear. (See also **23b**.)

UNCLEAR   Andrea, who had never had to deal with a hostile member of an audience before, showed composure, particularly considering the circumstances, which included an overheated room and inadequate lighting, when she answered the person's question quickly but politely and then went on to respond to other questions.

CLEAR   Andrea, who had never had to deal with a hostile member of an audience before, showed composure when she answered the person's question quickly but politely and then went on to respond to other questions.

Copyright © 1995 by Harcourt Brace & Company. All rights reserved.

Deduct 10 for each incorrect revision.

## Subordination and Coordination

Exercise 24–1

NAME _____ SCORE _____

DIRECTIONS   Combine each of the following groups of choppy sentences by using either subordination or coordination.

EXAMPLE
Most speakers will be given time to answer questions from the audience. People in the audience often want to have certain points clarified.

*Most speakers will be given time to answer questions from the audience since people often want to have certain points clarified.\**

1. Some of the questions people ask may sound silly. A good speaker never makes the person asking the question feel foolish.

   *Although some of the questions people ask may sound silly, a good speaker never makes the person asking the question feel foolish.*

2. Often a question may require a lengthy answer. In order to respond to as many people as possible, a speaker should keep track of the time.

   *Often a question may require a lengthy answer, so, in order to respond to as many people as possible, a speaker should keep track of the time.*

3. Speakers are sometimes asked questions outside their fields. Careful speakers do not pretend to be experts in all areas. They acknowledge their inability to answer those questions.

   *If asked questions outside their fields, careful speakers do not pretend to be experts in all areas but acknowledge their inability to answer those questions.*

4. Some people in an audience ask questions in an attempt to badger the speaker. A practiced speaker replies courteously and does not engage in pointless arguing.

   *Some people in an audience ask questions in an attempt to badger the speaker, but a practiced speaker replies courteously and does not engage in pointless arguing.*

\*Students may combine sentences effectively in ways other than those shown, in which case they should be given credit.

Copyright © 1995 by Harcourt Brace & Company. All rights reserved.

5. Other questioners give miniature speeches. These people may be trying to teach the speaker and the audience something. They may have a hidden agenda.

> When other questioners give miniature speeches, they may have a hidden agenda, and they may be trying to teach the speaker and the audience something.

6. A person may ask about material already covered. It may have been in the speech itself or in an answer to another question. The speaker's reply should be brief and courteous.

> The speaker's reply to a person asking about material already covered in either the speech or an answer to another question should be brief and courteous.

7. Some people ask for additional information. Conscientious speakers do what they promise to do. They mail it promptly to them.

> As they have promised to, conscientious speakers promptly mail additional information to those who ask for it.

8. Some speakers may use the question-and-answer period to expand on their original material. This additional information was perhaps too technical to include in the speech itself.

> Some speakers may use the question-and-answer period to expand on their original material with additional information that was perhaps too technical to include in the speech itself.

9. Well-prepared speakers anticipate many of the questions they are asked. They bring additional explanatory materials. These materials will help them answer such questions clearly.

> Well-prepared speakers anticipate many of the questions they are asked, and they bring additional explanatory materials which will help them answer such questions clearly.

Copyright © 1995 by Harcourt Brace & Company. All rights reserved.

10. Good speakers prepare for the question-and-answer period as well as for the speech itself. They enjoy this part of their presentation.

> Because good speakers prepare for the question-and-answer period as well as for the speech itself, they enjoy this part of their presentation.

Copyright © 1995 by Harcourt Brace & Company. All rights reserved.

## 25

**Keep related parts of the sentence together. Avoid dangling modifiers. Place modifiers carefully to indicate clearly their relationship with the words they modify.**

While most adverbial modifiers may be moved to various places in a sentence without affecting the clarity of the sentence, adjectival modifiers usually must be placed either just before or just after the words they modify. (See also **1d**.)

ADVERBIAL

*When you think about the number of hours you will spend working,* you realize how important a choice of careers is. [Notice that the *when* clause may be moved to the end of the sentence or to the middle —after the main verb *realize*—without affecting clarity.]

ADJECTIVAL

Most people *who hold full-time jobs* can expect to spend ten thousand days of their lives working. [Notice that the *who* clause cannot be moved anywhere else in the sentence without affecting clarity.]

ADJECTIVAL

*Optimistic about the future,* most high-school and college students expect to achieve recognition and status in their occupations. [Notice that the verbal phrase may be placed either before or after the word it modifies—*students*—but nowhere else in the sentence without affecting clarity.]

### 25a  Keep related parts of the sentence together.

MISPLACED

Fifty percent of all college seniors expected to become wealthy *who were interviewed in 1988.*

CLEAR

Fifty percent of all college seniors *who were interviewed in 1988* expected to become wealthy.

AWKWARD

You will find that most students are, *when you analyze their expectations,* determined to have successful careers. [Even an adverbial modifier should not be placed so that it awkwardly splits parts of the verb.]

CLEAR

*When you analyze their expectations,* you will find that most college students are determined to have successful careers.

INFORMAL

Perhaps students *almost* expect too much from their careers.

CLEAR

Perhaps students expect *almost* too much from their careers.

Copyright © 1995 by Harcourt Brace & Company. All rights reserved.

## 25b  Revise dangling modifiers.

Dangling modifiers do not refer clearly and logically to another word or phrase in the sentence. (Most dangling modifiers are misplaced verbal phrases.) To correct a dangling modifier, either rearrange and reword the sentence base so that the modifier clearly refers to the right word or add words to the sentence to make the modifier clear by itself.

| | |
|---|---|
| DANGLING | Not wanting to waste forty years of their lives, students' concern about their careers is not surprising.   [The verbal phrase illogically modifies concern.] |
| CLEAR | Not wanting to waste forty years of their lives, students, not surprisingly, are concerned about their careers. [The verbal phrase logically modifies students.] |

OR

Since most students do not want to waste forty years of their lives, their concern about their careers is not surprising.   [The verbal phrase is made into a clear subordinate clause with students as its subject.]

| | |
|---|---|
| DANGLING | Once unheard of, many people today change their careers. [The verbal phrase illogically modifies people.] |
| CLEAR | Although the practice was once unheard of, many people today change their careers.   [The verbal phrase is made into a clear subordinate clause.] |

OR

Once unheard of, changing careers is common today.   [The verbal phrase logically modifies changing.]

**Note:**   A dangling modifier usually cannot be corrected by simply moving it to the end of the sentence.

| | |
|---|---|
| DANGLING | Having mastered one job or skill, another one may be tried. [The verbal phrase illogically modifies one.] |
| DANGLING | Another one may be tried, having mastered one job or skill. [The verbal phrase still illogically modifies the subject, one.] |
| CLEAR | Having mastered one job or skill, a person may try another. [A subject, person, is supplied for the verbal phrase to modify.] |

Copyright © 1995 by Harcourt Brace & Company. All rights reserved.

Deduct 10 for each incorrectly rewritten sentence.

## Avoiding Misplaced Parts and Dangling Modifiers

NAME _____ SCORE _____

DIRECTIONS   In each of the following sentences either a misplaced part or a dangling modifier is in italics. Rewrite the sentence or add the words needed so that the reference is clear and logical.

EXAMPLE
Some things have changed during the last few years about the job market.

Some things about the job market have changed in the last few years.*

1. Liberal arts majors almost were certain to have a difficult time finding a job during the 1970s.

   Liberal arts majors were almost certain to have a difficult time finding a job during the 1970s.

2. Graduates with a general education were, during the late 1960s and 1970s, considered to be too plentiful.

   During the late 1960s and 1970s, graduates with a general education were considered to be too plentiful.

3. Not specifically trained for any one job, many businesses refused to hire these graduates.

   Many businesses refused to hire these graduates since they were not specifically trained for any one job.

4. Today many businesses are seeking liberal arts majors that did not hire them during the 1970s.

   Today many businesses that did not hire liberal arts majors during the 1970s are seeking them.

*Students may find various ways to eliminate the problems other than those shown, in which case they should be given credit.

Copyright © 1995 by Harcourt Brace & Company. All rights reserved.

5. Offering something valuable to the job market, the late 1980s began to appreciate graduates with a liberal arts education.

   Offering something valuable to the job market, graduates with a liberal arts education began to be appreciated during the late 1980s.

6. Liberal arts majors can be molded for particular jobs who have received a general education by the companies that hire them.

   Liberal arts majors who have received a general education can be molded for particular jobs by the companies that hire them.

7. Able to adapt themselves to different kinds of jobs, many companies now appreciate graduates with a general education.

   Because graduates with a general education are able to adapt themselves to different kinds of jobs, many companies now appreciate them.

8. Many career planning offices are, so that students will have greater job flexibility, advising them to train for more than one limited area of work.

   So that students will have greater job flexibility, many career planning offices are advising them to train for more than one limited area of work.

9. A field may be overcrowded by the time a student graduates that seems promising at the moment.

   A field that seems promising at the moment may be overcrowded by the time a student graduates.

10. Persons who only can do one thing may not be able to find a job in their area of specialization.

    Persons who can only do one thing may not be able to find a job in their area of specialization.

Copyright © 1995 by Harcourt Brace & Company. All rights reserved.

## 26

**Use parallel structure to express matching ideas.**

Parallel structure means that a grammatical form is repeated—an adjective is balanced by another adjective, a verb phrase is balanced by another verb phrase, a subordinate clause is balanced by another subordinate clause, and so on. Parallel structure can emphasize ideas (see Chapter **29**), make relationships clear, and contribute to coherence within and between paragraphs (see also Chapter **32**).

There are several connectives that frequently call for parallel structure: *and, but, or, nor*, and especially *not only . . . but also, either . . . or, neither . . . nor*, and *as well as*. These words and phrases—and sometimes *rather than* or *not*—can be used to give a balanced treatment to items in a list or series or to parts of a compound construction.

Examples in this section are given in outline form to show the parallel structure (printed in italics) and the connectives (printed in boldface).

Each year more and more women enter traditionally "male" professions.
|| *They become* civil or electrical engineers;
*they become* attorneys, public defenders, and judges;
   **and**
*they become* professors of physics and computer science.

### 26a For parallel structure, balance similar grammatical elements: nouns with nouns, prepositional phrases with prepositional phrases, clauses with clauses.

People no longer believe
|| *that it takes* brawn to design a skyscraper
   **or**
*that one needs* muscle to perform open-heart surgery.   [balanced subordinate clauses]

|| *Gaining equal recognition for equal responsibilities*
   **as well as**
*earning equal pay for equal work*
concerns women in the work force.   [balanced verbal phrases]

### 26b To make the parallel clear, repeat a preposition, an article, the *to* of the infinitive, or the introductory word of a long phrase or clause.

The number of women demanding equal opportunity is not likely
|| *to* decrease in the future
   **but**
*to* increase during the next decade.

A woman who enters a career wants to be seen
|| *as* a competent worker first
   **and**
*as* a woman second.

Copyright © 1995 by Harcourt Brace & Company. All rights reserved.   *319*

**26c  Use parallel structures with correlatives (*both...and; either...or; neither...nor; not only...but also; whether...or* ).**

**Both**  ‖  *women who work outside the home*
**and**  ‖  *women who remain home to raise children*
can be said to hold equally challenging jobs.

Copyright © 1995 by Harcourt Brace & Company. All rights reserved.

Deduct 7 points for each incorrect revision and 3 for each incorrect underlining.

**Parallel Structure**                                          Exercise 26–1

NAME _____  SCORE _____

DIRECTIONS   In the following sentences underline the connective(s) that call for parallel structure; then make the structure(s) parallel.

EXAMPLE

Today women not only <u>want</u> challenging careers <u>but also</u> ~~to have~~ *want* equal pay and esteem for

what they do.

1. In the 1970s the number of women attending college <u>and</u> ~~who held~~ *holding* jobs increased

   noticeably.

2. Since the early 1900s women's rights have expanded to include voting, education,

   <u>and</u> ~~that they could own~~ *ownership of* property.

3. Three major problems facing women are ~~to gain~~ *gaining* access to education, finding suit-

   able employment after graduation, <u>and</u> being paid equal salaries for equal work.

4. In the past, women had difficulty ~~to enroll~~ *enrolling* in certain educational curriculums <u>and</u>

   finding employment in certain professions.

5. Many women explored career paths that were very nontraditional; these women

   ~~want~~ *wanted* to be hired for their skills rather than as tokens.

6. Many people believed that women were physically unable to do such things as

   work in law enforcement, ~~cutting~~ *cut* trees, <u>or</u> fly commercial airplanes.

Copyright © 1995 by Harcourt Brace & Company. All rights reserved.

7. Current studies indicate that many women now start their own businesses, ~~working~~ *work* out of their homes, <u>or</u> freelance for a number of companies rather than follow more customary career paths.

8. Unlike women entering the job market in the 1970s <u>or</u> those ~~who looked~~ *looking* for work in even earlier times, young women today have many role models in almost all walks of life to look to for inspiration.

9. Women fly in space, hold elective office at all levels of federal, state, and local government, <u>and</u> ~~administering~~ *administer* many large corporations.

10. Ratification of the equal rights amendment would assure that all people have equal rights under the law <u>and</u> ~~for~~ *that* no one ~~to have~~ *has* her or his rights denied.

Copyright © 1995 by Harcourt Brace & Company. All rights reserved.

Deduct 20 for each incorrect revision. (Revisions will vary.)

**Parallel Structure—Continued**                           Exercise 26–2

NAME _____ SCORE _____

DIRECTIONS   To make a topic outline easily readable, a writer should use parallel structure for Roman-numeral and capital-letter headings. The following outline fails to use parallel structure in five places. Revise these five parts so that all divisions of the outline will be immediately clear to the reader.

Thesis:    The American worker is likely to experience at least three major kinds

of change in his or her job during the next twenty years.

I.  Changes in the work schedule

A.  Fewer hours

F
B.  ~~Working~~ flexible schedules

J
C.  ~~Companies will use~~ job sharing,

II.  Changes in the workplace

A.  Less stressful environments

B.  Recreational facilities

Elimination of routine chores
C.  ~~Many routine chores will be handled by robots and computers.~~

Changes in
III.  ~~There will be many new~~ fringe benefits,

A.  Educational opportunities

B.  Sabbaticals

O
C.  ~~Providing~~ on-site day-care centers

Copyright © 1995 by Harcourt Brace & Company. All rights reserved.

# 27

**Make grammatical structure, tone and style, and viewpoint consistent.**

### 27a Keep tense, mood, and voice consistent.

SHIFT IN TENSE     During the 1970s women all over the world *became* concerned about their status and *establish* organizations to work for improvements. [The verbs shift from past to present tense.]

CONSISTENT     During the 1970s women all over the world *became* concerned about their status and *established* organizations to work for improvements.

SHIFT IN MOOD     To understand the recent history of the women's movement, first *read* Betty Friedan's *The Feminine Mystique* and then you *should examine* what feminists in the 1970s and 1980s have said about women's rights. [*Should examine* is a shift to the indicative mood from the imperative (command) mood, *read*.]

CONSISTENT     To understand the recent history of the women's movement, first *read* Betty Friedan's *The Feminine Mystique*, and then *examine* what feminists in the 1970s and 1980s have said about women's rights .

SHIFT IN VOICE     First we *will read The Feminine Mystique*; then the writings of contemporary feminists *will be examined*. [The verbs shift from the active to the passive voice.]

CONSISTENT     First we *will read The Feminine Mystique*; then we *will examine* the writings of contemporary feminists.

Shifts in tense are especially troublesome. The tendency to shift tenses is particularly strong when you are referring to what others have written, since the customary practice is to speak of written observations in the present tense even though they were written in the past.

SHIFT     In *The Feminine Mystique* (1963) Betty Friedan *discusses* the lack of fulfillment modern women feel and *showed* that their sense of loss results from their inability to find meaningful occupations outside the home.

CONSISTENT     In *The Feminine Mystique* (1963) Betty Friedan *discusses* the lack of fulfillment modern women feel and *shows* that their sense of loss results from their inability to find meaningful occupations outside the home.

### 27b Be consistent in the use of person and number. (See also **6b**.)

SHIFT IN PERSON     *If you* study the history of the women's rights movement, *one* cannot help being startled by the changes that have occurred. [The pronouns shift from second to third person.]

Copyright © 1995 by Harcourt Brace & Company. All rights reserved.

CONSISTENT    If you study the history of the women's rights movement, you cannot help being startled by the changes that have occurred.

SHIFT IN NUMBER    Each woman fighting for equality in the working world feels that they have a valid cause.   [The pronouns shift from singular to plural.]

CONSISTENT    Each woman fighting for equality in the working world feels that she has a valid cause.

## 27c  Avoid needless shifts between indirect and direct discourse.

SHIFT    Women are now saying, "Give us the opportunity to enter the same professions men do" and that they want to be paid the same salaries as men.   [The sentence shifts from direct to indirect discourse.]

CONSISTENT    Women are now saying that they want the opportunity to enter the same professions men do and that they want to be paid the same salaries as men.

OR

Women are now saying, "Pay us the same salaries as men, and give us the same opportunity to enter the same professions."

Copyright © 1995 by Harcourt Brace & Company. All rights reserved.

Deduct 6 for each incorrect revision and 4 for each incorrectly filled blank.

## Avoiding Needless Shifts                                        Exercise 27–1

NAME _____ SCORE _____

DIRECTIONS    In each of the following sentences, indicate the kind of shift by writing 1 if the shift is in tense, mood, or voice; 2 if it is in person or number; or 3 if it is between indirect and direct discourse. Then revise the sentence to eliminate the needless shifts.

EXAMPLE

        *we*
When ~~one~~ looks back over history, we realize how much the role of women

in society has changed.                                                     __2__

1.  In most ancient societies, women remained at home, and no formal
*they received*

education was received by them.                                             __1__

2.  Biblical historians say, *that* Old Testament traditions dealt extensively

with the relations between husbands and wives, and that religious

authorities affirmed the dominant role of males.                           __3__

3.  Indeed, most of the world's religions questioned the equality of

women, and *their ability to* could they do any useful work other than housework

and child rearing.                                                         __1__

4.  Interestingly, Roman women had more legal rights and social

freedom than other European women did, but their status

*d*
decreases with the spread of Christianity.                                __1__

Copyright © 1995 by Harcourt Brace & Company. All rights reserved.

5. When you examine the course of the Industrial Revolution, ~~we~~ <sup>you</sup> find

   that one of its results was the emergence of women as a significant

   part of the work force.                                                      2

6. Before the 1800s, very few women in the United States worked out-

   side the home, and those who did often ~~do~~ <sup>did</sup> so out of necessity.     1

7. At first, the working conditions in textile mills and in other factories

   that employed women were reasonably good, but as time ~~goes~~ <sup>went</sup> by

   conditions ~~worsen~~ <sup>worsened</sup> and salaries drop <sup>ped</sup>.              1

8. The women's rights movement, which began during the first half of

   the nineteenth century, ~~makes~~ <sup>made</sup> significant progress in 1920 with the

   introduction of a constitutional amendment granting women the

   right to vote.                                                               1

9. Beginning in 1873 the amendment was brought before Congress

   every year until it finally ~~passes~~ <sup>passed</sup>.                          1

10. Each of the major wars fought by our country has also had ~~their~~ <sup>its</sup>

    effect on the role women could play outside their homes.                    2

Copyright © 1995 by Harcourt Brace & Company. All rights reserved.

## 28

**Make a pronoun refer unmistakably to its antecedent.** (See also **6b** and **19j**.)

A pronoun usually depends on an antecedent—a word it refers to—for its meaning. If the antecedent is not immediately clear so that the reader can understand without difficulty, we say that the *reference* of the pronoun is vague. Reference can be vague because *two* possible antecedents appear, because no specific antecedent has been provided, or because the pronoun refers to the general idea of the preceding sentence or sentences rather than to something more specific.

> *They* claimed that the standard work week would be only thirty-five hours by the middle of the 1980s. *They* said *this* because it had decreased continually since 1900.

There are three main ways to correct an unclear reference of a pronoun: (1) rewrite the sentence to eliminate the pronoun; (2) provide a clear antecedent for the pronoun to refer to; and (3) substitute a noun for the pronoun or, in the case of *this*, add a noun, making the pronoun an adjective.

> A *report produced by the American Institute for Research* claimed that the standard work week would be only thirty-five hours by the middle of the 1980s. *The researchers who worked on the report* made *this claim* because the *work week* had decreased continually since 1900.

### 28a  Make antecedents clear.

Recast the sentence to make the antecedent clear, or replace the pronoun with a noun.

AMBIGUOUS    John wrote to Oliver when *he* got *his* new job.

CLEAR       When John got his new job, he wrote to Oliver.
                             OR
      When Oliver got his new job, John wrote to him.

### 28b  Make references clear.

Recast the sentence to bring a pronoun and its antecedent closer together or substitute a noun for the obscure pronoun.

REMOTE    Oliver studied the job description. A variety of skills and a considerable amount of work experience were required. *It* convinced Oliver that he was not qualified for the position.

CLEAR      Oliver studied the job description. A variety of skills and a considerable amount of work experience were required. The *job description* convinced Oliver that he was not qualified for the position.

OBSCURE    When *Ms. Mazaki's* company was founded, she asked Oliver to join her staff. [A reference to an antecedent in the possessive case is unclear.]

CLEAR      When *Ms. Mazaki* founded her company, *she* asked Oliver to join her staff.

Copyright © 1995 by Harcourt Brace & Company. All rights reserved.     *329*

## 28c  Use broad or implied references only with discretion.

In general, avoid broad references—that is, the use of pronouns like *which*, *it*, and *this*—to refer to the general idea of a preceding sentence or clause.

| | |
|---|---|
| BROAD | Oliver was a skillful writer, and he used it to get ahead in the new company. |
| CLEAR | Oliver used his writing skill to get ahead in the new company. |
| BROAD | The new company sent out many proposals. This was Oliver's specialty. |
| CLEAR | The new company sent out many proposals. This type of writing was Oliver's specialty.  [One way to correct a vague *this* is to add a noun for the pronoun to modify.] |

OR

The new company's need to submit many proposals made use of Oliver's specialty.  [The vague *this* is eliminated by rewriting the two sentences as one.]

## 28d  Avoid the awkward use of *it* or *you*.

| | |
|---|---|
| AWKWARD | Although it was difficult for Oliver to get a new job, he decided to do it. [The use of the first *it*—an expletive—makes the meaning of the second *it*—a pronoun—unclear.] |
| CLEAR | Although it was difficult for Oliver to get a new job, he decided to do so. |
| AWKWARD | In the yellow pages it lists the names of all insurance companies in the area. [This construction is wordy as well as awkward.] |
| CLEAR | The yellow pages list the names of all insurance companies in the area. |

OR

In the yellow pages are the names of all insurance companies in the area.

| | |
|---|---|
| AWKWARD | In my business writing textbook they name two kinds of proposals. |
| CLEAR | My business writing textbook names two kinds of proposals. |

OR

The author of my business writing textbook names two kinds of proposals.

Copyright © 1995 by Harcourt Brace & Company. All rights reserved.

Deduct 7 for each incorrect revision and 3 for each blank incorrectly filled.

**Reference of Pronouns** Exercise 28–1

NAME _____ SCORE _____

DIRECTIONS   In the following discussion of leisure time, circle each pronoun whose reference is vague and write the pronoun in the blank. Then revise the sentence or sentences to clarify the meaning.

EXAMPLE

Because the
~~The~~ number of hours spent at work may lessen during the

                                                          will
coming decade, ~~which will cause~~ people ~~to~~ reevaluate their

idea of leisure time.*                                    _____which_____

1. The four-day work week, is used by some companies,

   ~~This~~ gives employees more leisure time.            _____This_____

2. Increased automation is bound to give employees more

   leisure time. It is hard to say what employees will do
        their additional leisure time.
   with it.                                               _____it_____

3. In Sebastian de Grazia's Of Time, Work, and Leisure, he

   explains the ancient and modern attitudes toward

   leisure.                                               _____he_____

*Give credit for correct revisions not shown here.

Copyright © 1995 by Harcourt Brace & Company. All rights reserved.

4. The ancient Greeks had a different notion of leisure

from ours. We think of using our leisure time to accom-

plish a definite task, like painting our house or washing

the Greeks,    leisure time
the car. To ~~them~~ ~~it~~ meant time to do something enjoy-

able for its own sake.                                   _____them; it_____

total dedication
5. Many Americans' ~~are totally dedicated~~ to the work

ethic, ~~This~~ causes them to take a second job if they have

very much spare time.                                    _____This_____

6. When Americans retire from their careers, they often

their time.
do not know what to do with ~~it.~~                      _____it_____

7. Although it has been a tradition in our country to retire

retirement
at the age of sixty-five, we are now unsure that ~~it~~ is a

good thing.                                              _____it_____

Because many
8. ~~Many~~ people find nothing to give them a sense of ful-

they become unhappy.
fillment outside their work, ~~which leads to personal~~

~~unhappiness.~~                                         _____which_____

Copyright © 1995 by Harcourt Brace & Company. All rights reserved.

9. Perhaps we need to adopt the ancient Greek attitude

   *The Greeks*

   toward leisure. ~~They~~ thought that just thinking, or even

   doing nothing, could be worthwhile.                    *They*

10. Extended lifespans may well allow us to have twenty or

    more years of retirement living. We must educate our-

    *our time*

    selves ~~to use~~ ~~this~~ creatively.                    *this*

Copyright © 1995 by Harcourt Brace & Company. All rights reserved.

*333*

## 29

**Construct sentences to emphasize important ideas.** (See also Chapters **20, 21,** and **24.**)

The following suggestions will help you stress the main ideas in your sentences and paragraphs.

### 29a Place important words at the beginning or end of the sentence—especially at the end.

| | |
|---|---|
| UNEMPHATIC | *Leisure time can be a problem*, sociologists tell us. |
| EMPHATIC | *Leisure time*, sociologists tell us, *can be a problem*. [Note how *problem* gains emphasis.] |

**Note:** The two strong (emphatic) positions to place important ideas within a sentence, a paragraph, a section, or an essay are the beginning and the end.

### 29b Occasionally use a periodic instead of a cumulative sentence.

In a cumulative or loose sentence, the main idea comes first and less important ideas or details follow. In a periodic sentence, however, the main idea appears last, just before the period.

| | |
|---|---|
| LOOSE | Some people find leisure time troublesome, causing them problems such as boredom, anxiety, and stress. |
| PERIODIC | Problems such as boredom, anxiety, and stress trouble some people faced with leisure time. |

**Caution:** Do not overuse periodic sentences; if you do, they will lose their effectiveness.

### 29c Occasionally arrange ideas in an ascending order of climax.

In this type of sentence, build your ideas from least to most important.

| | |
|---|---|
| UNORDERED | Some people regard leisure time as wasteful, as unhealthy, or as a nuisance. |
| ORDERED | Some people regard leisure time as wasteful, as a nuisance, or even as unhealthy. |

### 29d Rely on the active voice and forceful verbs.

The active voice emphasizes the *doer* rather than the *recipient* of the action of the sentence. Sentences in which the grammatical subject and the doer of the action are the same usually present your ideas strongly and directly.

Copyright © 1995 by Harcourt Brace & Company. All rights reserved.

| PASSIVE | Most people's leisure time is spent watching television. |
|---|---|
| ACTIVE | Most people spend their leisure time watching television. |

**Note:** When you wish to emphasize the recipient of an action over the doer, use the passive voice to make this emphasis clear.

Leisure time is spent by most people watching television.

### 29e  Repeat important words to gain emphasis. (See also Chapter **26**)

| UNEMPHATIC | The prospect of retirement has many unpleasant associations for people who have no interests outside work. It makes them think of boredom. And it may also bring to mind uselessness and loss of self-respect. |
|---|---|
| EMPHATIC | The prospect of retirement has many unpleasant associations for people who have no interests outside their work—associations such as boredom, uselessness, and loss of self-respect. |

### 29f  Invert the word order of a sentence occasionally to gain emphasis. (See also **30b**.)

| NORMAL ORDER | Most people need to feel that they contribute to their community in a productive way. |
|---|---|
| INVERTED ORDER | Feeling that they contribute to their community in a productive way is what most people need. |

**Caution:** If overused, this method of gaining emphasis will make your style seem stilted and contrived.

### 29g  Use balanced sentence construction to gain emphasis.

A balanced sentence uses grammatically equal structures—usually main clauses with parallel elements—to express contrasted (or similar) ideas. The balance emphasizes the contrast (or similarity).

To use leisure time well is to feel productive; to use leisure time ineffectively is to feel aimless.

### 29h  Abruptly change sentence length to gain emphasis.

[1]"Stopping out," or taking a temporary leave from college, is not a new phenomenon, but it is a practice that is gaining popularity among college students. [2]One national survey shows that 95 percent of all college students have seriously considered stopping out during their undergraduate years. [3]Many students would like to leave school temporarily to travel, to work, or just to find themselves. [4]They feel that what they learn during their absence from college will introduce them to the real world, will motivate them to become better students, and will enable them to set realistic goals for their futures. Certainly stopping out can accomplish all of these things.

  Copyright © 1995 by Harcourt Brace & Company. All rights reserved.

[6]College administrators and many students who have unsuccessfully tried stopping out warn about the disadvantages: getting permanently sidetracked from one's education, finding that travel plans and jobs do not always work out, being tempted to do nothing during the absence from college. [7]Thus, stopping out should not be tried on impulse. [8]It requires careful planning so that a student will not waste a semester or a year, and it requires informing advisors and filling out forms so that the college will know what the student will be doing during the leave and when he or she will return.

**Note:**   These two paragraphs also illustrate the use of the active voice—in all sentences—and parallel structure—in sentences 3, 4, and 6—to achieve emphasis.

Copyright © 1995 by Harcourt Brace & Company. All rights reserved.

Deduct 10 for each unemphatic sentence.

**Emphasis**                                              Exercise 29–1

NAME _____ SCORE _____

DIRECTIONS    In each of the following, write a sentence that achieves emphasis by means of the pattern given. Then underline the part of the sentence that you wished to emphasize.

EXAMPLE
Place important words at the beginning of a sentence.
How many people, one wonders, look forward to retirement?*

1. Use balanced sentence construction to emphasize the similarities between two ideas.


2. Emphasize your idea by repeating structures.


3. Use balanced sentence construction to emphasize the differences between two ideas.


4. Emphasize your ideas by repeating key words.


*Answers will vary.

Copyright © 1995 by Harcourt Brace & Company. All rights reserved.

5. Write a series of sentences in which the most important idea is contained in a sentence that is noticeably shorter than the others.

6. Place important words at the end of the sentence.

7. Emphasize ideas by arranging them in the order of climax, from the least to the most important.

8. Emphasize your idea by inverting the usual word order of the sentence.

9. Use the active voice.

10. Emphasize ideas by means of a periodic sentence.

Copyright © 1995 by Harcourt Brace & Company. All rights reserved.

## 30

### Vary the structure and length of your sentences to maintain the reader's interest.

A writer of essays is usually more concerned about variety than is a writer of business letters and reports. In occupational writing, quite understandably, the emphasis is on clarity and simplicity rather than on style. But to hold the reader's attention, even the occupational writer must avoid too many short, choppy sentences, strung-out compound sentences, or sentences that begin in the same way. In short, business and technical writers, as well as general writers, need to know how to vary their sentence structure to produce writing that is not only clear but also pleasing to read.

**30a Vary the length of your sentences; avoid a series of short simple ones.** (See also **29h**).

SIMPLE     A few companies have set up retirement clinics. These clinics help workers prepare for their retirement years.

COMPOUND   A few companies have set up retirement clinics, and these clinics help workers prepare for their retirement years.

COMPLEX    A few companies have set up retirement clinics that help workers prepare for their retirement years.

**30b Vary the beginnings of your sentences.**

**(1) Begin with an adverb or adverbial clause.**

*Gradually*, workers learned to cope with retirement.   [adverb]
*When they began dealing with this issue*, workers close to retirement felt apprehensive. [adverbial clause]

**(2) Begin with a prepositional phrase or a verbal phrase.**

*Through courses and counseling*, the clinics help people discover the talents they would like to develop.   [prepositional phrase]
*Studying their life-long interests* these new retirees discovered things they had always wanted to do but had postponed.   [participial phrase]
*To have the opportunity to pursue a life-long dream* became an exciting possibility to retirees.   [infinitive phrase]

**(3) Begin with a sentence connective—a coordinating conjunction, a conjunctive adverb, or a transitional expression.**

Retirees are naturally apprehensive about their future. *But* the changes they face can offer them exciting opportunities.   [coordinating conjunction]
Retirees are naturally apprehensive about their future. *However*, the changes they face can offer them exciting opportunities.   [conjunctive adverb]

Copyright © 1995 by Harcourt Brace & Company. All rights reserved.

Retirees are naturally apprehensive about their future. When they grow more confident, the changes they face can offer them exciting opportunities.   [transitional expression]

### 30c  Avoid loose, stringy compound sentences. (See also **24b**.)

To revise a loose, stringy compound sentence, try one of the following methods.

#### (1) Make a compound sentence complex.

COMPOUND   Many older executives have achieved high salaries, and so they are expensive to keep on the payroll, and so their companies force them to retire early.

COMPLEX   Many highly paid older executives, who are expensive to keep on the payroll, are forced by their companies to retire early.

#### (2) Use a compound predicate in a simple sentence.

COMPOUND   Often people plan ahead, and they save money, and they retire much earlier than the "standard" age of sixty-five.

SIMPLE   Often people plan ahead, save money, and retire much earlier than the "standard" age of sixty-five.

#### (3) Use an appositive in a simple sentence.

COMPOUND   Many people plan ahead, and they are prudent, and they invest wisely the money they are saving for retirement.

SIMPLE   Many people, prudent individuals, plan ahead and invest wisely the money they are saving for retirement.

#### (4) Use a prepositional or verbal phrase in a simple sentence.

COMPOUND   The economy is unpredictable, and people saving for retirement know they must take inflation into account.

SIMPLE   In an unpredictable economy, people saving for retirement know they must take inflation into account.

### 30d  Vary the conventional subject-verb sequence by occasionally separating subject and verb with words or phrases.

S–V–C   Some employees are retiring from their present jobs at the age of fifty-five to start a new career.

VARIED   Some employees, at the age of fifty-five, are retiring from their present jobs to start a new career.

OR

Some employees, eager to start a new career, are retiring from their present jobs at the age of fifty-five.

**Note:**   This kind of variety must be used with discretion because separating sentence parts too frequently makes the writer's style unnatural and even difficult to follow. (See also **25a**.)

   Copyright © 1995 by Harcourt Brace & Company. All rights reserved.

**30e Occasionally, instead of the usual declarative sentence, use a question, an exclamation, or a command.**

Retirement clinics are not commonplace today. In fact, only a very few companies supply them. But who can say how popular they may become in the next twenty years when the greatest percentage of workers in our history will be reaching retirement age?

Copyright © 1995 by Harcourt Brace & Company. All rights reserved.

Deduct 3 for each incorrect answer.

**Variety**                                                            Exercise 30–1

NAME _____   SCORE _____

DIRECTIONS   Analyze the ways in which the writer has achieved variety in the paragraphs below by answering the questions that follow. When the question asks, "Which sentence…?" use the sentence's number to identify your answer.

[1]Until recently most people believed that once they chose a profession as young adults they had to stick with it until they retired. [2]Now some of them are challenging this assumption. [3]Unlike their co-workers who never change fields these people are abandoning the security of a known routine to explore a new occupation.

[4]Why do professionals such as lawyers, teachers, administrators, and business executives "quit"? [5]Because they have decided that their comfortable salary and relatively secure position are less important than their desire to feel satisfied with their work. [6]In their professional occupations they feel bored. [7]They admit that they are unhappy. [8]So why not change? [9]In some respects they are only doing what all of us dream about: following our secret ambitions. [10]However these people—without any guarantee of success—have had the courage to put their dreams into action. [11]What finally has convinced them to risk the change is the thought that if they do not at least try, they will never know if they could have succeeded. [12]That is the best challenge of all. [13]They want and need to test themselves.

[14]These days there are even counselors who help professionals as they make this difficult decision to change their lives. [15]A switch from banking to weaving blankets is dramatic. [16]But if a banker is tired of three-piece suits and has always wanted to move to a mountain resort and restore antique furniture, a career counselor can help determine whether or not the change is likely to be for the best. [17]Of course, not everyone who considers changing careers will actually do so. [18]But for those who take the risk, a happier life may be waiting.

[19]I know how difficult it is to make the switch, but it can be done. [20]I live in a resort area where many people come to try out their secret ambitions. [21]My next-door neighbor used to be a social worker in Miami; now he weaves baskets. [22]A couple down the road taught school for years, until they decided that they would rather run a country

store. [23]And a former geological consultant raises Christmas trees and rhododendrons. [24]When I ask these people if the expense and the uncertainty of the change have been worth it, I always get the same answer. [25]"Yes!"

ANALYSIS

1. Which sentences are shortest? <u>2, 6, 7, 8, 12, 13, 15, 19, and 25</u>

   Why do you think the writer used them? <u>for emphasis</u>

2. How many simple sentences are there? <u>5</u>

   How many compound sentences? <u>2</u>

   How many complex sentences? <u>17</u>

3. How many sentences begin with something other than the subject? <u>12</u>

   Which sentences begin with an adverb or an adverb phrase? <u>1, 2, 5,</u>
   <u>9, 14, and 24</u>

   Which begin with an adverb clause? <u>3, 16, and 24</u>

   Which begin with a coordinating conjunction or transitional expression? <u>2,</u>
   <u>8, 10, and 23</u>

4. In which sentence is the usual subject-verb sequence interrupted by a word or phrase? <u>10</u>

5. Which sentences are not declarative sentences? <u>4, 8, and 25</u>

   What kind are they? <u>interrogative (4, 8) and exclamatory (25)</u>

 Copyright © 1995 by Harcourt Brace & Company. All rights reserved.

Deduct 10 for each incorrect sentence.*

**Variety—Continued**                                  Exercise 30–2

NAME _____ SCORE _____

DIRECTIONS   Write sentences to illustrate the techniques for achieving variety listed below. You may want to continue this book's theme of the world of work.

1.  a simple sentence containing a compound predicate

2.  a complex sentence

3.  a sentence beginning with an adverb clause

4.  a simple sentence containing a compound predicate

5.  two sentences, the second beginning with the coordinating conjunction

*Answers will vary.

Copyright © 1995 by Harcourt Brace & Company. All rights reserved.    *347*

6. a sentence beginning with a single-word modifier

7. a sentence in which the subject and verb are separated by an intervening word **or** words

8. a simple sentence containing at least one prepositional phrase

9. a sentence beginning with an adverb or an adverb phrase

10. a sentence beginning with a subordinate clause

Copyright © 1995 by Harcourt Brace & Company. All rights reserved.

**Mastering Variety: A Review**                    Exercise 30–3

NAME _____ SCORE _____

DIRECTIONS   Rewrite each of the following paragraphs so that the sentences flow more smoothly and the style is more varied. Use a transitional expression or two, vary the beginnings of some of the sentences, combine sentences, and omit or add words if you wish.

[1]In the last decade more and more people started their own businesses. [2]They grew tired of working for someone else. [3]These independent businesspersons frequently work out of their homes. [4]This trend is sometimes referred to as cottage industry. [5]It has its roots in the traditional arts and crafts practiced by people in remote rural areas. [6]The types of contemporary cottage industries operating today include much more than the production of handicrafts. [7]People working at home do such diverse things as develop computer software, make specialty products, and act as freelance consultants. [8]People working out of their homes like the freedom gained from being their own boss. [9]They gain satisfaction from creating and running their own businesses.

REVISION (sample revision)

In the last decade more and more people started their own businesses because they grew tired of working for someone else. These independent businesspersons frequently work out of their homes, a trend sometimes referred to as <u>cottage industry</u>. It has its roots in the traditional arts and crafts practiced by people in remote rural areas. But the types of contemporary cottage industries operating today include much more than the production of handicrafts. For example, people working at home develop computer software, make specialty products, and act as freelance consultants. People working out of their homes like the freedom gained from being their own boss and the satisfaction of creating and running their own businesses.

Copyright © 1995 by Harcourt Brace & Company. All rights reserved.

[1]We can find plenty of examples of worthwhile uses of leisure time in our society. [2]The arts are attracting many new participants and fans. [3]People are painting, writing, dancing, and making music as never before. [4]Small rural communities are being visited by symphony orchestras and art exhibitions. [5]Handicrafts are flourishing everywhere. [6]A majority of the citizens in some towns are involved in making things. [7]They are making things like pottery, furniture, and macramé items. [8]People are buying the works that are produced. [9]Artists of all types are able to make a living from their crafts.

REVISION (sample revision)

We can find plenty of examples of the worthwhile uses of leisure time in our society. For example, the arts are attracting many new participants and fans. People are painting, writing, dancing, and making music as never before. And small rural communities are being visited by symphony orchestras and art exhibitions. Handicrafts, especially, are flourishing everywhere. In some towns, a majority of the citizens are involved in making things like pottery, furniture, and macramé items. Because people are buying the works that are produced, artists of all types are able to make a living from their crafts.

Copyright © 1995 by Harcourt Brace & Company. All rights reserved.

# 31

**Learn to be a critical reader and to apply critical thinking as you write. Avoid logical fallacies.**

### 31a  Distinguish between fact and opinion.

As a reader, you should expect that the writer presents a case supported by *facts* more than merely by personal opinion. Facts are pieces of information that can be verified through independent sources or by repeating an experiment or observation; opinion, on the other hand, is subjective; that is, it is a judgment that may or may not be based on fact and represents one person's or one group's interpretation of observable data.

Learning to read critically and to think logically are important skills for any writer; by employing them you distinguish between reasonable claims and ideas and those that are less so. The critical reader evaluates what you have to say carefully, having learned that not everything they read is necessarily true. Most readers are reasonable people who will listen to what you have to say. How readily they will be persuaded to look at an issue from your point of view, however, depends on how well you present your case, how reasonable your argument is, and how convincing your supporting evidence is. In many respects, informing your reader about an issue is similar to a lawyer's presenting a case to a jury. The more logical the presentation—that is, the more clearly stated and reasonably argued—the more likely your reader will be to listen to your ideas. The more sense a piece of writing makes, the more confidence your reader will have that you know what you are talking about.

Critical reading and logical thinking are two of the most valuable skills a writer can develop since they help you to make reasonable choices in such things as how you structure a piece of writing, the evidence that you select to include, and the way in which you approach a topic to present to a particular reading audience.

### 31b  Read for evidence.

As a critical reader, you must expect writers to support their claims with sufficient, convincing evidence. The evidence you are given should be such that you can verify it for accuracy; although in some arguments conclusions are based on evidence drawn from *exceptional* cases or from a *biased* sample rather than from information representing the norm. *How much* evidence will be compelling depends on how great or innovative is the claim. If a writer takes a stance that differs greatly from the normal way people view the subject, that writer will need to provide more evidence than will one who explores an issue from a less controversial perspective.

Whether you write or read critically, look for evidence that is accurate, representative, sufficient, and verifiable.

Copyright © 1995 by Harcourt Brace & Company. All rights reserved.

## 31c  Evaluate for credibility.

As you read, or when you review your writing, ask yourself the following questions:

1. Does the writer support claims with evidence?
2. Does the writer reveal how and where the evidence was obtained?
3. Does the writer recognize that other points of view may also be legitimate?
4. Does the writer use sarcasm or make personal attacks on opponents?
5. Does the writer reach a conclusion that the evidence will support?

## 31d  Learn to use inductive reasoning in your writing.

Inductive reasoning uses examples and draws conclusions based on those instances.

When you reason inductively, you reach a conclusion based on the available evidence. For example, if you were writing a memorandum to argue that one of your company's customers should be refused further credit (your conclusion), you would base your recommendation on the customer's poor record of past payment (the evidence). You are reasoning that because the customer has repeatedly failed to meet his obligations in the past, he will probably fail in the future. Note that there is an element of probability, rather than certainty, in inductive reasoning. This requires that you present as much evidence as possible to support the conclusion you want the reader to accept. But, because successful inductive arguments rest on convincing evidence, the conclusions that they reach strike the reader as possible and believable.

Using evidence as the basis of its argument, inductive reasoning can be a powerful persuasive tool, lending strength and authority to any material you present. The evidence you present to your readers helps to convince them that the conclusions you reach are valid ones. It is, therefore, essential that you select with care the material that you present; insufficient evidence will make your conclusions look weak, while evidence clearly expressing exceptional cases or bias will cause readers to doubt your conclusions.

When you use induction, you can arrange your material in one of three ways: (1) present the evidence first and then draw the conclusions, (2) let the reader draw the conclusions, or (3) state the conclusion first and then develop the evidence that led you to form that conclusion. The first two methods are effective if you are writing for a reader who is likely to disagree with you; it is best to let this reader evaluate the evidence and then draw the conclusion along with you as you sum up or reach the conclusion that you, the writer, leave unstated. The third method, presenting the conclusion first and then discussing the evidence that supports it, works well for a reader who is likely to be receptive. Which strategy you select will depend on your audience and the effect you wish to produce.

## 31e  Learn how to use deductive reasoning in your writing.

The writer who uses deductive reasoning begins with generalizations (premises) and reaches a conclusion about a particular instance based on the generalizations. For example, if you know that DOS 6.0 is the version of a disk operating system installed on your home computer, and that your software package requires DOS 6.0 to operate, then you could conclude that this package will run on your computer. For a deductive

Copyright © 1995 by Harcourt Brace & Company. All rights reserved.

argument to be successful, your reader must accept as true the generalizations (premises) you use. In deductive reasoning the writer argues logically from principles (assertions of truths) rather than from evidence; if A is true and B is true then it follows that C must be true. This basic logical structure is called a syllogism. Syllogisms contain three parts: a major premise (usually a generalization), a minor premise (usually a specific fact), and a conclusion that fits both the major and the minor premises. In a deductive argument, you must carefully examine your premises to make sure that they are both true; for even if you reason logically you may reach a wrong conclusion if one of your premises is false. Finally, for your argument to be effective, you must be certain that your premises are ones that your reader can accept.

| | |
|---|---|
| MAJOR PREMISE | People doing the same job should be paid the same salary. |
| MINOR PREMISE | Both men and women work at this job. |
| CONCLUSION | Men and women doing this job should be paid the same salary. |

## 31f Learn how to use the Toulmin method.

Another way of viewing the use of logic is to see an argument as moving from accepted facts or evidence (data), to a conclusion (claim) by way of a statement (warrant) that establishes a reasonable relationship between the two.

For example in the argument,

> Since my computer has DOS 6.0, and since my software package requires 6.0 to run, my software package will run on my computer,

the claim is that my software program will run on my computer, and the data is that my software package requires DOS 6.0 to run. The warrant, my computer has DOS 6.0, ties the two statements together, making the conclusions follow from the data.

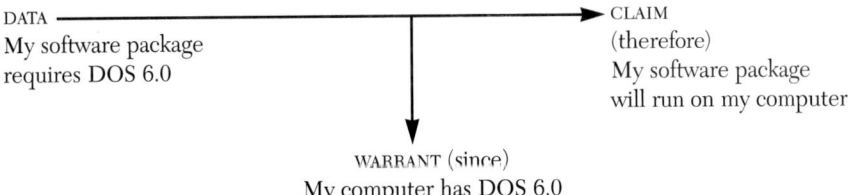

DATA ———————————————————————→ CLAIM
My software package                                    (therefore)
requires DOS 6.0                                       My software package
                                                       will run on my computer

WARRANT (since)
My computer has DOS 6.0

## 31g Recognize logical fallacies and avoid using them.

Fallacies are errors in arguments that have to do with false premises, faulty reasoning, insufficient or biased evidence, or other factors that distort or misrepresent the issues.

### (1) Ad Hominem:

Attacking the person who presents an issue rather than dealing with the issue itself.

> It may be true that my competitor makes a superior product, but what has he done for our community?  [The competitor's contribution to the community has no bearing on the quality of the product he sells.]

Copyright © 1995 by Harcourt Brace & Company. All rights reserved.

## (2) Bandwagon:

An argument that says in effect, "Everyone else is doing (or thinking or saying) this, so you should."

> Everyone likes this make of computer, and you will too.   [You will not necessarily *respond* in the same way as the majority.]

## (3) Begging the Question:

An assertion that restates the point just made. Such a statement is circular in that it draws as its conclusion a point stated in the premise.

> She habitually is late because she finds it impossible to be on time.   [Being late and finding it impossible to be on time mean the same thing.]

## (4) Equivocation:

An assertion that illogically relies on the use of a term in two different senses.

> You have a right to complain, so do what is right and complain.   [The word *right* means both "a just claim" and "correct."]

## (5) False Analogy:

Assuming that because two things are similar in certain ways they must be similar in other ways.

> Since this computer costs the same as the other model, it will perform all the functions the other does.   [Equal price does not necessarily indicate that the two products will do the same things.]

## (6) False Authority:

Assuming that an expert in one field can be a credible expert in another.

> The 2438 computer is the best one to meet our accounting needs, as our wellness coordinator has shown.   [Wellness coordination is unrelated to accounting.]

## (7) False Cause:

Assuming that because one event followed another, the second was caused by the first. Sometimes called *post hoc ergo propter hoc* ("after this, so because of this").

> Last week we redecorated our showroom, and already the number of customers has increased by 25 percent.   [The assumption that the redecoration *caused* the increase is not warranted.]

## (8) False Dilemma:

Asserting that there are only two options when other options exist.

> Our drop in profit last year leaves us with only two options: freeze wages or lay off 25 percent of our employees in order to give raises to the other 75 percent.   [In fact, other options exist.]

Copyright © 1995 by Harcourt Brace & Company. All rights reserved.

### (9) Guilt by Association:

An unfair attempt to make someone responsible for the beliefs or actions of others.

> This computer must be worthless because it is made by the same company that made the useless XE8765. [Different models can be manufactured by the same company without having the same design flaws.]

### (10) Hasty Generalization:

A generalization based on too little, exceptional, or biased information.

> People dislike changing to new products. [This may be true of some people, but certainly not of all people.]

### (11) *Non Sequitur:*

A conclusion that does not follow from the premise.

> This product outperforms its competitors; therefore, it will sell well. [Many superior products do not sell well.]

### (12) Oversimplification:

A statement or argument that leaves out relevant considerations about an issue.

> Because he is over sixty he cannot possibly be an effective administrator. [Assumes that all older persons are ineffective.]

### (13) Red Herring:

Bringing up an irrelevant issue in order to avoid the real issue.

> Never mind the workers' demands for better benefits; what we really need is an improved customer service department. [Improving customer relations has nothing to do with meeting workers' demands.]

### (14) Slippery Slope:

Assuming that if one thing is allowed it will only be the first step in a downward spiral.

> Using computers in college classrooms will ultimately lead to the replacement of professors with machines. [Assumes that the machines can do everything that a human teacher can.]

Copyright © 1995 by Harcourt Brace & Company. All rights reserved.

Deduct 5 for each incorrectly filled blank and 5 for each incorrect reason given.

## Arguing Logically

Exercise 31–1

NAME _____   SCORE _____

DIRECTIONS   Identify the logical fallacy that weakens each statement, and explain why it is falla-
cious. Refer to the list of fallacies in this section.

EXAMPLE
John has been an accountant for six years; therefore, he is

better at his job than the new man we hired last month.   _Non Sequitur_

Reason: Being in a job longer does not necessarily mean that a
person is more skilled than someone hired more recently.

1. We cannot grant your request for additional time

because we cannot approve extensions at this time.   _Begging the question_

Reason: Additional time and extensions mean the same thing.

2. She ordered a larger storage disk, so the material that

she saves will be better organized.   _Non Sequitur_

Reason: Larger storage disks do not guarantee that files will
be better organized.

3. John apologized to the customer for the late order,

telling her that one of the telephones in the office had

required extensive repairs during the week.   _Red Herring_

Reason: Repairs to one telephone most likely had nothing to
do with preparing the order.

4. There are only two ways to evaluate this situation: yours

and mine.   _False Dilemma_

Reason: More points of view are possible.

Copyright © 1995 by Harcourt Brace & Company. All rights reserved.

5. I put this new fax machine in our office, and in the last week sixteen transmissions have failed to get where we sent them.  <u>False Cause</u>

   Reason: The missing transmissions need not be the fault of the fax machine.

6. Women are disorganized.  <u>Hasty Generalization</u>

   Reason: Some women may be disorganized, but not all.

7. In a free enterprise system we should be free to do whatever we want to get business.  <u>Equivocation</u>

   Reason: The <u>free</u> in <u>free enterprise</u> has a limited meaning that the second <u>free</u> greatly exceeds.

8. All of the other executives wear three-piece suits, so should you.  <u>Bandwagon</u>

   Reason: What is appropriate for some may be inappropriate for others.

9. Why should I accept your evaluation of my work when you received a poor evaluation yourself?  <u>Ad Hominem</u>

   Reason: That one did not <u>receive</u> a good evaluation has no bearing on one's ability to <u>make</u> an evaluation.

10. These two training videos about hostile working environments run for sixty minutes, so either one will be good to show our supervisors.  <u>False Analogy</u>

    Reason: That the two videos run for the same time does not mean they contain the same material or are of equally good quality.

Copyright © 1995 by Harcourt Brace & Company. All rights reserved.

# THE PARAGRAPH ¶ 32

## 32

**Write paragraphs that are unified, coherent, and adequately developed.**

We recognize the beginning of a new paragraph in a composition by the indention—about an inch when handwritten and five spaces when typewritten. Although a paragraph may be only one sentence long, most paragraphs require several sentences to adequately develop the central, or controlling, idea. By the time we finish reading the paragraph, we expect to know what the writer's controlling idea is and to be able to recognize the relationship that each of the other sentences has to the sentence that states or suggests this controlling idea. Finally, we expect the sentences to flow along smoothly so we do not have to mentally fill in any words or phrases or stop reading after every sentence or two to refocus our attention.

### 32a Construct unified paragraphs.

The controlling idea is printed in italics in the first sentence of the following paragraph. Notice that the key word, *flextime*, is echoed in each of the other sentences in the paragraph. (The words that echo *flextime* are printed in boldface.)

> [1]*Flextime is here to stay.* [2]Surveys, like one conducted by *Psychology Today* in 1978, suggest that the American worker strongly approves of **flextime**; fully 78 percent of those questioned by *Psychology Today* wanted to have some say in the time they started and finished their workday. [3]Employers, while they acknowledge some problems with **individualized work schedules**, seem equally satisfied with the system; as proof, only two percent of the companies that have tried **flextime** have returned to eight- or nine-to-five schedules. [4]Based, then, on present trends, **flextime** seems certain to replace the rigid work schedules that people have followed since the beginning of the Industrial Revolution. [5]Looking ahead to the kind of workplace we will have in the year 2001, William Abbott, editor of the World Future Society's newsletter, *Careers Tomorrow*, says quite confidently, "Workers will schedule their own hours under **flextime**."

The unity of this paragraph would be destroyed by inserting a sentence that is not a part of the plan called for by the controlling idea. Try reading the paragraph with these sentences inserted between sentences 2 and 3: "People obviously have different biological rhythms. Some people go to bed early and awaken at 6:00 or 7:00 ready for a full day's work. Others cannot fall asleep before 12:00 or 1:00 a.m. and are not really prepared to face the workplace before 10:00 a.m." Although pertinent to the general subject of convenient work schedules, these three sentences, or even one of them, would shift the focus of the paragraph away from the specific controlling idea: *Flextime is here to stay.*

To maintain unity in a paragraph, then, you must be conscious of your controlling idea each time you add a sentence.

The sentence that states the controlling idea of a paragraph is called the *topic sentence*. Although a paragraph may have unity without an expressly stated topic

Copyright © 1995 by Harcourt Brace & Company. All rights reserved.

sentence, inexperienced writers will find that a clear, specific topic sentence in each paragraph helps them keep their writing well organized. Since the controlling idea gives direction to the other sentences in the paragraph, the topic sentence usually appears early in the paragraph—as the first or second sentence. But it may be placed elsewhere—for example, at the end if the writer wishes to build up to a dramatic closing.

To construct unified paragraphs, follow these suggestions:

(1) Make sure every paragraph has a main idea.

(2) Relate each sentence to the main idea of the paragraph.

### 32b Make paragraphs coherent by arranging ideas in a clearly understandable order and by providing appropriate transitions.

A coherent paragraph is one in which the relationship of any given sentence to the ones before it is clear and the transitions between the sentences are smooth. A coherent paragraph is easy to read because there are no jarring breaks—the sentences are arranged in a clear, logical order. The following patterns are ones most often used to achieve coherence in a piece of writing.

**(1) Arrange ideas in a clearly understandable order.**

(a) Chronological order

Follow a time sequence in your presentation of material.

(b) Spatial order

In descriptions you can start from a logical position and move from north to south, from near to distant, from left to right, and so on.

(c) General-to-specific or specific-to-general

Begin with a general statement or idea and support it with specific details, or begin with a striking detail or series of details and conclude with a summary statement.

(d) Topic-restriction-illustration

The paragraph begins with a general statement, narrows it to a specific aspect, and illustrates it.

(e) Question-answer

The first sentence asks a question that the supporting sentences answer.

(f) Problem-solution

The first sentence or two states the problem and the remainder of the paragraph details the solution.

**(2) Use appropriate transitions to link ideas together.**

A coherent paragraph also provides smooth transitions between sentences:

(a) Pronouns are used to refer to antecedents in preceding sentences.

(b) Key words, phrases, or ideas are repeated.

(c) Conjunctions or other transitional expressions are used.

(d) Parallel structures are used where appropriate.

**Note:** It is equally important to link paragraphs with clear transitions.

Copyright © 1995 by Harcourt Brace & Company. All rights reserved.

The following paragraph illustrates methods of achieving coherence. The sentences are arranged in order of climax (from least important to most important); the methods of making smooth transitions between sentences are indicated by numbers—2a through 2d—that correspond to those cited above.

> There is much evidence that the roles of the sexes are changing. [2c] First, and most noticeable, is the change in dress and appearance. Today many young men and women look much alike. [2a] Their hair may be similar in style. [2a, 2d] They may wear the same shirts and pants. [2a, 2d] They may in fact go to the same unisex hair stylists and boutiques. [2c, 2b] But more significant evidence of the shift in sex roles is apparent in the job market. While a generation ago no more than one out of ten women with young children was employed outside the home, today four out of five is so employed. [2c] And positions that were once considered appropriate only for men are now being filled by women. [2c, 2b] Conversely, many men today are training to be nurses, secretaries, and flight attendants— positions once considered unmistakably feminine.

### 32c  Develop the paragraph with details and examples.

The length of a paragraph varies with its purpose. Thus a one-sentence paragraph or even a one-word paragraph ("Yes" or "No") may say emphatically all that the writer needs to say. Paragraphs that report dialogue are usually short because a new paragraph must begin each time the speaker changes. Most paragraphs in expository writing tend to vary in length from about seventy-five to two hundred fifty words, the average length being about one hundred words. (And remember that when you write in longhand your paragraph looks much longer than it would if it were typed or set in print.)

#### (1)  Develop with specific details.

The use of details is the most common method of developing a controlling idea, and almost every paragraph makes some use of it. Pertinent facts and details about the changing roles of the sexes are used to develop the controlling idea of the paragraph illustrating coherence. Notice that the most significant fact is discussed last, a common type of arrangement for this method of development.

#### (2)  Develop with one striking example or several closely related examples.

A paragraph developed by examples is almost certain to hold the reader's attention. The success of one of the most popular books ever printed, Dale Carnegie's How to Win Friends and Influence People, depends primarily on the author's use of hundreds of examples. Because of the interest generated by a well-chosen example, many essays and speeches begin with this type of development. In his book Megatrends, John Naisbitt discusses what it takes for a company to be labeled "successful" and offers the following illustration:

> [1]But even among the most successful [companies], Tandem is remarkable. [2]The founder of the fast-growing $100-million-a-year company, James Treybig, emphatically states that the human side of the company is the most critical factor in reaching his goal— the $1 billion mark in annual sales. [3]Treybig frees up 100 percent of his personal time to spend on "people projects." [4]Tandem's people-oriented management style includes Friday-afternoon beer parties, employee stock options, flexible work hours (unlike Intel, where

Copyright © 1995 by Harcourt Brace & Company. All rights reserved.

everyone is expected to show up promptly at 8:15 a.m.), a company swimming pool that is open from 6:00 a.m. to 8 p.m., and sabbatical leave every four years—which all employees are required to take. [5]Review meetings occur spontaneously with no formal procedures.

—JOHN NAISBITT, *Megatrends*

Examples may be fully developed, like the one above, or simply listed in passing, like the series of examples in the following paragraph used to illustrate the characteristics of workaholics during childhood.

[1]Marilyn Machlowitz, a psychologist for New York Life Insurance Co., has spent the past eight years studying the obsessive worker—first for her doctoral dissertation at Yale, more recently for her book Workaholics: Living With Them, Working With Them. [2]From interviews with 165 apparent workaholics, she has found that most exhibit identical characteristics early in their lives. [3]They turn games into imitations of work and go about them with intensity. [4]They set up lemonade stands, run sidewalk carnivals and cash in returnable soda bottles. [5]Later, they sell more Girl Scout cookies, Christmas cards and magazine subscriptions than anyone else on the block. [6]And their teachers love them because they are such hard-working, attentive students.      —"Thank God, It's Monday," *Dun's Review*

## 32d  Use various strategies of paragraph development.

The controlling idea of a paragraph may be developed in a number of ways. Most experienced writers use several methods of development in each paragraph without having to think about what they are doing. But as an inexperienced writer, you may need to practice consciously the methods discussed below until you are able to use them automatically and naturally. A study of these methods will help you not only to think of things to say but also to organize your thoughts, since the method of development usually suggests a pattern of arrangements for the sentences in the paragraph. Keep in mind that the subject matter will also determine which method or methods of paragraph development will be most effective.

### (1)  Narrate a series of events.

Strong paragraphs are internally consistent—their ideas relate to each other logically. If you are describing an event or a sequence of events, one good way to ensure that your paragraph is strongly unified is to discuss those events in the order in which they occurred. The following paragraph describes the method one businessman employs to make his company successful. Note that the ideas are arranged in chronological order, that is, in the order in which they take place.

[1]When it comes to choosing between business and social activities, Howard Bronson knows where his priorities lie: with his job. [2]Bronson, who heads his own financial public relations firm, is up by four a.m. and has mapped out his day by the time he gets to his Manhattan office at 6:45. [3]He works at a furious pace, often skipping lunch, until about 6:30 in the evening. [4]Then, after dinner, he puts in another hour and a half of reading before turning in at 12:15.      —"Thank God, It's Monday," *Dun's Review*

### (2)  Describe to make a point.

The use of well-chosen descriptive details will help your reader to visualize what you are talking about and to share the experience more fully. Carefully chosen, concrete

Copyright © 1995 by Harcourt Brace & Company. All rights reserved.

details strengthen a paragraph, and you will want to be sure that the ones you use are relevant to the main purpose of the paragraph.

> [1]The fault ran straight through Culligan's ranch house, and had split its levels, raising the back twelve feet. [2]The tornado sound had been made by eighty million tons of Precambrian mountainside...half the mountain came falling down in one of the largest rapid landslides produced by an earthquake in North America in historical time. [3]People were camped under it and near it. [4]Among the dead were some who died of the air blast, after flapping like flags as they clung to trees. [5]Automobiles rolled overland like tumbleweeds. They were inundated as the river pooled up against the rock slide, and they are still at the bottom of Earthquake Lake, as it is called—a hundred and eighty feet deep.
>
> —JOHN MCPHEE, *In Suspect Terrain*

Present details in a clear order—from general to specific, from top to bottom, from near to far, from right to left. By doing so you provide a logical and orderly scheme for your reader to follow and help prevent confusion. Use appropriate descriptive details that appeal to all of the senses, not just sight.

### (3) Explain a process.

Paragraphs that are organized around a process explain how something is done or made. Like the narrative paragraph, this type of paragraph follows a series of events as they occur through time and thus employs a chronological arrangement. In fact, a reader would likely be confused by a process paragraph that violated the ordinary chronological sequence of a group of events as it described them.

In the following instructions for repairing faucets, the reader would more than likely find it difficult to repeat the process if the chronological order were jumbled.

> [1]Turn the handle [of the pipe cutter] to the right until there is no resistance. [2]Then separate the two wheels. [3]Hold the lower one fast and give the handle a fraction of a turn into the work. [4]Tighten the upper wheel against the lower. [5]Again turn the handle to the right. [6]In this way, the cutter removes a layer of metal.  —MAX ALTH, *Do-It-Yourself Plumbing*

### (4) Show cause and effect.

A cause and effect paragraph explains why a particular outcome has occurred. To use this method effectively you must supply enough evidence to convince your reader that you understand the cause or causes for a particular effect. The following two paragraphs rely primarily on comments from interviews to persuade us that the editors of *Newsweek* have correctly identified two causes for the American worker's lack of commitment to the work ethic.

> [1]The problem traces to two main factors: a younger work force—25 per cent of which is under 25 years old—and the nature of the work itself in a highly industrialized society. [2]"It's mainly a problem of this younger worker," said Benjamin Aaron, director of the Institute of Industrial Relations at UCLA. [3]"He doesn't want to work to get ahead; he wants to work to get enough money for a while and then he wants to drop out." [4]Or, as Jerry Wurf, president of the American Federation of State, County and Municipal Employees, put it: "The Depression is something they learned about in history class."
>
> [5]Once on the job, workers all too often find that, however good their wages and working conditions, work is a totally unsatisfying experience. [6]"People my age don't take much pride

Copyright © 1995 by Harcourt Brace & Company. All rights reserved.

in this work," says Victoria Bowker, a 27-year-old blueprinter at Lockheed Aircraft. [7]"In the old days, you used to start a job and you used to finish it. [8]Now things have become so diversified you can't see your product; you start something and it goes through 50 million other hands before it's completed." [9]Mike Eckert, a longtime Lockheed employee twice Miss Bowker's age, agrees that things have changed. [10]"Today's management doesn't have any compassion for the person that's down the line," he says. [11]"They treat you like a machine...and you can't treat human nature that way." [12]And when a worker begins feeling like a machine, he'll probably resort to one of two alternatives: goldbrick, or start looking for another job. [13]"I'll tell you how attitudes are," UAW vice president Ken Bannon summed up last week. [14]"You will find people who say they would rather work in cleanup and take a cut of 15 cents an hour than work the assembly line. [15]At least on cleanup you have the choice of sweeping the pile in the corner or sweeping the pile by the post."

—"Too Many U.S. Workers No Longer Give a Damn," *Newsweek*

**(5) Compare and contrast to develop an idea.**

In everyday conversation you often explain or evaluate something by comparing or contrasting it with something else. In compositions, too, comparison or contrast is often useful. In general, the people, ideas, or objects to be compared or contrasted should belong to the same class (one type of roommate is compared or contrasted with another type of roommate, not with some other type of person).

The following paragraph compares the importance of three values—work, family, and leisure.

[1]Along with family life, work and leisure always compete for people's time and allegiance. [2]One or the other is usually the center of gravity, rarely does the individual strike an equal balance among all three. [3]For the New Breed, family and work have grown less important and leisure more important. [4]When work and leisure are compared as sources of satisfaction in our surveys, only one out of five people (21 percent) states that work means more to them than leisure. [5]The majority (60 percent) say that while they enjoy their work, it is not their major source of satisfaction. [6](The other 19 percent are so exhausted by the demands work makes of them that they cannot conceive of it as even a minor source of satisfaction.)　　—DANIEL YANKELOVICH, "The New Psychological Contracts at Work"

**(6) Use classification and division to develop an idea.**

Classification organizes things and ideas by placing them in larger groups that share certain common characteristics. Division, on the other hand, separates objects and ideas into smaller subclasses according to some dividing principle. For example, the following paragraph on "alternate work schedules" breaks its subjects down into the four categories of compressed time, flextime, part-time, and shared time.

[1]Alternate work schedules are rapidly replacing the rigid eight- or nine-to-five workdays of the past. [2]For example, the 10-hour, four-day workweek has been used in industry for many years. [3]This type of compressed-time job schedule allows the worker to enjoy a regular three-day weekend. [4]But surpassing compressed-time scheduling in popularity with workers is flextime, which lets them choose their own hours to begin and end their workdays so long as they work a certain numbers of hours a week and so long as they are on the job during the mid-day core period. [5]Also, part-time work, which involves one out of every six workers in this country, continues to gain in popularity as people, especially the young,

Copyright © 1995 by Harcourt Brace & Company. All rights reserved.

begin to value leisure as much as they do money. [6]And shared-time work schedules, whereby two employees share one full-time position, are saving employers as well as employees from massive lay-offs in an increasingly automated society.

Classifications and division often work together in the same paragraph or set of paragraphs.

### (7) Formulate a definition.

Sometimes you may need to compose a paragraph or even an entire essay to define a difficult term or a term that you want the reader to understand in a special way. The essayist Jon Stewart uses two paragraphs to define a silicon chip for a general audience of readers who may be unfamiliar with the workings of microprocessors and computers.

> [1]The revolution, of course, is that wrought by the silicon chip, that virtually invisible, spiderlike network of tiny electronic circuits etched on a flake of silicon (sand) less than half the size of the fingertip. [2]In the form of microprocessors, or miniature computers, it is invading every aspect of American life—the way we play, work, even think.
>
> [3]This computer-on-a-chip, with amazing powers of memory and computation, has immediate applications almost everywhere from universities to automobile engines, from corporate offices to farms, from hospitals to satellites. [4]Virtually any routine work can be taken over by the devices, which have shrunk to less than 1/30,000 the size of their original predecessors, those giant room-size computers of yesterday. [5]And they grow smaller and more versatile almost daily. [6]IBM recently announced that it can now produce a chip containing 256,000 bits of information, four times as many as are crammed onto the most highly integrated chip today.
>
> —JON STEWART, "Computer Shock: The Inhuman Office of the Future"

### (8) Use a combination of strategies.

The various methods of developing a controlling idea have been listed and illustrated separately, but almost every paragraph makes use of more than one method. For example, the paragraph developed by cause and effect (see **(4)** above) also uses details, and the paragraph developed by classification (see **(6)**) also uses definition and examples to explain the types of alternate work schedules given.

**Note:** Since paragraphs do not often include more than twelve sentences, you do not need a detailed or complicated outline to follow. But you may find it useful to jot down the controlling idea and the main points of development before you begin to write a paragraph.

Copyright © 1995 by Harcourt Brace & Company. All rights reserved.

Deduct 4 for each incorrect answer.

**Analyzing Paragraphs**  Exercise 32–1

NAME _____  SCORE _____

DIRECTIONS   Analyze the unity, coherence, and development of the following paragraph by answering the questions that follow it. When the question asks, "Which sentence…?" use the sentence's number to identify your answer.

¹During the 1980s and 1990s both men and women have registered complaints about the role of women in the work force. ²Obviously, a possible reason for women's unhappiness with their jobs relates to their salaries: women generally earn far less than men for the same kind of work. ³Employers who pay women less than men offer many excuses for doing so. ⁴They assert that women are absent from work more frequently than men. ⁵And they claim that women are less dependable at work than men. ⁶Yet many employers have found these prejudices to be untrue. ⁷When placed in positions of responsibility women are as capable of handling the work as their male counterparts. ⁸Furthermore, women supervisors seem to be able to handle uncooperative workers more easily than male authority figures do. ⁹Finally, employers have found that female administrators are capable problem solvers. ¹⁰Although the job market is more open to women than it was one hundred years ago, many working women still find it difficult to advance as rapidly as men holding the same job, despite the increased opportunities.

ANALYSIS

1.  Which sentence states the controlling idea of the paragraph?  1

2.  What is the major method of development used in the paragraph?  Use of relevant details

3.  Which sentences show the use of comparison or contrast?  4, 5, 7, and 8

4.  What is the key term that is repeated throughout the paragraph?  women

5.  Which sentences use transitional expressions?  2, 5, 6, 8, and 9

6.  Which two sentences are linked by parallel structure?  4 and 5

Copyright © 1995 by Harcourt Brace & Company. All rights reserved.

7. Which sentence is the shortest one in the paragraph? _4_

   What is its purpose? _It introduces the main point of the_

   _second half of the paragraph._

8. Which sentence is the clincher, the one that repeats the controlling idea? (Not all

   paragraphs have this kind of sentence.) _10_

9. What is the basis for the arrangement of the sentences in the paragraph: is it by

   time, from general to specific, by order of climax, or by location of what is being

   described? _general to specific_

10. Which two sentences use an introductory phrase to vary from the usual word order

    of placing the subject first? _1, 7, 9, and 10_

    Which sentence begins with a single adverb? _2 (or 8 or 9)_

    Which sentence uses an introductory subordinate clause? _10_

Copyright © 1995 by Harcourt Brace & Company. All rights reserved.

Deduct 8 1/2 for each incorrectly filled blank.

## The Controlling Idea and the Methods of Development    Exercise 32–2

NAME _____    SCORE _____

DIRECTIONS    For each of the following four paragraphs list (1) the number of the sentence that states the controlling idea; (2) the main method of development used to support the controlling idea; and (3) an additional method of development used in the paragraph.

PARAGRAPH ONE

[1]Psychologists are also starting to unravel the mystery of why some people turn out to be workaholics while others do not. [2]It is becoming increasingly apparent that the process begins in early childhood. [3]Psychiatrist Lawrence Susser, who treats workaholics on his yacht in New Rochelle, New York, claims that workaholics are the product of "controlling parents"; that is, parents who, rather than simply supporting or setting guidelines for their children, are constantly pushing them to excel. [4]The children fear that unless they live up to these expectations, love will be withheld. [5]Eventually they develop a sort of "inner voice" that prods them in the same manner as their parents did. [6]This voice can be very demanding, Dr. Susser says. [7]It does not let them relax. —"Thank God, It's Monday," *Dun's Review*

1. Controlling idea   *2*_____

2. Main method of development   *cause/effect*_____

3. Additional method of development   *details*_____

PARAGRAPH TWO

[1]Many people mistakenly think that creativity is the ability to think thoughts that no one else has ever thought. [2]In fact, creativity is just a way of looking at the ordinary in a different way. [3]Alex Osborn, one of the pioneers in the study of creativity and imagination, discovered that almost everyone is more creative than he [or she] thinks. [4]We usually don't recognize our good ideas as creativity in action. [5]For example, in a large midwestern city a gang of thieves had worked out a coordinated routine that was so smooth and fast that they could break into a clothing store, sweep the clothes off the racks, and be gone before the police could answer the

Copyright © 1995 by Harcourt Brace & Company. All rights reserved.

alarm. [6]Then a young detective got an idea. [7]He asked all the clothing merchants in the area to alternate the way they placed the hangers on the rack. [8]He told the store owners: "Turn one hook toward the wall and the next one toward the aisle. Do it that way throughout the store." [10]When police answered the next alarm they found the frustrated thieves removing the garments one at a time. [11]Everyday "shirtsleeve creativity" is simply the adaptation of existing ideas—taking another look at all the pieces of the situation from a new perspective.

—DALE O. FERRIER, "Shirtsleeve Creativity"

1. Controlling idea    *2*

2. Main method of development    *definition or example*

3. Additional method of development    *example or definition*

PARAGRAPH THREE

[1]Of course, not everyone who works long hours is a workaholic. [2]Many people simply have more work than they can handle on a normal schedule. [3]Others work for companies where long hours are part of the job. [4]Some Wall Street law firms, for example, are notorious for expecting associates to work late into the night; and young lawyers, even when they have no work to do, frequently remain at their desks until their superiors have left the office. [5]There are also a number of people who reluctantly moonlight because they need the money.

—"Thank God, It's Monday," *Dun's Review*

1. Controlling idea    *1*

2. Main method of development    *classification*

3. Additional method of development    *comparison/contrast*

*or example*

Copyright © 1995 by Harcourt Brace & Company. All rights reserved.

PARAGRAPH FOUR

[1]Even in the past decade, the average U.S. farm worker's productivity has increased 185 percent, while the manufacturing worker has upped productivity by 90 percent. [2]Those figures may not be as high as in the past, or in other parts of the world today, but they certainly compare favorably with the performance of U.S. office workers. [3]In the past 10 years, according to studies done by the Massachusetts Institute of Technology and others, the white-collar worker's productivity has increased a mere four percent. [4]This figure is reached by measuring time spent on work tasks, as well as by counting units (letters typed, reports written, cases handled) where possible. [5]Four percent is the total for the whole past 10 years, not an annual rate of productivity increase.

—RAYMOND P. KURSHAN, "White-collar Productivity"

1. Controlling idea _2_

2. Main method of development _comparison/contrast_

3. Additional method of development _details_

Answers will vary.

**Paragraph Practice: Examples**                    Exercise 32–3

NAME _____ SCORE _____

DIRECTIONS    Using several closely related examples or one striking example as the method of development (see **32c(2)**), write a paragraph on one of the subjects listed below or one of your own or your instructor's choosing. First, plan the paragraph, writing out the controlling idea and making a list of three or more examples that will develop it. Then compose the sentences in your paragraph. You may use examples from this book (rephrased in your own words, of course), examples from your own knowledge, or, if your instructor permits, examples gathered from research.

SUBJECTS

1. the ideal job for you

2. writing in your chosen profession

3. a useful internship for your chosen career

4. a good supervisor/supervisee relationship

5. managing stress

CONTROLLING IDEA


DEVELOPMENT

1.

2.

3.

4.

5.

Copyright © 1995 by Harcourt Brace & Company. All rights reserved.                    *373*

PARAGRAPH

Copyright © 1995 by Harcourt Brace & Company. All rights reserved.

Answers will vary.

**Paragraph Practice: Process Analysis**                    Exercise 32–4

NAME _____ SCORE _____

DIRECTIONS    Using process analysis as the method of development (see **32d(3)**), write a paragraph on one of the subjects listed below or one of your own or your instructor's choosing. First, plan the paragraph, writing out the controlling idea and making a list of three or more examples that will develop it. Then compose the sentences in your paragraph. You may use examples from this book (rephrased in your own words, of course), examples from your own knowledge, or, if your instructor permits, examples gathered from research.

SUBJECTS

1. how to select a major

2. the best way to prepare for your chosen career

3. how you found a summer job

4. how to construct an effective résumé

5. how to ask someone for a recommendation

CONTROLLING IDEA

DEVELOPMENT

1.

2.

3.

4.

5.

Copyright © 1995 by Harcourt Brace & Company. All rights reserved.

PARAGRAPH

Copyright © 1995 by Harcourt Brace & Company. All rights reserved.

Answers will vary.

**Paragraph Practice: Cause and Effect**                    Exercise 32–5

NAME _____ SCORE _____

DIRECTIONS    Using cause and effect as the method of development (see **32d(4)**), write a paragraph on one of the subjects listed below or one of your own or your instructor's choosing. First,
plan the paragraph, writing out the controlling idea and making a list of three or more examples
that will develop it. Then compose the sentences in your paragraph. You may use examples from
this book (rephrased in your own words, of course), examples from your own knowledge, or, if
your instructor permits, examples gathered from research.

SUBJECTS

1. the effects of on-the-job stress

2. the causes of students changing their major

3. the effects of a sluggish economy on soon-to-be graduates' attitudes about finding
   a job

4. the causes of students seeking internships in their chosen field

5. the effects of computerization on the modern office or on your chosen profession

CONTROLLING IDEA

DEVELOPMENT

1.

2.

3.

4.

5.

PARAGRAPH

Copyright © 1995 by Harcourt Brace & Company. All rights reserved.

Answers will vary.

**Paragraph Practice: Comparison or Contrast**    Exercise 32–6

NAME _____ SCORE _____

DIRECTIONS    Using comparison or contrast as the method of development (see **32d(5)**), write a paragraph on one of the subjects listed below or one of your own or your instructor's choosing. First, plan the paragraph, writing out the controlling idea and making a list of three or more examples that will develop it. Then compose the sentences in your paragraph. You may use examples from this book (rephrased in your own words, of course), examples from your own knowledge, or, if your instructor permits, examples gathered from research.

SUBJECTS

1. compare or contrast your major with the major of a friend

2. compare or contrast the roles of men and women in your chosen profession

3. compare or contrast a smoker's versus a non-smoker's reaction to a ban on smoking in the workplace

4. compare or contrast being self-employed and working for a large corporation in your chosen profession

5. compare or contrast the benefits of majoring in a specific professional field (such as accounting) with majoring in a liberal art (such as history)

CONTROLLING IDEA

DEVELOPMENT

1.

2.

3.

4.

5.

Copyright © 1995 by Harcourt Brace & Company. All rights reserved.

PARAGRAPH

Copyright © 1995 by Harcourt Brace & Company. All rights reserved.

Answers will vary.

**Paragraph Practice: Classification**                    Exercise 32–7

NAME _____ SCORE _____

DIRECTIONS    Using classification as the method of development (see **32d(6)**), write a paragraph on one of the subjects listed below or one of your own or your instructor's choosing. First, plan the paragraph, writing out the controlling idea and making a list of three or more examples that will develop it. Then compose the sentences in your paragraph. You may use examples from this book (rephrased in your own words, of course), examples from your own knowledge, or, if your instructor permits, examples gathered from research.

SUBJECTS

1. methods for preparing for an interview

2. types of career tracks in your chosen major

3. ways of dealing with stress

4. types of sexist behavior in the work place

5. types of writing demanded in your chosen profession

CONTROLLING IDEA

DEVELOPMENT

1.

2.

3.

4.

5.

Copyright © 1995 by Harcourt Brace & Company. All rights reserved.

PARAGRAPH

Copyright © 1995 by Harcourt Brace & Company. All rights reserved.

Answers will vary.

**Paragraph Practice: Definition**                    Exercise 32–8

NAME _____ SCORE _____

DIRECTIONS    Using extended definition as the method of development (see **32d(7)**), write a paragraph on one of the subjects listed below or one of your own or your instructor's choosing. First, plan the paragraph, writing out the controlling idea and making a list of three or more examples that will develop it. Then compose the sentences in your paragraph. You may use examples from this book (rephrased in your own words, of course), examples from your own knowledge, or, if your instructor permits, examples gathered from research.

SUBJECTS

1. the perfect boss

2. the meaning of career

3. the meaning of sexual harassment

4. the meaning of technical writing

5. the meaning of on-the-job stress

CONTROLLING IDEA

DEVELOPMENT

1.

2.

3.

4.

5.

Copyright © 1995 by Harcourt Brace & Company. All rights reserved.

PARAGRAPH

Copyright © 1995 by Harcourt Brace & Company. All rights reserved.

Answers will vary.

**Paragraph Practice: Combination of Methods**         Exercise 32–9

NAME _____         SCORE _____

DIRECTIONS   Write a paragraph on one of the subjects listed below. First, plan the paragraph, writing out the controlling idea and making a list of three or more examples that will develop it. Then compose the sentences in your paragraph, listing in the margin the type or types of development you have used. Underline the controlling idea of your paragraph, and make a list of the traditional devices you have used to achieve coherence. Consult the material in this Chapter (**32**) freely as you complete this exercise.

SUBJECTS

1. an aspect of relations between a supervisor and supervisee

2. proof that our society values work too much (or too little)

3. an aspect of being self-employed

4. an aspect of the connection between exercise and on-the-job productivity

5. an aspect of your major that is particularly attractive to you

CONTROLLING IDEA

DEVELOPMENT

1.

2.

3.

4.

5.

PARAGRAPH

 Copyright © 1995 by Harcourt Brace & Company. All rights reserved.

# 33

**Plan, draft, and revise your writing effectively.**

### 33a Consider your purpose, audience, occasion, and tone.

No matter what type of writing you do, you engage in a process of developing a subject for presentation to a specific audience. As you focus on your subject, you develop a thesis statement which will help you determine what material to include in your essay and the order in which you will present your ideas. This writing process is not a "straight line" that runs from the initial conception of a topic to a final draft. Rather, most writers find they must revise their original draft many times to make it a clear, well-unified piece of writing.

As you write, you process ideas, explore and answer questions, rethink strategies, stop in the middle of discussing one idea to take up another that has just occurred to you and so on. You may decide that your original thesis is not specific enough—or that it is not appropriate for your audience. The writing process is a dialogue between you (the writer) and your ideas; having new ideas grow out of the ones that you are currently working on is not a sign that you are a poor writer or that you do not know what you want to talk about. Rather, it indicates that you are working toward an understanding of exactly what you want to say. For this reason your first draft will probably need reorganizing and polishing before all the ideas can work together in a unified way.

### (1) Clarify your purpose.

The first question you will need to ask yourself is, "What do I want to accomplish in what I am about to write?" The purpose of or motivation for writing will determine how you organize your material, the tone you adopt, and even the length of sentences and the complexity of the vocabulary you use. All nonfiction writing has a purpose—for example, to express a point of view, to inform, or to persuade your reader. Be sure you have your purpose firmly in mind as you begin planning and writing.

*Expressive* writing emphasizes the writer's feelings and reactions to the world as in reminiscences, personal letters, and journals and diaries.

*Expository* or *referential* writing focuses your reader's attention on the world of events, ideas, and objects rather than on your feelings or attitudes about them as in news stories, laboratory and scientific reports, textbooks, and articles in professional journals.

*Persuasive* writing attempts to influence your reader's attitudes and actions as in a position paper or your résumé, an attempt on your part to make a future employer see you as a competitive applicant for a job.

*Literary* writing focuses on the imaginative use of language, to express something in an original way through the medium of language; forms of literary writing include fiction, poetry, drama, and humor.

Copyright © 1995 by Harcourt Brace & Company. All rights reserved.

## (2) Clearly define your audience.

You will also need to ask yourself for what sort of readers are you writing. Will they be familiar with the topic you have selected? What areas of the topic may need explaining? What level of technicality will your readers be able to understand? Are there aspects of your audience that you need to keep in mind, such as age or attitude toward the subject? What tone will best appeal to your audience? Will your readers "be on your side" or will you need to convince them to think about your topic from your point of view? Will you be writing for one or multiple audiences?

A specialized audience will have considerable knowledge of the subject about which you write and will be interested in reading what you have to say. General audiences, on the other hand, will not be experts on your topic but should be willing to read what you have to say. Even so, you can still identify shared characteristics about a general audience that will enable you to write effectively to them. It is often helpful for a writer to imagine the ideal person representing the general audience, with a typical background and expectations, and then adjust your selection of detail and tone accordingly. You may also write for multiple audiences, in which case you must take into account the special needs of each group of readers.

## (3) Understand the occasion.

You will also need to take into account the occasion for which you are writing. For example, an essay would be structured differently than a letter to the editor of a newspaper or a talk addressed to a group.

## (4) Set the appropriate tone.

The purpose, audience, and occasion will determine the tone that you use in your writing. Tone reflects your attitude about the subject and varies in level of formality depending on the particular writing situation. For example, the tone you would adopt in a letter thanking a company for an interview would be quite different from the tone you would use in writing to a friend about your experiences in that same interview. The tone of the first letter would be formal and perhaps reserved; the tone of the letter to your friend, however, would be more relaxed and candid.

## 33b Find an appropriate subject.

The appropriateness of a topic depends on the writer, the reader, and the occasion. You must know and care enough about the topic to have something interesting to say. But you must also be sure that the topic is acceptable to your intended reader or readers and suitable to the occasion on which it will be read.

If your subject is already assigned, or if your situation controls what you will write about, you will be able to begin your work with a consideration of your audience. However, in college writing your instructors may often ask you to select the subject you will write about, which is for some people the most difficult aspect of the writing process.

One way to find a subject to write about is to draw on your own experience, attitudes, or knowledge. What do you like to do with your time? What issues interest you? What

Copyright © 1995 by Harcourt Brace & Company. All rights reserved.

has happened recently that made you stop and examine your own attitudes about the subject? Is there a particular event, place, or person you could share with a reader? Being able to select your own topic usually means that you can write a more interesting paper because it will deal with something about which you care.

Often, however, the subject you are asked to write about will be one that is unfamiliar to you. For example, you may be required to write a paper for a European history class; the purpose of the paper will be to demonstrate your command of the subject to your instructor. In few papers of this kind will it be appropriate for you to write an essay which focuses on your personal opinions. However, writing about an aspect of the subject that interests you will help you write a stronger essay. To select such a topic, review your notes and the chapters in your textbook for issues that catch your attention, look in the subject catalog, or browse through books and articles on the topic in the library. If you are still unable to settle on a topic, discuss the assignment with other students or talk it over with your instructor.

Many times you will be required to write a paper bound by other constraints as well. For example, although you may be allowed to select your topic, your instructor may give you a length limit of six to eight pages. In this case, you would need to make certain that the topic you choose provides you with enough material to satisfy that requirement. Whatever the restrictions, it will be up to you to choose a topic that meets the requirements.

### 33c  Explore and focus the subject.

#### (1)  Explore your subject.

Writers use a variety of methods to explore a subject: freewriting, listing, questioning, and applying perspectives are some of the common ones.

**Freewriting**    If you are having difficulty getting started on a subject, this technique can be helpful: write nonstop for a brief period of time about whatever aspect of your subject first occurs to you; then examine what you have written for productive starting points.

**Listing**    Often when you begin working on an essay, you will have so many ideas that they will become disorganized if you try to review them all in your mind. Put this surplus information to work for you: make a list of everything that occurs to you about your topic. At this stage of the writing process you should not worry about imposing any order on your ideas. Just jot them down as rapidly as they come to mind and in whatever order they occur. What matters at this point is that you record the ideas themselves; grammar, spelling, and organization are all things you can concern yourself with after you have some material to work with.

As you write your list, one idea will often lead naturally to another. Jot it down. Interrupt your current train of thought if you suddenly think of an important, new aspect of your topic. Experiment until you learn how the listing method can work most effectively for you.

Copyright © 1995 by Harcourt Brace & Company. All rights reserved.

**Questioning**    Another way to explore your topic is to ask yourself the journalist's questions "who? what? when? where? why? and how?" Investigate your topic by answering these questions may help you to see your topic more clearly as well as to consider its various aspects. You will force yourself to consider who is concerned about the material you are developing, how something works the way it does, why an event happened as it did, and so forth.

**Applying Perspectives**    You may also want to try looking at your subject from someone else's point of view or in another light; the three ways most often employed are seeing the subject as static, dynamic, and relative.

The static perspective asks you to look at your subject as it is: defining it, describing its characteristics, analyzing its parts or main uses, or referring to specific examples that highlight the nature of the subject.

The dynamic perspective focuses on action and change: looking at your topic as it evolves through time, for instance, or as it works as a process.

Finally, the relative perspective examines relationships and systems; how, for instance, your subject is a part of a larger system or itself represents a system or compares to other systems.

**Strategies for Development**    Finally, consider which development strategies can best help you explore your topic (discussed fully in **32d**). These strategies parallel the ways in which we think about almost any subject: narration (retelling an event); process (how to do something or how something works); cause and effect (why something happened); description (what something is like); definition; classification and division (placing things into larger categories or breaking something down into its component parts); analysis (why something happened or is a particular way); example; and comparison and contrast (how things differ from and resemble each other). These strategies can serve as prompts to help you think about the various aspects of your topic.

### (2)  Limit and focus your subject.

Once you have explored your topic you must decide which aspects of it to discuss; that is, you must limit and focus your topic. The following analogy will help you understand the importance of this step. When you use a microscope, you first decide what you want to view under the lens, select the appropriate slide, and place it in the viewing field. Next, you use the rough focusing wheel to bring the object into view, turn the light up or down to sharpen or soften the contrasts in the image, and move the slide around on the viewing stage until the segment you wish to concentrate on is under the lens. Finally, you use the fine focusing wheel to bring this segment into sharp focus.

Focusing and limiting your subject works in much the same way. You must find those parts of the topic that meet the requirements of your reading audience. If, for example, you are writing an essay for your history class about the ways in which medieval monasteries preserved manuscripts, you will not want to include information about the architecture of a typical cloister or about the rivalries among the different monastic orders. Such material might be interesting, but it has little bearing on the subject you have chosen.

Copyright © 1995 by Harcourt Brace & Company. All rights reserved.

The particular focus you employ will be determined by your purpose, your audience, the length of your essay, and the amount of time you have in which to write it.

### 33d  Establish a thesis.

After limiting and focusing the subject of your writing, you will have done quite a bit toward identifying and developing an idea that controls the content of your text and the approaches you use to develop your ideas.

A thesis statement can make the focus of your essay clear to your reader. It will help you to think more exactly about your topic and to avoid straying from the topic as you write. The thesis statement is to the essay what the controlling idea is to the paragraph. As you discuss the various aspects of your topic, refer to your thesis statement from time to time to make sure that what you are saying relates to your main idea. Furthermore, if you have difficulty developing specific material that relates to your topic, a clear thesis statement can often help you organize your thoughts and explore new aspects of the topic. Finally, once you have formulated a thesis statement you should not think that you cannot change it. As you write you may find that you wish to explore a different or modified version of your topic, in which case you will need to rethink and revise your thesis statement.

Most frequently, thesis statements appear in the beginning paragraph; however, they may appear at whatever point in your essay best suits your purpose. For example, if the conclusion is one which you must prepare your reader to accept, your thesis will appear in the conclusion. Or, if you first need to give your reader background information about the broad aspects of your subject, your thesis statement could appear several paragraphs into your paper. In other types of essays—such as narrative or descriptive writing—a thesis statement is often omitted; in still others, it is only implied. Yet no matter what tactic you choose, a thesis statement can help you give direction to your writing—even if it never appears in the finished essay. Use your thesis statement to help you select the information you will include in your essay.

### 33e  Choose an appropriate method or combination of methods to arrange ideas.

A working plan can help you write your first draft more efficiently. The strategies for organizing paragraphs (see **32d**) and exploring ideas (see **33c**) are the same as those you will use to organize and develop your essay. The methods you finally use will be determined by your purpose, audience, occasion, subject, and focus; and you may find that a combination of methods will be most useful for organizing your material. But, no matter what method or methods you choose, you will probably want to create a written guide to follow as you work on your first draft. Some writers like to create a highly structured, formal outline and use it almost like a map; other writers feel that such a detailed outline inhibits them, that it stifles the development of their ideas. For these writers, jottings or informal lists work better. The formal outline or the formal arrangement are helpful, however, if you are working on a long or a complex project. Try all three ways; then use whichever one works best for you.

Copyright © 1995 by Harcourt Brace & Company. All rights reserved.

**Informal Working Plans**   Your informal working plan can be simply an organized list of the topics you plan to discuss. This list may resemble the one you generated as you initially explored your subject (see **33c**) with one important difference—in this new list you will arrange the topics in the order you wish to discuss them. As you generate your working plan, your ideas may overlap; arrange and refine the entries on the list until you have a good picture of the general structure of your essay. Like the other methods for arranging ideas, a working plan can be changed at any time—before or as you write.

**Outlines**   Roman numerals mark the headings that set forth the main points used to develop the thesis statement. The subheadings (signaled by capital letters) present the specific proof for the main headings. If the composition is very long—ten pages or more—further subheadings (signaled by Arabic numbers and then by lower-case letters) may come under the capital letter divisions.

The outline may or may not have an introduction and a conclusion. If during the planning stage you have in mind a way to introduce your thesis statement, write it down as a part of the outline. Likewise, if an idea for a conclusion or a concluding sentence occurs to you while planning the outline, record it at the time.

## TOPIC OUTLINE

How Not to Choose a Career

Thesis:  Students have four major misconceptions about how to choose a career.

I.   That the decision must be made alone, without the help of others
  A. Qualified friends and family members
  B. High-school and college counselors
  C. Employment agencies

II.   That the decision must be based entirely on reason
  A. The importance of emotions in decision making
  B. Examples of unhappy workers in occupations that seemed to be logical choices

III.   That the decisions must never be changed
  A. Changing job market
  B. Realization of a wrong choice

IV.   That the decision must make a person constantly happy
  A. The good and the bad side of all decisions
  B. The importance of other aspects of life
  C. The likelihood of emotional setbacks

## SENTENCE OUTLINE

How Not to Choose a Career

Introduction: The choice of a career is one of the most important decisions a person makes in life. Yet many people are poorly prepared for this decision.

Thesis: Students have four major misconceptions about how to choose a career.

Copyright © 1995 by Harcourt Brace & Company. All rights reserved.

    I.   They think they must make the decision unaided.
- A. Qualified friends and family members can be helpful.
- B. High-school and college counselors have special training to guide students in selecting their careers.
- C. Employment agencies can help students find the jobs that fit their skills and talents.

   II.   They think that their decisions must be based entirely on reason.
- A. Emotions are important in career planning.
- B. There are many examples of unhappy workers in occupations that seemed to be logical choices.

 III.   They think that their decisions must never be changed.
- A. The changing job market often necessitates a change in career plans.
- B. Actual work experience often reveals a wrong decision.

 IV.   They think that their decision must make them constantly happy.
- A. There is a good and a bad side to all decisions.
- B. Other aspects of life also influence happiness.
- C. In any job there is the likelihood of an emotional setback.

Conclusion: If students are aware of these common misconceptions about how to choose a career, they will be better prepared to make one of life's most important decisions.

Note these points about sentence and topic outlines:

(1)  The thesis is stated as a sentence regardless of the type of outline.

(2)  The introduction and the conclusion may or may not be included in the outline.

(3)  In both the sentence and the topic outlines, there must be at least two headings at each level (two Roman numerals, two capital letters) for the development to be adequate.

(4)  In the sentence outline, only sentences are used; in the topic outline, parallel structure is used.

(5)  In any outline, proper indention is maintained to make the outline easy to read.

Avoid making these four errors in outlines:

(1)  Overlapping headings. If information in one heading (for example, in II.B.) overlaps information in another (for example, in I.A.) or restates it in different words, then the essay will be repetitious.

(2)  Misarranged headings. The headings show the order of presentation. If the arrangement is not logical the paper cannot be coherent. (See also **32b**.)

(3)  Inadequately developed headings. Usually three main headings (Roman numerals) and at least two subheadings (capital letters) are necessary to supply adequate development.

(4)  Needless shifts in tense or number. This weakness is more noticeable in the sentence outline than in the topic outline. Usually a needless shift in the outline is carried over to the composition.

Copyright © 1995 by Harcourt Brace & Company. All rights reserved.

## FORMAL (OR CLASSICAL) ARRANGEMENT

You may follow a formal arrangement pattern when your main purpose is expository or persuasive:

Introduction    Announce the subject, set the tone, and gain the reader's attention.

Background    Provide any background information that the reader may need.

Definition of Terms and Issues    Define technical terms and stipulate meanings for ambiguous ones.

Development or Proof    Develop thesis.

Refutation    Answer disagreements or questions that your reader might have.

Conclusion    Summarize the main points. You may repeat the thesis considered in a wider context or ask the reader to take action or reconsider an accepted point of view.

Depending on the type of essay that you are writing, you may not need to include all of these parts, and you may emphasize certain parts more than others.

### 33f  Write the first draft.

Once you have created your informal working plan or formal outline, let it guide you as you write the first draft of your essay. Your most important goal is to get all of your material down on paper; do not worry if the sentences are not as polished as you would like them to be or if you misspell words or make grammatical mistakes. You will concentrate on eliminating the weak spots later on as you revise. Write as rapidly as you can; refer periodically to your working plan or outline to check your progress: Have you strayed from the main focus? Are you covering all the points you wished to consider? Your working plan or outline can also serve as a prompting tool when you cannot think of what to say next. You may want to stop occasionally to look over what you have already written; doing so will help you to gain a better perspective on the overall progress of your essay as well as to reassess the points you plan to cover next. Once you have completed your draft, set it aside for a time—preferably for a couple of days—so that you will be able to look at it from a less biased perspective when you begin to revise.

A composing process that works well for one writer may be a disaster for another. There is no one right way to generate a working draft. Some writers like to "blurt out" the entire essay at one sitting, while others work best when they write their compositions a portion at a time and wait till the revision stages to piece the parts together in a logical sequence. Become familiar with your own writing process so that you can use whatever method enables you to produce the best results most efficiently.

The following is an example of the first page of a rough draft for a composition on "How Not to Choose a Career."

    Copyright © 1995 by Harcourt Brace & Company. All rights reserved.

## How Not to Choose a Career

As ^small^ children most of us ^easily^ find our careers in a row of buttons: doctor, lawyer, teacher, police officer, fire fighter, astronaut, dancer. Ten years or so later, when what we want to be in life is a real question, many of us continue to be arbitrary in our choice of careers. We may, ^decide^ ~~be certain that we want~~ to be accountants even though we have never been good at mathematics, or we may choose to be nurses even though we cannot tolerate the sight of an open wound or an infected eye. ~~We sometimes make the most important decision of our lives without any reasonable guidelines.~~ It is not surprising, ^to learn^ ~~then~~ that many of us, ^will be^ ~~are~~ unhappy with our work, for we, ^approach^ ~~have approached~~ the choice of a career with a variety of misconceptions.

The first and perhaps most serious misconception ~~that~~ ~~many of us have~~ about career choices is that, ^many of us think^ we must make the decision alone, unaided. Actually there are many people who ~~not only want to help us make the decision but who~~ can ~~also~~ help us make the right decision: friends, family members, teachers, ^and^ guidance counselors.

Copyright © 1995 by Harcourt Brace & Company. All rights reserved.

### 33f(1)  Write an effective introduction.

In the average-length student paper—three hundred to five hundred words—the introduction and the conclusion need not be long. The introduction gets the reader interested in the body of the paper and may need to be no more than the thesis statement or a sentence that suggests the thesis statement. Students may use as an introduction a striking example, a shocking statement that is later explained, or a question that leads into the thesis.

### 33f(2)  Write an effective conclusion.

The conclusion of your essay should wrap up the points you have made. It may be no more than a restatement, in different words, of the thesis; or, if the thesis is only suggested in the introduction, the conclusion may be the first forthright statement of the thesis. A writer strengthens the conclusion by suggesting a solution to a problem presented in the essay. In the conclusion the writer should avoid raising a new point that is not to be explored, nor should the writer apologize for reaching the conclusion that he or she has stated.

### 33f(3)  Choose an appropriate title.

Usually a title will occur to you during the planning or the writing of the essay. Certainly you should not spend the time you need for writing your paper sitting and thinking about a title. If you have not thought of a title by the time that you finish the composition, however, use the topic or some form of it—for example, "Common Misconceptions About Career Choices." Rereading your introduction and conclusion and examining key words and phrases in the essay will also help you to identify possible titles.

When time permits, though, give attention to the title. Choose one that is provocative, that will make a reader want to read your essay. But never sacrifice appropriateness for cleverness; above all else, the title should suit the content of the essay. In general, it is best to avoid long wordy titles or declarative-sentence titles that tell the reader too much about the essay.

Many instructors prefer the title on a separate page, along with your name, the course name and section number, the date, and the paper number. Remember that the title should not be punctuated with quotation marks or italics (underlining) unless you are referring to a literary or artistic work and that the title should be followed by an end mark of punctuation only if it is a question or an exclamation.

## 33g  Revise, edit, and proofread your writing.

Many inexperienced writers make the mistake of thinking that revising is the same thing as proofreading, which it is not. Very few people can produce a well-written text in only one draft. In fact, most writers will find that they revise in one way or another throughout all the stages of the writing process: they reorganize their writing plan as they jot down ideas; they consider and discard ideas and topics even before they begin to write; they rephrase or refocus their thesis statement, and so forth. But the majority of your revisions will be made once you have completed the first draft of your writing;

Copyright © 1995 by Harcourt Brace & Company. All rights reserved.

in fact, some writers will tell you that they spend more of their time revising than creating a working draft.

After you have let your draft cool off (at least overnight if not longer), look at it first for overall concerns, since you would be wasting your time to correct mechanics, word choice, sentence structure, spelling, and the like in material that may very well be changed as you reorganize your composition. Have you established the focus of your essay early on? Are the sections of the text organized in the most logical order? Have you strayed at times from your main point or raised issues that do not pertain to your thesis? As you work on these global revisions, check also to see that you have kept your audience in mind.

Next, apply the same perspective to your paragraphs. Are they well focused? Do they use transitions to move smoothly from one idea to the next and from one paragraph to the next? Have you varied sentence structure and length to provide variety, eliminate choppiness, and improve clarity? Look to see if you have maintained a consistent tone, style, level of diction, and point of view.

After you are satisfied with the order in which your paragraphs appear and with their general content, turn your attention to the sentences themselves. Are they clear? If not, examine the structure of each, the words you have used, and the relationship of the ideas to the other sentences in the paragraph. Identify those sentences that use the passive voice and make them active. Look for weak repetitions of words and phrases, for clichés, for redundancy; strengthen these weak spots with more effective words and phrases. Make certain that the words you use are appropriate for your audience and occasion and that you have defined technical and unfamiliar words. Finally, edit each of your sentences for errors in punctuation, mechanics, and spelling, and proofread for typographical errors. Make certain that your manuscript has a neat, professional appearance.

Approached in this manner, revision will be a powerful tool that can help you make your writing forceful and persuasive. In fact, many writers feel that revision is the most important part of the writing process, the part where they clarify, sharpen, and strengthen their writing—deleting, adding, and reorganizing again and again until their text communicates their ideas clearly to a specific audience. The following suggestions for proofreading may help you to revise your composition:

(1) Wait at least one day, if possible, before you revise and edit your first draft. Then you will be more likely to spot weaknesses and mistakes.

(2) Proofread at least three times: once for organization; a second time, out loud, for style; and a third time for grammar, punctuation, and spelling. If you have serious problems with grammar, punctuation, or spelling, proofread still another time for the error or errors you most frequently make.

(3) When proofreading for errors, slow your reading down. To make yourself go more slowly, actually point to each word with your pencil as you read. If you have real difficulties with spelling, try reading each line from right to left instead of the usual left to right so that you will notice words individually.

(4) Read your writing assignment to someone else and ask your listener to stop you when something does not make sense or does not sound right.

Copyright © 1995 by Harcourt Brace & Company. All rights reserved.

(5) Type your written work. Even if you do not type well enough to make the final copy, type at least one draft of your work. Typing the manuscript forces you to take a close look at what you have written. (Many writers do most of their editing while they are typing.)

You may wish to use a word processor instead of a typewriter, both to create or to work on your rough drafts and to produce the final copy of your writing. A word processor will allow you to draft, revise, and edit your work in a variety of sophisticated ways. Before using one, however, be sure to check with your instructor to see if it is all right to do so, particularly to see if the type style of your printer is acceptable. If possible, use a printer that will allow you to select a near-letter-quality mode, a setting that produces print closely resembling that of a typewriter.

Use the following checklists to help streamline the revising and editing processes.

## Revising Checklist

### The essay as a whole

1. Is the purpose of the work clear (**33a[1]**)? Does the work stick to its purpose?
2. Does the work address the appropriate audience (**33a[2]**)?
3. Is the tone appropriate and consistent (**33a[4]**)?
4. Is the subject focused (**33b**)?
5. Is the thesis sharply conceived (**33d**)? Does your thesis statement (if one is appropriate) clearly suggest the position and approach that you take? Do the ideas expressed in the work show clear relationships to the thesis?
6. Are the paragraphs arranged in a logical, effective order (**33e**)?
7. Does the work follow an effective method or combination of methods of development (**33e**)?
8. Is the reasoning sound in the writing as a whole and in individual paragraphs and sentences (**31**)?
9. Will the introduction arouse the reader's interest (**33f[1]**)? Does it indicate what the work is about?
10. Does the work come to a satisfying close (**33f[2]**)?

### Paragraphs

1. Are all paragraphs unified (**32a**)? Are there ideas in any paragraph that do not belong?
2. Is each paragraph coherent (**32b**)? Are sentences within each paragraph arranged in a natural and deliberate order? Are the sentences connected with effective transitions?
3. Are the paragraphs linked effectively with easy and natural transitions (**32b[6]**)?
4. Is each paragraph purposefully and effectively developed (**32c–32d**)?

Copyright © 1995 by Harcourt Brace & Company. All rights reserved.

## Editing Checklist

**Sentences and diction**

1. Are ideas related effectively through subordination and coordination (**24**)?
2. Are all sentences unified (**23**)?
3. Do any sentences contain misplaced parts or dangling modifiers (**25**)?
4. Is there any faulty parallelism (**26**)?
5. Are there any needless shifts in grammatical structures, in tone or style, or in viewpoint (**27**)?
6. Does each pronoun refer clearly to its antecedent (**28**)?
7. Are ideas given appropriate emphasis within each sentence (**29**)?
8. Are the sentences varied in length and in type (**30**)?
9. Are there any fragments (**2**)? Are there any comma splices or fused sentences (**3**)?
10. Do all verbs agree with their subjects (**6a**)? Do all pronouns agree with their antecedents (**6b**)?
11. Are all verbs in their appropriate forms (**7**)?
12. Are any words overused, imprecise, or vague (**20a**)? Are all words idiomatic (**20b**)?
13. Have all unnecessary words and phrases been eliminated (**21**)? Have any necessary words been left out by mistake (**22**)?
14. Is the vocabulary appropriate for the audience, purpose, and occasion (**19, 33a**)?
15. Have all technical words that are unfamiliar to the audience been eliminated or defined (**19g**)?

Copyright © 1995 by Harcourt Brace & Company. All rights reserved.

**The Essay**                                                    Exercise 33–1

DIRECTIONS   Choose a topic from the list of suggested subjects in Exercises 32–3 through 32–9 or a topic of your own for an essay of three hundred to five hundred words. (If you choose to write about work, you may find the facts and ideas presented in this workbook useful in planning your essay.) You may use the following page for a working plan or outline as your instructor directs. Then write a first draft of the composition. Revise it carefully according to the suggestions in **33g**. (Save your rough draft for future reference.) Follow your instructor's directions with regard to the placement of your title, and number the pages of the paper, using Arabic numerals, beginning in the upper right-hand corner of page 2.

TOPIC

WORKING PLAN OR OUTLINE

Copyright © 1995 by Harcourt Brace & Company. All rights reserved.

## The Essay: Revising

Exercise 33–2

NAME _____ SCORE _____

DIRECTIONS    Exchange a revised draft version of the essay you are working on in Exercise 33-1 with a classmate. Using the revising and editing checklists on pages 398–399 of this section, evaluate your classmate's text, recording your specific revising, editing, and proofreading suggestions at the appropriate places in that text. Then write a summary evaluation—including helpful suggestions—in the space below.

Copyright © 1995 by Harcourt Brace & Company. All rights reserved.

## 35

### Write effective letters, résumés, and memos.

Success in business depends a great deal on good communication skills, both person-to-person and written. Many times the only way that a business associate or client will know you will be on paper, so it is essential that what you write communicates clearly and sounds professional. Misunderstandings resulting from poorly written business documents cost money and lose clients. In addition, many business documents are legally binding, and for this reason it is essential that they say clearly and precisely what you mean. Finally, effective business communication eliminates extra work; no one who is busy wants to spend extra time trying to figure out what the writer of a letter, memo, or report "really meant." In the world of work, effective writing pays off: it fosters good will; it creates a favorable impression of the company; and, ultimately, it results in increased profits.

### 35a(1)* Write effective, well-formatted letters and résumés.

**Format**    Business letters are usually typed on only one side of white, unlined, $8^{1}/_{2} \times 11$ inch paper. Standard business envelopes measure about $3^{1}/_{2} \times 6^{1}/_{2}$ inches or $4 \times 10$ inches. (Letterhead stationery and envelopes vary both in size and color.)

Check to see if your company or organization has a policy about letter format. Most companies use either full block (see p. 405) or modified block (see p. 407) for regular correspondence, though an indented format is often used for personal business correspondence such as thank-you notes, congratulations, and the like.

A business letter has six parts: (1) heading, (2) inside address, (3) salutation, (4) body, (5) closing, which consists of the complimentary close and signature, and (6) added notations.

The *heading* gives the writer's full address and the date. If letterhead stationery is used, the date is typed beneath it flush left, flush right, or centered, depending on your format. If plain stationery is used, the address of the writer followed by the date is placed toward the top of the page—the distance from the top arranged so that the body of the letter will be attractively centered on the page—flush with the left- or right-hand margin, as in the letters on pages 405 and 407. Notice that the heading has no end punctuation.

The *inside address*, typed two to six lines below the heading, gives the name and full address of the recipient.

The *salutation* (or greeting) is written flush with the left margin, two spaces below the inside address, and is followed by a colon.

When the surname of the addressee is known, it is used in the salutation of a business letter, as in the following examples.

*The numbering in Chapter 35 does not correspond to that of the Handbook.

Copyright © 1995 by Harcourt Brace & Company. All rights reserved.

| | |
|---|---|
| Dear Dr. Davis: | Dear Mayor Rodriguez: |
| Dear Mrs. Greissman: | Dear Ms. Joseph: |

**Note:** Use Miss or Mrs. if the woman you are addressing has indicated a preference. Otherwise use Ms., which is always appropriate and which is preferred by many businesswomen, whatever their marital status.

In letters to organizations, or to persons whose name and gender are unknown, such salutations as the following are customary:

| | |
|---|---|
| Dear Sir or Madam: | Dear Mobil Oil: |
| Dear Subscription Manager: | Dear Registrar: |

For the appropriate forms of salutations and addresses in letters to government officials, military personnel, and so on, check an etiquette book or the front or back of your college dictionary.

The body of the letter should follow the principles of good writing. Typewritten letters are usually single-spaced, with double spacing between paragraphs. The first sentence of each paragraph should begin flush with the left margin (in full block or modified block) or should be indented five spaces (in indented format). The subject matter should be organized so that the reader can grasp immediately what is wanted, and the style should be clear and direct. Do not use stilted or abbreviated phrasing:

| | | | |
|---|---|---|---|
| NOT | The aforementioned letter | BUT | your letter |
| NOT | Please send it to me ASAP. | BUT | Please send it to me as soon as possible. |

The closing is typed flush with the left-hand margin in full-block style. In modified block and indented style, it is typed to the right of the letter, in alignment with the heading. Here are the parts of the closing:

Complimentary close: This conventional ending is typed, after a double space, below the last paragraph of the body of the letter. Among the endings commonly used in business letters are the following:

| FORMAL | LESS FORMAL |
|---|---|
| Very truly yours, | Sincerely, |
| Sincerely yours, | Cordially, |

Typed name: The writer's full name is typed four lines below the closing.

Title of sender: This line, following the typed name, indicates the sender's position, if he or she is acting in an official capacity.

Manager, Employee Relations
Chairperson, Search Committee

Signature: The letter is signed between the complimentary close and the typed name.

Notations are typed below the closing, flush with the left margin. They indicate, among other things, whether anything is enclosed with or attached to the letter (enclosure or enc., attachment or att.); to whom copies of the letter have been sent (cc: AAW, PTN); and the initials of the sender and the typist (DM/cll).

Copyright © 1995 by Harcourt Brace & Company. All rights reserved.

**MODEL BUSINESS LETTER: full block format (all parts flush with the left margin)**

LETTERHEAD CONTAINING    ALICE'S NURSERY
RETURN ADDRESS         Route 1 Box 156      HEADING
                       Brewster, WA 98865

January 25, 1994

Customer Service Representative
Interface Computing Service
2001 Halvorsen Drive       INSIDE ADDRESS
Diablo, TX 75643

Dear Customer Service Representative:    } SALUTATION

I run a small nursery business with a fairly complicated inventory. For years I have kept track of my nursery stock on paper; now I would like to use a microcomputer and inventory software program to simplify my operations. Could you please tell me more about your <u>Invent</u> inventory software package, which I saw advertised in last month's issue of <u>Seeds</u> magazine.

I would appreciate it if you could answer the following questions:

1. What is the price of this software package?
2. Can you customize it for a nursery business, and, if so, how much more would that cost?
3. Will the <u>Invent</u> program run on a Computec 2000 computer?
4. Can you give me the name, address, and phone number of your nearest sales representative?
5. I would like to keep track of the different varieties of nursery stock I sell (seeds, trees, bushes and shrubs, vegetables, roses, and so on). Will I be able to subdivide the inventory categories by both variety and Latin name?

BODY

Because I will be placing my spring stock orders within the next month, I would like to have an inventory software package set up and running before the end of March so that I can work out all of the bugs before the spring rush begins. I would be grateful if you could send me the information I have requested within the next two weeks so that I can place my order soon.

Sincerely yours,       COMPLIMENTARY CLOSE

*Alice L. Getz*       SIGNATURE      CLOSING

Alice L. Getz       TYPED NAME
Owner               TITLE

ALG/ff    } NOTATION

Copyright © 1995 by Harcourt Brace & Company. All rights reserved.

## MODEL BUSINESS ENVELOPE

**Alice's Nursery**
Route 1 Box 156
Brewster, WA 98865

> Customer Service Representative
> Interface Computing Service
> 2001 Halvorsen Drive
> Diablo, TX 75643

### 35a(2) Write effective application letters and résumés.

The first real business writing that you do may be the letter and résumé you prepare when you look for a job. Obviously, you will want to take particular care that these documents represent you well; a future employer will judge you on the basis of how professionally you present yourself in these samples of your written communication skills.

Both your application letter and your résumé should show the reader that you are suited to fill the job for which you are applying. The letter first identifies the exact job for which you wish to be considered, then discusses your skills as they relate to the requirements of the job itself, and finally requests an interview. Your letter should refer to the company by name several times in the body and should call your reader's attention to the résumé that you will have enclosed.

Never send an application letter without an accompanying résumé or a résumé without an application letter. These two documents work together to persuade the reader to ask you to come for an interview. Be especially careful to make your letter and accompanying résumé look professional; do not send out material that contains corrected typographical errors or that looks poorly arranged on the page. Neither your résumé nor your application letter should exceed one page in length (unless you have been working for a long time and have a great deal of experience related to the job for which you are applying).

**Note:** It is thoughtful to send a thank-you letter after an interview (see p. 437).

Copyright © 1995 by Harcourt Brace & Company. All rights reserved.

**MODEL APPLICATION LETTER: modified block format (heading and closing may be placed in the center or near the right margin)**

Box 743 Wellborn Hall
Washington State University
Pullman, WA 99163
November 9, 1994

Mr. Thomas McLaughlin
Personnel Manager
Laser Corporation
2183 Davis Drive
Seattle, WA 98250

Dear Mr. McLaughlin:

IDENTIFY POSITION
SOUGHT AND HOW
LEARNED ABOUT

I believe that my background—a degree in Marketing and Management, experience in retail sales, and familiarity with computer software—qualifies me to be a productive member of the Laser Corporation's sales department. Please consider my application for the position of field representative trainee, which you advertised in the October 1994 issue of <u>On-Line</u>.

INDICATE MAJOR
QUALIFICATIONS
FOR JOB

A double major in Marketing and Management, along with a minor in Computer Science, have provided me with a strong and diverse background for sales work. In particular, I have learned to apply theory to the practical use of computer technology in small business management. My training will enable me to show my clients how to make the best use of Laser's software packages such as <u>FastCalc</u> and <u>Ready Ledger</u>.

REFER TO RÉSUMÉ
INDICATE FURTHER
QUALIFICATIONS
FOR JOB

My activities and work experience show that I enjoy working with people and can handle responsibility effectively. From my résumé you can see that I have learned to adapt to and work effectively in different situations: counseling marketing majors, designing efficiency surveys, and working as a sales representative. That I worked to pay all of my college expenses demonstrates my initiative and determination to meet the goals that I set for myself. I will bring this same hardworking attitude to the Laser Corporation.

REQUEST
INTERVIEW

I would appreciate the opportunity to meet with you and discuss the ways I can fill Laser's needs. Since you will be on the Washington State University campus the week of January 25, could you please contact me at the above address or phone me at (505) 555-9817 after 3 p.m. to schedule an interview?

Sincerely yours,

*Marie Bear*

Marie Bear

Enclosure: Résumé

Copyright © 1995 by Harcourt Brace & Company. All rights reserved.

## The Application Letter

DIRECTIONS    Using the full or modified block style, write an application letter for a job in your field. Plan your letter in the space provided below; but, if possible, type or word process your letter on good quality paper.

PLANNING SPACE

Copyright © 1995 by Harcourt Brace & Company. All rights reserved.

## The Application: Peer Review

DIRECTIONS   Exchange your application letter with a classmate. On the letter mark sections, sentences, and words that need additional revision, editing, proofreading, or formatting. Make comments in the margin about ways in which the letter can be made stronger. Write a summary evaluation of your classmate's letter.

Copyright © 1995 by Harcourt Brace & Company. All rights reserved.

**The Application Letter: Rewrite**     Exercise 35–3

DIRECTIONS    Revise your application letter in light of your classmate's comments and summary evaluation. Write a summary indicating how you changed your original version of your application letter and why.


NOTES FOR SUMMARY COMMENTS

Your résumé gives a brief overall picture of your qualifications for the job you are seeking. It provides more specifics than you can, or should, discuss in your application letter. Although a résumé may be organized in a number of ways depending on which material you wish to emphasize, it should cover the following categories:

1. Personal Data: name, mailing address, and phone number (with area code)
2. Educational Background
3. Work Experience
4. Honors and Activities
5. References

The material you include in your résumé should illustrate the ways in which you are qualified to fill the position for which you are applying. Do not try to list everything about yourself; pick and choose carefully. Consider designing a résumé specifically aimed at the particular job for which you are applying. A customized résumé stands out when it is reviewed because it addresses the employer's particular needs. It shows that you have thought carefully about the job and the company.

An excellent way to put together an effective résumé is to make lists of all your qualifications using a separate sheet of paper for each category. Write down everything you can think of about yourself—jobs held, classes taken, honors, activities, and so forth. Then go back and fill in details: dates, supervisors' names, job responsibilities. After you complete your brainstorming. Then go back and mark those items that you want to include in the résumé you are developing for this particular job. Within each category, arrange information in order, with the most recent first: May 1994–present, December 1993–May 1994, and so forth.

Type a neat first draft of your résumé to see how it looks on the page. Do not crowd material too closely together; let information stand out by surrounding it with some blank space so that the reader can easily pick out each important aspect of your background. Finally, type a clean copy; if you make an error, do not correct it but retype the page until everything is perfect. Errors and corrections make a résumé look sloppy and unprofessional. Especially if you are not an excellent typist, you may want to have your résumé professionally printed. Choose good stationery—white or a dignified off-white shade such as beige or light gray—and consider buying matching blank paper and envelopes for your application letter.

The following tips will help you prepare a well-organized résumé.

### TIPS ON RÉSUMÉ WRITING

1. Do not forget to include your name, address, and telephone number; unless relevant to the job, personal data such as age and marital status are better left out.
2. Mention your degree, college or university, and pertinent areas of special training.
3. Think about career goals but generally reserve mention of them for the application letter or interview (and even then make sure they enhance your appeal as a candidate). Your interest should be to match your qualifications to the employer's goals.
4. Even if an advertisement asks you to state a salary requirement, any mention of salary should usually be deferred until the interview.

Copyright © 1995 by Harcourt Brace & Company. All rights reserved.

5. Whenever possible, make evident any relationship between jobs you have had and the job you are seeking.
6. Use an acceptable format and make sure the résumé is neat, orderly, and correct to show that you are an efficient, well-organized, thoughtful person.
7. Be sure to ask people's permission before listing their names as references.

Copyright © 1995 by Harcourt Brace & Company. All rights reserved.

## MODEL RÉSUMÉ

MARIE BEAR

<u>College Address</u>
Box 743 Rankin Hall
Washington State University
Pullman, WA 99163
Phone (505) 555-9817
Before May 14, 1995

<u>Permanent Address</u>
Route 1 Box 966
Davis, CA 91304
Phone (916) 555-1954
After May 14, 1995

<u>Position Sought</u>

Entry-level position as sales representative with a computer firm.

<u>Education</u>

Bachelor of Science Degree in Marketing and Management
Washington State University, expected May 1995

Grade Point:   3.53/4.00
Major Courses:   Consumer Behavior, Managerial Strategies, Business Law, Accounting
Minor Courses:   COBOL, PASCAL, FORTRAN
Related Courses:   Business Communications, Technical Writing

<u>Employment</u> (provided 100% of college expenses)

<u>Programming Intern</u>, ReadyWare Software, Davis, CA
Debugged specialized accounting packages
Developed application recordkeeping package for dentists
Advised clients
May–August 1994

<u>Sales Representative</u>, Brandes ComputerWorld, Sacramento, CA
Demonstrated various software packages to the public
Developed efficiency evaluation survey
October 1992–May 1994

<u>Honors and Activities</u>

Phi Kappa Phi Scholastic Honorary
Alpha Lambda Delta Freshman Honorary
TRW Scholarship 1991
Team leader, College of Business orientation, 1992–present
District Five Representative, Faculty-Student Senate, Washington State University, 1993–1994

<u>References</u>

Placement Bureau
Bryan Hall
Washington State University
Pullman, WA 99163

Copyright © 1995 by Harcourt Brace & Company. All rights reserved.

## The Résumé                                       Exercise 35–4

NAME _____     SCORE _____

DIRECTIONS   Write a résumé for a summer job, a permanent job, or an internship. Tailor your résumé to meet the specific requirements of the job for which you are applying. Use the space below to list your qualifications, to list the job requirements, and to write a rough draft of your résumé. Type or word process a final copy of your résumé on white bond paper.

JOB REQUIREMENTS

Copyright © 1995 by Harcourt Brace & Company. All rights reserved.

MY QUALIFICATIONS

Copyright © 1995 by Harcourt Brace & Company. All rights reserved.

ROUGH DRAFT OF RÉSUMÉ

Copyright © 1995 by Harcourt Brace & Company. All rights reserved.

## The Résumé: Peer Review

NAME _____  SCORE _____

DIRECTIONS   Exchange your résumé with a classmate. Using the checklist on pages 413–414 as a guide, mark places that need additional revision, editing, proofreading, or formatting. Make comments in the margin about ways in which the résumé can be made stronger. Write a summary evaluation of your classmate's résumé.

NOTES FOR SUMMARY EVALUATION

Copyright © 1995 by Harcourt Brace & Company. All rights reserved.

**The Résumé: Rewrite**                                    Exercise 35–6

NAME _____ SCORE _____

DIRECTIONS    Revise your résumé in light of your classmate's comments and summary evaluation. Write a summary indicating how you changed the second version of your résumé and why.

NOTES FOR SUMMARY COMMENTS

Copyright © 1995 by Harcourt Brace & Company. All rights reserved.

**35a(3)  Write effective business letters.**

**Letter of Inquiry**    Many business letters are requests for information. Such letters should be direct and should give sufficient background so that the person you write to can answer your questions fully. If you need the information by a certain date, be sure to say so (and, in any case, a date will help motivate your reader to get back in touch with you promptly). A stamped, self-addressed envelope can also speed up the reply.

The first paragraph of a letter of inquiry should begin with the most important question. It should also give any background information necessary for the reader to understand why you are asking for the information and to focus their answers accordingly. For example, if you were inquiring about stereo systems for your home, you would probably want to mention the price range you have in mind and the options that you want in the system. Otherwise, the reader might not tell you about the right sort of equipment.

The middle section of your letter contains any questions of a specific kind. Arranging them in a numbered list may make them easier for your reader to answer.

Use the final section of the letter to express appreciation (but avoid the phrase "thank you in advance," which is wordy and might strike your reader as presumptuous). This final paragraph is also the place to mention the date by which you need to receive the information.

Copyright © 1995 by Harcourt Brace & Company. All rights reserved.

## MODEL INQUIRY: full block format

5602 King Street
Bangor, ME 17895
December 21, 1994

Ms. Loretta Katz
Shady Brook Kennels
2886 Laurel Lane
Cincinnati, OH 65432

Dear Ms. Katz:

ASK YOUR MOST
IMPORTANT
QUESTION FIRST,
GIVE SOME
BACKGROUND
INFORMATION

Will it be possible for me to board my Welsh Corgi from January 28 to 31? Your kennel was recommended to me by my brother-in-law, Paul Klinghammer, who has boarded his retriever with you many times.

I will be visiting the Cincinnati area and will be unable to keep my dog with me while there. Tigger is a five-year-old male who is very docile; however, he is an active dog and it is important that he have an outdoor run where he can exercise.

Could you please tell me:

ASK THE REST
OF YOUR
QUESTIONS

1. If you have room for my dog?
2. What your kennel facilities are like?
3. The cost for the four days?
4. If you have a groomer and how much it would cost to have my dog bathed?

REQUEST A
REPLY AND GIVE
A DATE

Because I will be leaving Bangor on January 15, I would appreciate hearing from you as soon as possible so that I can complete my plans.

Sincerely yours,

Edwin T. Arnold

Copyright © 1995 by Harcourt Brace & Company. All rights reserved.

## The Letter of Inquiry

Exercise 35–7

NAME _____ SCORE _____

DIRECTIONS    Using a full or modified block style, write a letter of inquiry about a product that you would like to purchase by mail (use a catalog advertisement or the "For Sale" column of a newspaper or magazine for the product information). Do your planning of the letter in the space provided below, but, if possible, type or word process your letter on good quality paper.

PLANNING SPACE

Copyright © 1995 by Harcourt Brace & Company. All rights reserved.

## The Letter of Inquiry: Peer Review

Exercise 35–8

NAME _____   SCORE _____

DIRECTIONS   Exchange your letter of inquiry with a classmate. Using the information on page 423 for things to call to the writer's attention and then mark places that need additional revision, editing, proofreading, or formatting. Make comments in the margin about ways in which the letter can be made stronger. Write a summary evaluation of your classmate's letter of inquiry.

NOTES FOR SUMMARY EVALUATION

Copyright © 1995 by Harcourt Brace & Company. All rights reserved.

## The Letter of Inquiry: Rewrite

NAME _____ SCORE _____

DIRECTIONS   Revise your letter of inquiry in light of your classmate's comments and summary evaluation. Write a summary indicating how you changed your second version of your letter of inquiry and why.

NOTES FOR SUMMARY COMMENTS

Copyright © 1995 by Harcourt Brace & Company. All rights reserved.

**Claim and Adjustment Letters**   Claim and adjustment letters are letters that you write to ask someone to resolve a problem for you. These letters are similar to inquiries in that you must explain what you want done and must use specific details so your reader will understand exactly what you want. However, the claim letter requires special diplomacy: remember that even though you may be annoyed by the problem you are writing about, you must not offend or anger your reader. A calm reader is more likely to do what you ask. If you must "blow off steam," do it in your rough draft; then edit out all impolite or accusatory tone as you revise. Appealing to your reader's sense of business integrity and fair play will gain a better response than calling names.

The claim or adjustment letter briefly states the problem in the first paragraph, uses the middle paragraphs to give supporting details, and concludes by outlining what you wish the reader to do. As in the inquiry letter, asking that the problem be resolved by a particular date may speed up the reply process.

In writing a letter of this type, details are important. For instance, if a jacket that you ordered prepaid has not yet arrived, send a copy of the cancelled check, give the date on which you placed your order, and list the item number, size, color, and price. Or, if the manufacturer refuses to fix a tape deck still under warranty, provide the model name and number and the date of purchase, and send copies of your receipts and warranty registration cards (keep the originals for your records). Be sure to mention each enclosure in the text of your letter so that your reader will know what to look for.

Copyright © 1995 by Harcourt Brace & Company. All rights reserved.

## MODEL CLAIM LETTER

Route 5, Box 87
Charlotte, NC 27654
May 5, 1994

Customer Service Manager
Efficient Electrix, Inc.
P.O. Box 765
Manhattan, KS 57744

Dear Customer Service Manager:

STATE THE
PROBLEM

I have always found your appliances to be reliable; that's why I purchased your model 543 pop-up toaster last December. But recently the bread will not come out of the toaster the way that it should.

DESCRIBE WHAT
HAPPENED

Starting a week ago, whenever I put a piece of bread in the slot and pushed down the handle one of two things happened: the bread stuck to the wires, refused to pop up, and burned; or the bread flew about 18 inches out of the toaster and landed on the floor. Needless to say, I'm unhappy about the mess and the waste.

STATE WHAT YOU
WOULD LIKE
DONE

Because I followed your "Care and Maintenance Suggestion" that came with my 543, I believe the problems stem from a mechanical malfunction rather than from neglect on my part. For this reason, I believe that my toaster should be repaired at no expense to me, especially since it is still covered by the warranty. The enclosed copy of my receipt indicates that I have owned this appliance for less than six months.

ASK FOR A
RESPONSE: GIVE
A DATE AND A
REASON FOR
NEEDING IT BY
THAT DATE

Would you please tell me where to send my toaster to be repaired and how to make sure that I am not charged for the service? Since I use this appliance every day, I would appreciate hearing from you within the next two weeks so that I can have my 543 back in working order soon.

Sincerely yours,

*Thelma M. Braker*

Thelma M. Braker

SEND ALONG
COPIES OF
NECESSARY
INFORMATION

Enclosure: sales slip

Copyright © 1995 by Harcourt Brace & Company. All rights reserved.

## The Claim or Adjustment Letter

NAMES _____     SCORE_____

DIRECTIONS    As a part of a two- or three-student team, work collaboratively to write a letter of complaint about a product you bought that is not working properly. Use the full or modified block style. Divide responsibilities up: take turns drafting, revising, editing, proofreading, and checking format. In the space below (1) record your planning of the letter and (2) note who worked on which aspects of the letter. If possible, type or word process your letters on good quality paper.

PLANNING SPACE

Copyright © 1995 by Harcourt Brace & Company. All rights reserved.

## The Claim or Adjustment Letter: Peer Review         Exercise 35–11

NAMES _____     SCORE _____

DIRECTIONS   As a part of the same or a different two- or three-student team, work collaboratively to evaluate another group's claim letter from Exercise 35–10. Use the information on page 429 for things to call to the writers' attention and also mark places that need additional revision, editing, proofreading, or formatting. Divide responsibilities up: take turns reviewing the letter for different concerns. Make comments in the margin about ways in which the letter can be made stronger. (1) Write a collaborative summary evaluation of your classmates' claim letter and (2) note who worked on which aspects of this evaluation.

NOTES FOR SUMMARY EVALUATION

Copyright © 1995 by Harcourt Brace & Company. All rights reserved.         *433*

## The Claim or Adjustment Letter: Group Rewrite          Exercise 35–12

NAMES _____    SCORE_____

DIRECTIONS    As a group, revise your complaint letter in light of your classmates' comments and summary evaluation. Again, divide responsibilities up: take turns revising, editing, proofreading, and checking format. (1) Write a collaborative summary indicating how your group changed its second version of the claim letter and why and (2) note who worked on which aspects of this rewrite. Turn in all materials with your final draft.

NOTES FOR SUMMARY COMMENTS

Copyright © 1995 by Harcourt Brace & Company. All rights reserved.

**Thank-you Letter** Frequently in business it will be appropriate for you to write a thank-you letter; these types of letters make the reader see you as a considerate person and build goodwill for your company or organization. When someone has done you a favor, has been more than ordinarily helpful or generous, or has entertained you as a guest, a letter of thanks is in order.

In addition, it is always a good idea to write a thank-you letter to someone who has interviewed you for a job. Not only will such a letter remind the reader who you are, but it will also convey your sincerity and good business sense. It is appropriate to reiterate briefly some important point you made in your interview, but do not belabor the issue. Keep a thank-you letter brief.

Copyright © 1995 by Harcourt Brace & Company. All rights reserved.

## MODEL THANK-YOU LETTER

534 Valley Crucis Road
Fargo, SD 44678
April 15, 1994

Ms. Edelma Huntley
Oakley Inc.
P.O. Box 12543
Lafayette, LA 75902

Dear Ms. Huntley:

Thank you for taking the time to talk to me about my qualifications for the position of sales representative with Oakley Inc. I enjoyed learning more about the job and about the new product line that Oakley will be marketing this fall.

During our meeting you said that you were looking for a person with at least two years' sales experience after college. Although I recognize that such experience can be valuable, I would like you to consider as equivalent training my two years as advisor for the local Junior Achievement Club and my volunteer work as a fund raiser and coordinator of sales for the campus-wide Fight Hunger Drive.

The extensive travel that the job requires is anything but a discouragement to me; on the contrary, I would welcome the opportunity. I enjoy meeting new people and seeing new places and would be glad to have the chance to do both as a field representative for Oakley Inc.

I look forward to hearing from you soon about your decision.

Sincerely yours,

*Eugene Miller*

Eugene Miller

Copyright © 1995 by Harcourt Brace & Company. All rights reserved.

## The Thank-you Letter

NAME _____ SCORE _____

DIRECTIONS    Using the full or modified block style, write a thank-you letter to a personnel officer at a company that has interviewed you; if you have not yet had the experience of being interviewed, invent an interview to talk about. Do your planning of the letter in the space provided
below, but, if possible word process or type the letter.

PLANNING SPACE

Copyright © 1995 by Harcourt Brace & Company. All rights reserved.

## The Thank-you Letter: Peer Review

**Exercise 35–14**

NAME _____ SCORE _____

DIRECTIONS    Exchange your thank-you letter with a classmate. On the letter mark sections, sentences, and words that need additional revision, editing, proofreading, or formatting. Make comments in the margin about ways in which the letter can be made stronger. Write a summary evaluation of your classmate's letter.

NOTES FOR SUMMARY EVALUATION

Copyright © 1995 by Harcourt Brace & Company. All rights reserved.

**The Thank-you Letter: Rewrite**                    Exercise 35–15

NAME _____ SCORE _____

DIRECTIONS    Revise your thank-you letter in light of your classmate's comments and summary evaluation. Write a summary indicating how you changed your second version of your letter and why. Turn in all materials with your final draft.

NOTES FOR SUMMARY COMMENTS

Copyright © 1995 by Harcourt Brace & Company. All rights reserved.                    *443*

## 35b  Write effective memos.

While business letters generally go to people outside your company, a memo is the standard way to share information within the firm. Clear, effective writing is just as important for people within your firm as for people outside it. Not only is clear communication essential to the company's operation, but what you write will be evaluated by people who are in a position to affect your future.

Often the tone of a memo can be less formal than that of a letter sent to someone outside your company; let the situation itself govern the level of formality you use. When in doubt, it is generally best to be slightly more formal since familiarity can offend some readers, even though they may be people whom you see every day at the office. This is particularly true if you are relatively new in your job or are a trainee.

Memos can be short or lengthy, depending on their purpose, but the basic format remains the same; most companies have printed forms for memos. The heading of a memo lists the names (and usually the titles) of the recipient and the writer, the subject, and the date.

TO:        Henry W. Wills, Vice President

FROM:      Sarah O. Jenkins, Quality Control Supervisor

DATE:      November 24, 1994

SUBJECT    Product Endurance Test Results

If a memo is long, headings should be used to label the sections. In fact, some reports may be written in memo form; these begin with a general statement of purpose followed by a summary section outlining what will follow. The remaining sections discuss various aspects of the topic in greater detail. If the content warrants it, a memo report concludes with a recommendation or conclusion section which states what should be done, by whom, and when. The fairly standard structure of most reports is designed to help busy readers grasp the purpose and important points as easily as possible.

Copyright © 1995 by Harcourt Brace & Company. All rights reserved.

**MODEL MEMO**

INTEROFFICE MEMORANDUM

# Reliable Plastics

**TO:**   M. Andrew Simons, Sales Manager

**FROM:**   Jacob Lenz, Production Manager   *J.L.*

**DATE:**   June 10, 1994

**SUBJECT:**   The Missing Pipe Insulators

Thank you for forwarding Mr. John Rollins's letter about the Rollins Company's incomplete order #234987. I have investigated the problem of the 5,000 missing 3/4" x 8' styrofoam pipe insulators, stock no. 46612. As I understand it, Rollins received the lengths of PVC pipe but not the insulators.

We have experienced production delays this month caused by a malfunctioning foam extruding tube in our Gary plant. We are currently three weeks behind schedule on filling standing orders for all varieties of pipe insulators. Apparently Shipping and Receiving ran the standing orders for July through the computer, sent out what was available, and neglected to inform some of our customers, including the Rollins Company, about the current delay.

The remainder of the order can be shipped on August 15 in time for the deadline the Rollins Company specified in their order last December. Because we plan to run overtime until we are caught up, we can guarantee that Rollins will receive the pipe insulators by the middle of August.

Please tell Mr. Rollins when he can expect his shipment.

JML/mb

Copies to:
Shipping and Receiving:   Carmean
Production:   Wellborn
Sales:   Durham

Copyright © 1995 by Harcourt Brace & Company. All rights reserved.

## The Memo

NAMES _____    SCORE _____

DIRECTIONS    As a part of a two- or three-student team, work collaboratively to write a memo to new students at your school informing them about how to register for next term's classes. Divide responsibilities up: take turns drafting, revising, editing, proofreading, and checking format. (1) Record your planning of the memo and (2) note who worked on which aspects of the memo. If possible, type or word process your memo.

PLANNING SPACE

Copyright © 1995 by Harcourt Brace & Company. All rights reserved.

**The Memo: Peer Review**                    Exercise 35–17

NAMES _____  SCORE _____

DIRECTIONS   As a part of the same or a different two- or three-student team, work collaboratively to evaluate another group's memo from Exercise 35-16. Use the information on page 445
for things to call to the writers' attention and also mark places that need additional revision, editing, proofreading, or formatting. Divide responsibilities up: take turns reviewing the memo for
different concerns. Make comments in the margin about ways in which the memo can be made
stronger. (1) Write a collaborative summary evaluation of your classmates' memo and (2) note
who worked on which aspects of this evaluation.

NOTES FOR SUMMARY EVALUATION

Copyright © 1995 by Harcourt Brace & Company. All rights reserved.

# The Memo: Group Rewrite

NAMES _____  SCORE _____

DIRECTIONS    As a group, revise your memo in light of your classmates' comments and summary evaluation. Again, divide responsibilities up: take turns revising, editing, proofreading, and checking format. (1) Write a collaborative summary indicating how your group changed its second version of their memo and why and (2) note who worked on which aspects of this rewrite. Turn in all materials with your final draft.

NOTES FOR SUMMARY COMMENTS

Copyright © 1995 by Harcourt Brace & Company. All rights reserved.

# APPENDIX

| Parts of Speech | Uses in the Sentence | Examples |
|---|---|---|
| **1. Verbs** | Indicators of action or state of being (often link subjects and complements) | Tom *hit* the curve. Mary *was* tired. He *is* a senator. |
| **2. Nouns** | Subjects, objects, complements | *Kay* gave *Ron* the *book* of *poems*. *Jane* is a *student*. |
| **3. Pronouns** | Substitutes for nouns | *He* will return *it* to *her* later. |
| **4. Adjectives** | Modifiers of nouns and pronouns | *The long* poem is *the best*. |
| **5. Adverbs** | Modifiers of verbs, adjectives, adverbs, or whole clauses | sang *loudly* a *very* sad song *entirely too* fast *Indeed,* we will. |
| **6. Prepositions** | Words used before nouns and pronouns to relate them to other words in the sentence | *to* the lake *in* a hurry *with* no thought *beside* her |
| **7. Conjunctions** | Words that connect words, phrases, or clauses; may be either coordinating or subordinating | win *or* lose in the morning *and* at night We won today, *but* we lost last week. Come *as* you are. |
| **8. Interjections** | Expressions of emotion (unrelated grammatically to the rest of the sentence) | *Woe* is me! *Ouch!* *Imagine!* |

Copyright © 1995 by Harcourt Brace & Company. All rights reserved.

## Common auxiliaries (helping verbs)

| | | |
|---|---|---|
| am | do | might |
| am (is, are, etc.) | does | must |
|   going to or | had | ought to |
|   about to | had to | shall |
| are | has | should |
| be | has to | used to |
| been | have | was |
| can | have to | were |
| could | is | will |
| did | may | would |

## Forms of the verb to be

| | | |
|---|---|---|
| am | have been | will OR |
| are | is |   shall be |
| had been | was | will OR |
| has been | were |   shall have been |

## Common indefinite pronouns—*those usually considered singular*

| | | |
|---|---|---|
| another | everybody | nothing |
| anybody | everyone | one |
| anyone | everything | somebody |
| anything | neither | something |
| each | nobody | |
| either | no one | |

## —*those usually considered plural*

| | | |
|---|---|---|
| all | more | none |
| any | most | some |

## Relative pronouns

| | | |
|---|---|---|
| that | who | whomever |
| what | whoever | whose |
| which | whom | |

Copyright © 1995 by Harcourt Brace & Company. All rights reserved.

## Common prepositions

| | | |
|---|---|---|
| across | for | over |
| after | from | through |
| as | in | to |
| at | in front of | under |
| because of | in regard to | until |
| before | like | up |
| beside | near | with |
| between | of | |
| by | on | |

## Subordinating conjunctions (OR *subordinators*)

| | | |
|---|---|---|
| after | if | until |
| although | in order that | when |
| as | since | whenever |
| as if | so that | where |
| as though | that | wherever |
| because | though | while |
| before | unless | |

## Coordinating conjunctions (OR *coordinators*)

| | | |
|---|---|---|
| and | nor | yet |
| but | or | |
| for | so | |

## Conjunctive adverbs

| | | |
|---|---|---|
| accordingly | hence | moreover |
| also | henceforth | nevertheless |
| anyhow | however | otherwise |
| besides | indeed | still |
| consequently | instead | then |
| first, second, third, etc. | likewise | therefore |
| furthermore | meanwhile | thus |

Copyright © 1995 by Harcourt Brace & Company. All rights reserved.

## Common transitional phrases

| | | |
|---|---|---|
| as a result | in addition | on the contrary |
| at the same time | in fact | on the other hand |
| for example | in other words | that is |
| for instance | | |

## Principal Parts of Some Troublesome Verbs

| Present | Past | Past Participle |
|---|---|---|
| begin | began | begun |
| blow | blew | blown |
| break | broke | broken |
| burst | burst | burst |
| choose | chose | chosen |
| come | came | come |
| do | did | done |
| draw | drew | drawn |
| drink | drank | drunk |
| drive | drove | driven |
| eat | ate | eaten |
| fly | flew | flown |
| freeze | froze | frozen |
| give | gave | given |
| grow | grew | grown |
| know | knew | known |
| lay | laid | laid |
| lie | lay | lain |
| raise | raised | raised |
| ring | rang | rung |
| rise | rose | risen |
| run | ran | run |
| see | saw | seen |
| set | set | set |
| sit | sat | sat |
| speak | spoke | spoken |
| steal | stole | stolen |
| swim | swam | swum |
| take | took | taken |
| wear | wore | worn |
| write | wrote | written |

Copyright © 1995 by Harcourt Brace & Company. All rights reserved.

## Case of pronouns

| Subjective | Objective | Possessive |
|---|---|---|
| I | me | my, mine |
| you | you | your, yours |
| he, she, it | him, her, it | his, her, hers, its |
| we | us | our, ours |
| they | them | their, theirs |
| who OR whoever | whom OR whomever | whose |

Copyright © 1995 by Harcourt Brace & Company. All rights reserved.

# Individual Spelling List

Write in this list every word that you misspell—in spelling tests, in themes, or in any other written work. Add pages as needed.

| NO. | WORD (CORRECTLY SPELLED) | WORD (SPELLED BY SYLLABLES) WITH TROUBLE SPOT CIRCLED | REASON FOR ERROR° |
|-----|--------------------------|------------------------------------------------------|-------------------|
|     |                          |                                                      |                   |
|     |                          |                                                      |                   |
|     |                          |                                                      |                   |
|     |                          |                                                      |                   |
|     |                          |                                                      |                   |
|     |                          |                                                      |                   |
|     |                          |                                                      |                   |
|     |                          |                                                      |                   |
|     |                          |                                                      |                   |

°See pages 255–273 for a discussion of the chief reasons for misspelling. Indicate the reason for your misspelling by writing a, b, c, d, e, f, or g in this column

a = Mispronunciation  
b = Confusion of words similar in sound and/or spelling  
c = Error in adding prefix  
d = Error in adding suffix  

e = Confusion of ei and ie  
f = Error in forming the plural  
g = Error in using hyphens  
h = Any other reason for misspelling  

Copyright © 1995 by Harcourt Brace & Company. All rights reserved.

## Individual Spelling List (cont.)

| NO. | WORD (CORRECTLY SPELLED) | WORD (SPELLED BY SYLLABLES) WITH TROUBLE SPOT CIRCLED | REASON FOR ERROR |
|-----|--------------------------|-------------------------------------------------------|------------------|
|     |                          |                                                       |                  |
|     |                          |                                                       |                  |
|     |                          |                                                       |                  |
|     |                          |                                                       |                  |
|     |                          |                                                       |                  |
|     |                          |                                                       |                  |
|     |                          |                                                       |                  |
|     |                          |                                                       |                  |
|     |                          |                                                       |                  |
|     |                          |                                                       |                  |
|     |                          |                                                       |                  |
|     |                          |                                                       |                  |
|     |                          |                                                       |                  |
|     |                          |                                                       |                  |

Copyright © 1995 by Harcourt Brace & Company. All rights reserved.

## Individual Spelling List (cont.)

| NO. | WORD (CORRECTLY SPELLED) | WORD (SPELLED BY SYLLABLES) WITH TROUBLE SPOT CIRCLED | REASON FOR ERROR |
|---|---|---|---|
| | | | |
| | | | |
| | | | |
| | | | |
| | | | |
| | | | |
| | | | |
| | | | |
| | | | |
| | | | |
| | | | |
| | | | |
| | | | |
| | | | |

Copyright © 1995 by Harcourt Brace & Company. All rights reserved.